923.1
Aj1

GEORGE WASHINGTON
By Gilbert Stuart
The Gibbs-Channing-Avery Portrait

THE PEOPLE'S CHOICE

FROM WASHINGTON TO HARDING

A Study in Democracy

BY

HERBERT AGAR

Boston and New York

HOUGHTON MIFFLIN COMPANY

The Riverside Press Cambridge

The Riverside Press
CAMBRIDGE · MASSACHUSETTS
PRINTED IN THE U.S.A.

TO

ELEANOR CARROLL CHILTON

PREFACE

THE lives of the American Presidents call attention, with dramatic sharpness, to a problem in their country's history. No one can consider the careers of these twenty-nine men without wondering why it is that, whereas six out of the first seven were men of great ability, only four out of the remaining twenty-two are above the common average of politicians. The answer to the question — which is one of the chief subjects of this book — involves a discussion of the whole history of the United States.

Under the first six Presidents the Government was an oligarchy, dominated by a little group of privileged and public-spirited men. About the time of Andrew Jackson, the seventh President, the country became a democracy, or rather three separate democracies: a thorough-going social and political democracy in the new Western States, where conditions of life reduced inequality to a minimum; a Greek democracy in the South, based on slave labour and accepting the leadership of the educated class; and lastly, in the Northeast (where the new industrialism had brought wealth and power), a democracy of city mobs bossed by politicians who took their orders from the rich. The last Presidents of this second period were Lincoln and Jefferson Davis, representatives of the Western and Southern forms of democracy. Both forms were destroyed by the Civil War, which left the country in the hands of the plutocrats. Theodore Roosevelt and Wilson stood for a protest against the drift of events. The effectiveness of the protest is suggested by the fact that the last President on the list is Harding.

A shocking tale loses force if told too often, which explains why I have closed with the death of Harding. The two Presidents who succeeded him merely proved, with growing unpleasantness, the need for a new order in American political life. Possible forms of that new order, in the light of history and the present trend of events, are discussed in the Conclusion to this book.

HERBERT AGAR

June, 1933.

THE PRESIDENTS AND THEIR TERMS OF OFFICE

1.	George Washington	1789–1793; 1793–1797
2.	John Adams	1797–1801
3.	Thomas Jefferson	1801–1805; 1805–1809
4.	James Madison	1809–1813; 1813–1817
5.	James Monroe	1817–1821; 1821–1825
6.	John Quincy Adams	1825–1829
7.	Andrew Jackson	1829–1833; 1833–1837
8.	Martin Van Buren	1837–1841
9.	*William Henry Harrison	1841–
10.	John Tyler	1841–1845
11.	James K. Polk	1845–1849
12.	*Zachary Taylor	1849–1850
13.	Millard Fillmore	1850–1853
14.	Franklin Pierce	1853–1857
15.	James Buchanan	1857–1861
16.	*Abraham Lincoln	1861–1865; 1865
17.	Jefferson Davis	1861–1865
18.	Andrew Johnson	1865–1869
19.	Ulysses S. Grant	1869–1873; 1873–1877
20.	Rutherford B. Hayes	1877–1881
21.	*James A. Garfield	1881
22.	Chester A. Arthur	1881–1885
23.	Grover Cleveland	1885–1889; 1893–1897
24.	Benjamin Harrison	1889–1893
25.	*William McKinley	1897–1901; 1901
26.	Theodore Roosevelt	1901–1905; 1905–1909
27.	William H. Taft	1909–1913
28.	Woodrow Wilson	1913–1917; 1917–1921
29.	*Warren G. Harding	1921–1923

* Died in office.

CONTENTS

MAPS

THE PEOPLE'S CHOICE
PART ONE
OLIGARCHY

INTRODUCTION

AMONG the airy nothings to which historians have given a local habitation and a name, the most airy of all is the picture of the American Revolution as a popular uprising against tyranny. This is not only false in itself, but it leads to a misreading of the first forty years of the country's history, and it prevents an understanding of the mind and character of Washington.

The story of the American Revolution must be traced from 1763, when the Seven Years War came to an end in Europe. The North American phase of the war brought a time of profits and high prices, when quartermasters were spending with lavish pleasure the money of the English taxpayer. The war was a success; the French were driven from North America; the imperial patriotism of the colonists was as notable as their prosperity. This patriotism might have stood the strain of the post-war depression, had not the British Government chosen in 1763 to inaugurate a new and efficient policy of colonial administration.

England had always looked upon her colonies as a source of raw materials and a market for finished products — a view which was expressed in a complicated system of trade acts. The acts had caused little friction, for they had been laxly applied. But in 1763 England was feeling poor, so she decided to enforce the trade laws, and at the same time to raise extra money from the colonists by means of a stamp tax, imposing heavy duties on legal papers, liquor licenses, pamphlets, newspapers, etc. In London, this seemed a sensible way of making the colonists contribute their share toward the cost of a war which had freed them from the French menace. Unfortunately for the Empire, however, the stamp tax was a burden on the two most vocal classes in the community: the lawyers and the journalists. And the decision to enforce the trade laws was a burden on the New England merchants and shippers, who had long made good profits from smuggling.

Neither of these burdens afflicted the people; neither had anything to do with freedom or the rights of man. But it so happened that when the powerful merchant-lawyer-journalist group began to protest against the Stamp Act and the suppression of smuggling, they found that various other groups throughout the colonies had old grievances of their own. First, the Southern planters were many of them in debt to their London agents, who paid poor prices for tobacco and overcharged for the goods they shipped in return. Second, the frontier farmers were angry because England had prohibited the printing of paper money (for the agrarian debtor has always had faith in the wealth-making powers of the printing press), and also because of the Proclamation of 1763, which forbade settlers from crossing the Appalachian Mountains into the Indian country beyond. Third, the artisans and labourers in the cities, many of them out of work because of the post-war business depression, resented their economic plight, and were ready to believe that the blame for their poverty and insecurity should be put on King George rather than on the local ruling class.

As a result of all this discontent, the response to the campaign against the Stamp Act surprised Americans as much as it surprised Parliament. Many of the wealthy colonial merchants were more surprised than pleased; for the city labourers formed themselves enthusiastically into bands known as 'Sons of Liberty,' and showed their horror of taxation without representation by pillaging and rioting in New York, Boston, Philadelphia, and Charleston. At once the more conservative merchants and professional men saw that here, at home, was a greater danger to their property than any that was threatened by King or Parliament. They quickly drew back, giving their support to no further agitations. But they had helped start a movement which they could not control, and which was to end in their own ruin and exile.

It is seldom realized how few of the upper class in the colonies were in favour of the break with England. Professor Van Tyne, the leading authority on the Loyalists, writes: 'After the Revolution passed the bounds of peaceful resistance, it was (except in Virginia) distinctly a movement of the middle and lower classes. A new set of leaders came forward, hitherto unknown, less educated, and eager for change. The very public documents became more illiterate. To the aristocratic and cultured class it seemed that the unlettered monster was unchained, and while they waited for British power to restore the old order they withdrew for the most part from what seemed an undignified contest.'

In Virginia, however, the conservative, prosperous group continued to oppose British policy — the reasons being, first, the tobacco-planters' debts to their London agents; second, the fact that in Virginia there were no cities, so that the 'Sons of Liberty' did not give warning of what anti-English agitation might bring; and third, the Quebec Act. This Act — which was passed in 1774 — was decisive. It illustrates that ignorance of American affairs for which Burke ridiculed the Government: in order to control the Indians, and to preserve the fur trade, the Province of Quebec was extended south to cover the great triangle between the Ohio and Mississippi Rivers, and settlers were prohibited from that region. The Proclamation of 1763 had been generally disregarded; but here was a new — and apparently a more serious — threat, which not only gave the Western farmers and pioneers a true grievance (to add to their false grievance over paper money), but which turned the richest and most influential planters of Virginia into enemies of England. Most of these planters were land-speculators, who already had interests in the Ohio country; and it was a strange blindness (or an unusual love of justice) which led Parliament to neglect their claims in favour of the claims of the red man.

It is worth mentioning that the Quebec Act also angered the freedom-loving New-Englanders, because it allowed French Canadians to continue an open, barefaced practice of their religion.

2

The story of the Boston Tea Party shows the mixture of real grievances, insincere appeals to liberty, and rioting, that led to the War of Independence.... The East India Company was on the verge of bankruptcy, and Parliament came to the rescue with the Tea Act of 1773, designed to help the company sell its surplus tea. The Act allowed the company to send tea to the American colonies in its own ships, and to sell the tea through its own agencies. And instead of paying the English tax of a shilling, such tea had only a duty of threepence at the American ports. The result was a drop of ninepence in the price of tea. American merchants who had bought their stocks legally in London (and even the more enterprising merchants who had smuggled their stocks from Holland) could now be undersold by the East India Company, while shipowners and sailors who lived on the tea-smuggling trade would be out of a job. These groups were naturally grieved; but it is hard to see what interest the 'Sons of Liberty' had in the quarrel. Nevertheless, a little more talk about 'no taxation without representation,' a few more quotations from Locke, and the mob was stimulated into boarding East Indiamen in Boston Harbour and flinging overboard a large consignment of tyrannously cheap tea.

In this story there appear the main causes for the War of Independence: first, Parliament was acting stupidly, or worse — for if it favoured other English trading houses in the same fashion, it might end by ruining most of the American merchants, and all of the smugglers; second, the merchant-lawyer class replied by organizing violence among the common people (who were discontented with the growing power of wealth, and who, through the popular assemblies, had long been demanding such radical legislation as paper money, bankruptcy acts in the interest of debtors, and free settlement of the Western lands); third, the common people responded to the unexpected assurance that they were, by nature, free, equal, and benign, by a joyful destruction of property.

The result of this brief unnatural alliance between the proper-
tied classes and the poor was a social and economic revolution.
A by-product of this revolution was the War of Independence —
an event so dramatic that it has distracted attention from the fact
that between the outbreak of hostilities with England in 1775
and the inauguration of Washington as President under the new
Constitution in 1789, agrarian radicals controlled the colonies.
They issued paper money at a disastrous rate; they annulled the
Proclamation of 1763, and disregarded the Quebec Act; they
confiscated the Crown domains and the estates of most of the
wealthy Tories; they abolished entails in every State but two; in
many States they extended the suffrage; they disestablished the
Church in four of the States. The alarm of the conservative
classes is expressed by General Knox, in a letter written to Washington in October, 1786: 'Their creed [i.e., the creed of the
populist majority in the Massachusetts legislature] is, that the
property of the United States has been protected from the confiscation of Britain by the joint exertions of all, and therefore
ought to be the common property of all.... This dreadful situation, for which our government have made no adequate provision,
has alarmed every man of principle and property in New England.
They start as from a dream, and ask what can have been the
cause of this delusion? What is to give us security against the
violence of lawless men? Our government must be braced,
changed, and altered to secure our lives and property.'

The change demanded by Knox was soon to come. Within
two and a half years of the writing of that letter, Washington
became President of a government that re-established most of
the conservative economic policies once maintained by Great
Britain. Primogeniture, entails, and an established church, however, were not restored; and American merchants and manufacturers remained free from foreign control. American farmers
and labourers, on the other hand, found that their last state was
much the same as their first, that they were expected to forget the catch-phrases out of Locke, or out of Jefferson's Declara-

tion of Independence, and to remember that man is born to sorrow as the sparks fly upward.

Radicals accused Washington of betraying his cause when he became head of a government formed to safeguard the rights of property — Tom Paine, for example, addressing him as follows, in an open letter: 'As to you, sir, treacherous in private friendship... and a hypocrite in public life, the world will be puzzled to decide whether you are an apostate or an impostor; whether you have abandoned good principles, or whether you ever had any.' And the American democrats abused Washington with similar violence, calling him 'crocodile,' 'hyena,' 'traitor.' Washington, however, had not changed sides. He was fighting for the same cause still, though some of his former followers were just beginning to discover what that cause was. Washington had no illusions about the virtues, or the abstract rights, of mankind. He believed in discipline and authority. His attitude toward the militia (the 'embattled farmers' of American heroic tradition) shows his cold realism: 'The militia,' he wrote, 'come in you cannot tell how, go out you cannot tell when; consume your provisions, exhaust your stores, and leave you at last in a critical moment.' And as for democracy: 'Mankind,' wrote Washington to Henry Lee, 'when left to themselves, are unfit for their own government.' Between 1775 and 1789, American mankind had been left so much to themselves that they interfered with the rights and privileges of property more ruthlessly than Parliament had ever done. So Washington returned to the fray, becoming the first President of what was intended to be an aristocratic Republic.

There were just under four million people in the United States of which Washington became President — the large majority of them still living in a little fringe of land along the coast. Although farming was the chief occupation throughout the country, trade was not negligible — exports, during the first decade of the new government, amounting to forty-four million, and imports to fifty-five million, dollars. The first political problem to face the United States was whether the government was to be run in the interests of the large farming class or of the small but powerful business community — a problem that remained un-settled until the Civil War. And before the end of Washington's presidency a second problem had arisen, namely, whether the government was to remain an oligarchy, or whether, under the influence of French ideas and of social equality in the Western frontier districts, it was to become a democracy. This problem was settled in 1829, by which year the first period of American history was ended, the oligarchy created by Washington's genera-tion was dead.

THE PEOPLE'S CHOICE

.:.

CHAPTER I

WASHINGTON

I

THE Washingtons, in Virginia, were of the second order of importance. Descended from respectable landowners in North-amptonshire, they remained respectable landowners in the colony; but none of them had ever been brilliant, or learned, or even very rich. Washington's father was married twice, George being the eldest child of the second marriage. When he was eleven, his father died, leaving little property for the six children of his second wife. So George's education was rudimentary; but his family connections saved him from the more cramping effects of poverty. His half-brother Lawrence owned the estate of Mount Vernon and was married to a daughter of the Fairfaxes, the richest landowners of Virginia. George spent much of his boyhood at Mount Vernon, and at the neighbouring Fairfax estate.

Thomas, Lord Fairfax, the head of the family, had recently left England to spend his disgruntled old age in Virginia. He took to Washington, and when the boy was sixteen Lord Fairfax gave him the job of surveying the six million acres of Fairfax estates in the Shenandoah Valley, to the west of the Blue Ridge Mountains. This gave Washington his first view of those western lands which led him to dream an imperial future for America, and to speculate most wisely for himself. It also gave him a hard, outdoor life which developed his full physical powers. He was six feet two inches tall, lean, muscular, and with a square, massive jaw and strong hands. He had large features, grey-blue eyes, and brown hair. His lips were generally firmly closed, which gave his face a stern expression.

Three years later, when he was nineteen, Washington went with his brother Lawrence to the West Indies, where he caught smallpox, which left him marked for life. Lawrence, who was travelling in search of health, died the following year, making George the guardian to his estates, and the heir to them in case Lawrence's daughter should die. This the daughter promptly did; so in 1752, at the age of twenty, Washington became a moderately wealthy landowner and the lord of Mount Vernon.

If an attentive Providence had been shaping the young man's career, there are few respects in which his life, up to this point, could have been improved. Born into a ruling class, but into a subordinate position within that class, he was made to feel from childhood that much was expected of him. At the same time it was clear that if he was to justify his birth and become one of the important men of Virginia, he would have to do so by his own efforts. He lived in surroundings where he could acquire an education in men and manners; but his ambition was never lulled by the knowledge that even if he failed to make anything of himself his life would be smooth and comfortable. At the age of sixteen he began to earn his own living in what was then, in that land-hungry Virginian society, the respectable profession of surveying. His job took him at once out of his accustomed world, into the unknown, exciting West.

There was nothing romantic about Washington's imagination; he responded to the West, and the red Indian, with the practical interest of an empire-builder. Washington became the first 'American,' in that he was the first colonial leader to think, and act, nationally; and it is probable that an important reason for this is his early experience with the world across the mountains It was too vast and rich a world for its future to be considered in terms of Virginia; and early in his life Washington came to the belief that Providence intended a new and splendid nation to arise among these so novel and so favourable conditions....

Finally, when his ambition had been strengthened and his imagination enlarged, Washington became financially independent, and could give his life to public service when the occasion should arise.

Formal education was the one thing lacking in Washington's training. The sons of the very rich, in colonial Virginia, were sent to college in England; the sons of the well-to-do went to William and Mary, in Virginia, or else to one of the Northern colleges; the sons of the poorer gentry had to learn what they could from the local clergyman, and from the libraries in their fathers', and their neighbours', houses. In this manner Washington learned practical mathematics (for his work as a surveyor), and while staying with Lord Fairfax he read English history and the *Spectator* essays. His military education was provided by two old soldiers, who taught him tactics, manual of arms, and fencing. After this preparation he became, at the age of twenty, an adjutant-general of Virginia, with the rank of major.

Washington had a perfunctory religious life. As a Virginia gentleman, he was brought up in the Church of England; and in later life, he usually went to church about once a month, presumably out of respect for the institution. In his letters and in his diary there is much mention of Providence — but in the sense of Destiny rather than of the Christian God. After Washington's death, his friend Bishop White wrote that he had never heard Washington discuss a religious subject, and that he had never seen him kneel down in church. The Bishop added, however, that Washington was 'attentive' in church.

In 1753, at the age of twenty-one, Washington had his first military employment. The French and Indian War (the North American phase of the Seven Years War) was already brewing. The French were laying claim to land along the Ohio River, and the Governor of Virginia sent Washington into this disputed country to order a French commander to leave. The order was delivered, but not obeyed. The next year Washington was sent back, with one hundred and fifty men, to seize the fork of the Monongahela and Allegheny Rivers. He attacked a small French force, killing the commander, Monsieur de Jumonville. Later he was attacked by a superior French force and compelled to capitulate. In the articles of capitulation, signed by Washington, there were two references to the 'assassination' of M. de Jumonville — who, according to the French, was on a peaceful errand when attacked by Washington. Washington claimed that he was misled by his interpreter and did not know he was signing a self-indictment. The French word was *assassinat* — not a hard word to translate.

On this expedition, Washington's tiny command had been joined by another group of about one hundred and fifty men, under a Captain McKaye. Washington was a lieutenant-colonel in the Virginia regiment, but McKaye held a royal commission and refused to take orders from Washington — for any officer with a royal commission took precedence over any officer with a colonial commission. This angered Washington, who protested, vainly, to the Governor of Virginia. In 1755, therefore, when General Braddock arrived from England with two regiments, to lead a joint English and colonial attack against the French in the Ohio Valley, Washington refused to join the expedition. Because of his knowledge of the country, however, and his reputation as a man of decision, Braddock offered him an unofficial position on the staff, without pay. Washington accepted, and thus was present at the famous ambush on the Monongahela, where the French and Indians routed the British force, inflicting casualties of almost seventy per cent. Washington, one of the few officers to be unhurt, distinguished himself for bravery. He was clearly one of the men whom danger rouses to a 'fierce and far delight.' His bravery was not a triumph of spirit over body, but a positive, whole-souled pleasure in the excitement of danger. After his first brief battle, with Jumonville, Washington wrote to his brother: 'I heard the bullets whistle, and, believe me, there is something charming in the sound.' The sentence was published in the *London Magazine*, and George II commented, 'He would not say so if he had been used to hear many.' Washington lived to hear very many, yet for him the sound remained charming to the end.

In his report of the Monongahela action, sent to Governor Dinwiddie of Virginia, Washington magnified the good behaviour of the Virginia troops, giving the English regulars a poor character. 'In short,' he wrote, 'the dastardly behaviour of the English Soldiers expos'd all those who were inclined to do their duty to almost certain Death.' Doubtless this was Washington's opinion; but it was not the fact, and it may be that Washington's scorn for the English soldiers was a result of his spleen on the subject of colonial and royal commissions. For this matter continued to rankle.

After Braddock's defeat, Washington was made colonel of the Virginia regiment, and Governor Dinwiddie tried to get him a royal commission. In this, Dinwiddie was joined by the Governor of Pennsylvania and by the Council and House of Burgesses of Virginia; yet the request was refused.... Washington's concern over the issue is shown by the following facts: a Captain Dagworthy, who had held a royal commission under Braddock, was now, with a Maryland commission, in command of thirty men at Fort Cumberland. He refused to take orders from Colonel Washington, whereupon Washington set out from Virginia to ride to Boston, where he could lay the whole matter before the English General Shirley. With two aides-de-camp and two servants, he rode the five hundred miles to Boston, where General Shirley decided that, except when in the presence of regular troops, Captain Dagworthy should take rank as a provincial officer.

In 1758, Washington became engaged to marry Martha Dandridge Custis, a rich widow. For some years past, Washington had been in love with Sally Fairfax, the wife of his friend George William Fairfax. After his engagement, Washington wrote to

Mrs. Fairfax, indicating, in roundabout and guarded fashion, that he was in love with her, but that he could not, in honour, tell her so. Sally Fairfax and Washington had known each other since 1749; they had acted in amateur theatricals together, and Mrs. Fairfax is reputed to have encouraged Washington to read. This is the most important passion of Washington's life, and although he suppressed it except for the one guarded statement, he never forgot Sally Fairfax. In 1798, the year before he died, he wrote to her in Bath, and after remarking on the many important events in the quarter-century since the Fairfaxes had left America, he added: 'None of which events, however, nor all of them together, have been able to eradicate from my mind the recollection of those happy moments, the happiest in my life, which I have enjoyed in your company.'

This almost complete suppression of his emotions is characteristic of Washington. The cold, impressive strength that was his in later life was not come by accidentally; it was the result of long control. A portrait-painter, after studying Washington's face, said it was the face of a man with tremendous passions. These passions were subdued to Washington's will, with the result that when he set his heart on something, he pursued it with a concentration of purpose that could not be withstood. And when on rare occasions he relaxed his lifelong vigilance and gave way to anger, the result was terrifying. We have a few descriptions of such scenes. In the summer of 1781, Washington was expecting the French fleet under de Grasse to make for New York. His plans were completed for what he thought would be a decisive battle. Suddenly the news came that de Grasse was making for the Chesapeake, thus destroying Washington's hopes for ending the war. It was the last of many disappointments from the French fleet, and Washington gave way to fury. Colonel Pickering and Robert Morris, arriving for a conference, found him striding up and down the room in such a storm of excitement that he would not notice them. They left the room. Half an hour later they were sent for, and found Washington his usual cold self. He discussed his plans and disappointments with an almost frightening calm.

Years later, when Washington was President, he sent an expedition of two thousand men under General St. Clair against the Indians along the Wabash River. St. Clair was surprised and routed by a small force of Indians. The news came to Washington while at dinner. He glanced through the dispatches, giving no sign of emotion; but when all the guests were gone he burst out before his secretary: 'Here, on this very spot, I took leave of him. "You have your instructions," I said.... "I had a strict eye to them and will add but one word — Beware of a surprise! I repeat it — *beware of a surprise....*" He went off with that as my last solemn warning thrown into his ears. And yet, to suffer that army to be cut to pieces, hacked, butchered, tomahawked! [1]... O God, O God, he's worse than a murderer!' Within five minutes the storm was over. 'This must not go beyond this room,' said Washington. 'General St. Clair shall have justice. I will receive him without displeasure; I will hear him without prejudice; he shall have full justice.'

These rare tornadoes of wrath show with what a strong hand Washington ruled himself during most of his life. With such a temperament he might have dissipated himself in frothy swashbuckling, or in any other form of easy passion; instead, he trained himself to a disciplined, forbidding strength. The bottled-up, denied passion that such discipline implies may explain why Washington, from young manhood on, gave so many strangers the impression that he was destined for greatness.

Washington's decision to marry may have been strengthened by his desire to put an extra barrier between himself and Sally Fairfax. In any case, he was not romantically in love with Martha Custis — the letters to Mrs. Fairfax, written after Washington's engagement, prove that.... Whatever his motives for deciding to marry, Washington made a suitable match. Mrs. Custis was

[1] It would be interesting to know whether, during those wild moments, Washington recalled his youthful strictures on Braddock's English regulars.

among the richest women in Virginia, and Washington had a keen affection for property. The marriage proved a simple, un-dramatic success. By her first husband, Martha Custis had borne four children — two of whom died in infancy. She and Washington had no children — a state of affairs for which he apparently held her responsible, for years later, in a characteristic letter to a nephew to whom he had left land in his will, Washington wrote that the boy might as well begin to build on the land at once, since, 'if Mrs. Washington should survive me, there is a moral certainty of my dying without issue; and if I should be the longest liver, the matter, in my opinion, is hardly less certain; for while I retain the faculty of reasoning, I shall never marry a girl; and it is not probable that I should have children by a woman of an age suitable to my own.'

3

Washington was married in January, 1759. Thereafter, he took no further part in the French and Indian War. For the next sixteen years he lived at Mount Vernon, looking after his estates, buying new farms, speculating in Western lands, taking a seat in the Assembly, fox-hunting, improving the breed of his fox-hounds, entertaining his neighbours, shooting wild fowl, playing cards and billiards, attending the race meetings at An-napolis, and dancing at Assembly balls — the typical life of the wealthy Virginian of his day. That Washington was not unduly excited by the first signs of the quarrel with England is suggested by the fact that the only entry in his diary on May 30, 1765 — after he had listened, at the House of Burgesses, to Patrick Henry's famous 'if this be treason' speech — is the tranquil statement, 'Peter Green came to me a gardener.' The next day, having had time to ponder the words of the orator, his entry was equally succinct: 'Cut my Clover for Hay.'

This does not mean, however, that Washington was interested in nothing but his own crops, and hounds, and private life; it merely means that he was uninterested in politics. So long as his own affairs, and what he regarded as the natural development of the colonies, were not persistently thwarted, Washington would take no leading part in public life. His practical mind would not bother with political theory except when forced to do so by events; he had no ability as a public speaker, and no ambition to contend for popular favour. Nevertheless, his energy could not be satisfied with caring for his own estates. It sought an outlet, and the outlet it found was Western land development. This satisfied his two great passions: for property, and for the growth and fruition of what he believed should be a new and happier form of society. As early as 1770, Washington was planning for a canal to connect the Ohio and the Potomac Rivers, the great central valley and the Atlantic seaboard. Once that was accomplished and the Indians suppressed, settlement across the mountains would become practical and profitable, and North America would see the prosperous agricultural empire of Washington's desire. If there had been no War of Independence, Washington would have won a place in history as the first North American to see this vision in its larger implications, and to take practical steps to make the vision real.

The first important move that Washington made in this direction brought him hard against the interference of the English. This was unfortunate for the British Empire. To thwart the merchant-smugglers of Boston, and the lawyers and journalists of the whole Atlantic seaboard, was rash though not necessarily unwise; but it was fatal to thwart this calm, passionate Virginia planter, to teach him that he could not forward his new world until he had destroyed an old loyalty. The War of Independence was made by a few hundred men, and fought by a few thousand, but it could not have been won without George Washington.

When he first met British obstruction in the West, Washington was not inclined to take it seriously. In 1763 — the very year of the unfortunate Proclamation — he sent his land agent into the Ohio country, directing him to buy 'some of the most valuable lands in the King's part, which I think may be accomplished after a while, notwithstanding the proclamation that restrains it at present, and prohibits the settling of them at all; for I can never look upon that proclamation in any other light (but this I say between ourselves), than as a temporary expedient to quiet the minds of the Indians.' In 1774, however, came the Quebec Act, depriving the colonies of their hope to expand into the great triangle between the Ohio, the Lakes, and the Mississippi. The menace of the new English policy could no longer be dismissed as a 'temporary expedient.'

In considering Washington's motives for siding with the patriots against the English, it must be remembered that his Western land schemes not only turned him against the British Empire, but turned him toward the idea of an American nation, since that world across the mountains was too huge for one colony to exploit. If Washington's canal was to be built, if the West and the East were to become an economic unit, it was clear that they must become a political unit as well. So when Washington made his tardy appearance on the political stage, he made it as the first American — though he did not, in the beginning, see any need to leave the British Empire. As late as October, 1775, after he had become Commander-in-Chief of the rebel army, he was still opposed to independence. But from the moment when he decided to fight England rather than allow her to hamper colonial development, he began to think of the thirteen colonies as a unit, with a common destiny. He was opposing the British Empire, not to protect Virginian lawyers from a stamp tax, but to create the Western empire of his dreams. And to do that he had need of a united America.

Presumably, there were other and less stirring motives that inclined Washington to the side of the rebels. His resentment against the English attitude toward colonial officers was bitter and must have influenced his decision. The fact that Virginia society as a whole tended to side with the rebellion must also have affected him. But none of this would account for his sudden nationalism; so it seems fair to suppose that the larger reason was the dominating one.

Late in 1774 Washington attended the Continental Congress as a member of the Virginia deputation. He was the one member of the Congress to attend in uniform, from which it has been assumed that he was making a bid for the post of Commander-in-Chief. It seems more likely that he merely wished to draw attention to the fact that when, or if, the Congress got round to doing anything, he wanted a military and not a political post. Washington was never interested, or adroit, in political manœuvres, and he was unlikely to have foreseen the complicated calculations that led John Adams to have him nominated for Commander-in-Chief. Washington may have thought that the post would be given to the man of most military experience, which was certainly not himself. But John Adams knew better. The rebellion, up to this point, had been chiefly the work of New-Englanders, and Adams knew there would never be effective Southern support for a war waged under a New England general. Massachusetts would accept a Virginian, since Massachusetts was already committed to the war (the battles of Lexington and Concord were fought in April, 1775; the Commander-in-Chief was not appointed until June); but Virginia would not return the compliment. Also, the Commander-in-Chief had to be a rich man. New York, quaintly enough, had instructed her delegates that the general, in this war for man's inalienable rights, must be a man of fortune, in order 'that he may rather communicate lustre to his dignities than receive it, and that his country in his property, his kindred and connections, may have some pledge that he will faithfully perform the duties of his office.' Lastly, in addition to being rich and a Southerner, it was desirable that the general should have had some military experience. Washington had commanded as many as a hundred and fifty men in action; he had been an unofficial member of Braddock's staff; and in boyhood he had received instruction in tactics and swordsmanship from two old soldiers.

4

Washington was forty-three when he became Commander-in-Chief; he had reached full maturity, but had not yet lost any of his physical strength or hardihood.... The question of Washington's purely military capacities will probably never be settled, for his was not a strictly military task. He seldom had an army with which he could oppose the enemy in decisive battle, and he never had a united country behind him. His job was to keep an army of some sort in the field, and wait for the English to lose the war. This the English did, in spite of the fact that it often seemed impossible.

Taking the colonies as a whole, the active, militant patriots probably did not comprise more than a third of the white population of two and a half millions. Even so, the military effort made by this little group is not impressive. Hardly ever did Washington have more than ten thousand effectives under his command. For particular occasions, as at Saratoga, the militia would turn out in surprising numbers; but they could not be counted on in advance. It is no wonder, then, that the Tories throughout the colonies were inclined to overconfidence, that they felt there was no need for them to exert themselves, since the English army and navy would soon put down this rioting. The price they paid for their faith in the English army was impoverishment and exile.

The first reason for English failure was that the minister responsible for the war was Lord George Germain. This is the man who, under the name of Lord George Sackville, had disgraced himself at the battle of Minden, and had then been court-martialled and dismissed from the army as 'unfit to serve his Majesty in any military capacity whatsoever.' He had since changed his name, but not his character.... A second reason for failure was that the brothers Howe (one an admiral and one a general) were put in charge of operations. It was Admiral Howe who, when the Loyalists in America wished to fit out privateers to fight the privateers of the rebels, indignantly asked, 'Will you never have done oppressing these poor people?' It was General

Howe who, in 1776, having Washington's whole army at his mercy at New York, deliberately allowed it to escape with its wounded, its stores, and its artillery — apparently from a family distaste for 'oppressing these poor people.' The American General Putnam, who was present, wrote to the Governor of Connecticut, 'General Howe is either our friend or no General.' Presumably, he was a little of both. In the subsequent retreat across New Jersey, Washington could have been destroyed by any competent or active English commander. Washington's own comment was, 'Nothing was more easy to them, with a little enterprise and energy, than to dissipate the remaining force which still kept alive our expiring opposition.'

Howe's exploits in 1776, however, were good generalship compared to the display made by Howe, Clinton, Burgoyne, and Lord George Germain in the summer of 1777. A sensible plan of campaign had been worked out for that summer. General Burgoyne was leading an army south from Montreal to Albany; and General Howe, from New York, was expected to advance north to Albany, thus securing the Hudson Valley and the country to the north of it, isolating New England from the South, and preparing the way for a quick end to the war. Washington foresaw the plan, and admitted it would prove 'fatal to the interests and liberties of the United States'; but he had no force with which to oppose it. He need not have worried, however. Howe, and his subordinate Clinton, were jealous of Burgoyne, who they feared would take all credit for a victory to himself. The way to avoid this danger was to make sure that there would be no victory. Germain had already done his best to see to this by refusing to allow Burgoyne liberty of action in case he found the direct north-and-south route impenetrable. Then Howe made assurance doubly sure by putting his troops on board ship and sailing south, for the Chesapeake Bay, just when Burgoyne expected him to march north for Albany.[1] Howe (who was fol-

---

[1] The tradition, popularized by Mr. Shaw in the Preface to *The Devil's Disciple*, that Howe never received word of Burgoyne's movements, or of the plan for the

lowed south, on land, by a perplexed Washington) left General
Clinton in charge at New York, with the suggestion that he might
do something to help Burgoyne. Clinton waited until it seemed
safely too late; then, on the third of October, he started north
with three thousand men. By that time Burgoyne, at Saratoga,
was in a bad plight. He sent word to Clinton that he could not
hold out beyond October 12. Clinton, on the sixth of October,
captured the only fortified place that stood between him and the
army of General Gates, who was opposing Burgoyne. He thereupon wrote Burgoyne, 'I sincerely hope this little success of ours
may facilitate your operations' — and turned back toward New
York! On October 14, Burgoyne surrendered his entire army.
The victory of Saratoga brought France to the side of the Americans. England's colonies were lost. Lord George Germain was
subsequently made a viscount.

It was the treacherous slackness of the English commanders
that led to the defeat which induced France to enter the war;
but it was the prestige of Washington that made France willing
to co-operate in an efficient way. Had she merely sent troops,
but kept them jealously under control from Paris, the result
would have been the vain bickering and bad feeling that arose
between the English and the colonials during the French and
Indian War. But the French trusted Washington, and gave him
complete control of their men. Rochambeau's instructions read,
'It is left entirely to General Washington to dispose as he pleases
of the auxiliary troops sent to America,' and, 'All projects or plans
for the campaign or for private expeditions should be decided
upon by the American general'; but it was added that if the
French troops were not under Washington's personal command,
then it should be arranged that the French and American officers,
though acting in concert, should not give each other orders. The
French even went so far as to propose to send the money they

Hudson Valley campaign, is false. By July 5, at the latest, Howe knew what was
afoot. Germain had, however, neglected to send him hard-and-fast orders, so on
July 23, he sailed for the Chesapeake.

were lending America to Washington personally, rather than to Congress. This economical plan, however, was vetoed by Franklin, who knew it would not do to affront the already jealous Congress.

The French confidence in Washington, though obviously justified, is hard to understand. How did they know enough about him to have such trust? He had accomplished little up to this time. A few brilliant skirmishes, much perseverance, much fortitude in defeat — that was his war record up to 1778; and his pre-war record (aside from the *assassinat* of M. de Jumonville) was not one that would have attracted attention across the Atlantic. Yet Washington was already becoming a legend in France. Just as in his extreme youth he gave people the feeling that some unusual greatness was in store for him, so now, as the leader of a dwindling and much-defeated army, he impressed the French as a man to whom troops and money could wisely be trusted.

Another respect in which the French showed their wisdom is in the order from the Ministry of War that 'the French troops being only auxiliaries, should on this account yield precedence and the right to the American troops... [and] the American officers with equal rank and the same date of commission shall have the command.' Remembering the evil effect on colonial officers of the English stand in regard to military rank, this French order is seen to be a triumph of good sense. The French were obviously in the war for a purpose, and were more interested in encouraging the Americans to fight than in putting them in their places. In fact, with the arrival of the French troops, the English felt that an ugly note of professionalism was creeping into the war. These people were fighting to win, and not for the fun of the thing, or for the incidental horseplay (such as making a fellow-general look pretty silly by losing his army). The English refused to adapt themselves to these unsportsmanlike conditions, with the result that in the end, in spite of every advantage of men, supplies, ships, and experience, they managed to lose another army, under Cornwallis, at Yorktown. It was not so difficult to lose this army as it had been to lose Burgoyne's; but even so, the job could not have been done if the British navy had not contributed some rich mistakes. After Yorktown, in 1781, the game was up, although peace was not concluded for over a year.

Not even the sloth and jealousy of the British commanders could have lost the war unless there had been an American army by whom, from time to time, the English could get themselves beaten. And Washington alone was responsible for the existence of this army — that is, for the nucleus of regular troops without which nothing could have been accomplished. At Saratoga the regular army was helped by a swarm of local militia; but the militia would not have turned up for the crisis if the regular army had not been there. Similarly, at Yorktown, the French army (which numbered 7800, to 8800 Americans) could not have been there if Washington had not kept some sort of American army in the field. How he did so is one of the puzzles of history. His troops were unpaid, except for worthless paper and promises of distant land in a distant future. They were never properly clothed, and were at times shoeless. They were inadequately fed; and often they were faced with the discouraging knowledge that the farmers in the country where they were encamped resented selling them food in exchange for their bad Continental money, because they hoped to sell it to the English for real cash. It was this background of indifference — at times of hostility — that made Washington's task so hard. It is difficult to rouse men to enormous effort, at great personal sacrifice, for a country that does not care. What Washington really did was to rouse the men to make their effort for him personally. He would never have put it that way, but the men felt it that way; and because they felt it, there remained an American army.... Another thing that helped Washington to support the Revolution almost single-handed was his deep self-confidence. Although, throughout the war, he painted conditions in dark colours in his reports to Congress (since the facts admitted of no other colours being used), he seems really to have found it hard to believe that the cause he represented would not triumph. For example, during the terrible winter of 1777–78, when the remnant of Washington's army was in winter quarters at Valley Forge and it seemed certain that the rebellion was being starved and frozen into defeat, Washington wrote to his stepson, 'Lands are permanent — rising fast in value — and will be very dear when our independency is established.'

5

Toward the close of the War of Independence, the American States finally agreed upon a loose form of union, defined in the Articles of Confederation. This was little more than a league of independent States, for the central government had no direct authority, and could only petition the States for money, could only request them to carry out the provisions of such treaties as it was able to make with foreign powers. One result of this anarchic union was that the radical agrarian groups were able, in most of the States, to control their local governments and run them without regard to the interests of the country as a whole — and especially without regard to the interests of commerce and finance. Business suffered; foreign trade declined; and the value of every form of property, except farm property, was threatened with destruction. Since, however, the vast majority of Americans were farmers, it was hard to rouse the country to much concern over the plight of business. It seemed as if agrarian radicalism were uncontrollable, as if the rule of the Left must continue until the existing foundations of society were destroyed. Men of property and culture were soon regretting the comparative security of English rule. It was under these conditions, in 1787, that Washington was induced to emerge from the retirement into which he had gone so thankfully in 1783, and to become the guarantor of a counter-revolution.

To Washington, with his unpolitical mind, the movement he was now enticed into by the young economic genius, Alexander Hamilton, would never have presented itself as a counter-revolution. He was merely aware that the destiny he foresaw for the United States could not come about until the country had a strong government, and that Hamilton and his friends were working for such a government. So Washington was persuaded to work with them. 'Strong government,' as it was interpreted by the Hamiltonians, meant government by, and in the interests of, the business and professional classes (as opposed to government by, and in the interests of, the farmers and mechanics); but these underlying economic realities were not at first clear to Washington. This fact is shown by his attempt to organize his administration on a non-party basis, by his surprise when he found that Hamilton and Jefferson could not work together. When Washington joined the group demanding a stronger federal government, he considered that he was merely finishing the work he had begun when he joined the rebellion against England; he did not observe that at the same time he was undoing the work that certain other people had begun when they fomented the rebellion against England.

It was, significantly, an interference with his plans for Western land development that caused Washington to take action in support of the Federalists (as the supporters of a strong central government came to be called). In 1784, a year after resigning his commission as Commander-in-Chief, Washington set out on a trip through the Ohio and Kanawha River country to look into the condition of his own lands and to find out the best trade routes from the Ohio Basin to the east. This trip convinced him of what he had long believed, namely, that the whole vast country west of Virginia, between the mountains and the Mississippi, would be open to development the moment the Ohio River was connected by canal with the Potomac and the James. If some such connection were not made, the Western country would soon fill up with settlers anyway (indeed, it was already doing so); but with no outlet to the east, the Mississippi would become their trade route. And the mouth of the Mississippi, as well as the whole right bank, was in the hands of Spain. Washington foresaw the menace to his American dream if the time came, as it soon might, when Spain could offer the Westerners trade and prosperity, whereas the young United States could not.

The first step toward Washington's cherished canal scheme was to secure the co-operation of Virginia and Maryland, since the Potomac River was the boundary between these States and trade on the river could never run freely until the States agreed on duty charges, etc. In 1785, delegates from the two States met at Mount Vernon, and an agreement was reached. This meeting led to an effort to establish similar agreements between all the States of the Confederation (many of whom had been erecting tariff barriers against one another); and this, in turn, led to a Convention, in 1787, for the purpose of revising the Articles of Confederation. It was at this Convention, over which Washington presided, that the new Constitution of the United States was devised. Once again, therefore, Washington's concern with Western land development had led him to take part in a movement with far-reaching results.

Ever since peace had been made with England, Washington had desired a stronger union between the States. In 1783 he wrote to Hamilton, 'It is clearly my opinion, unless Congress have powers competent to all general purposes, that the distresses we have encountered, the expense we have incurred, and the blood we have spilt, will avail us nothing.' Washington did not, however, intend to take part in a political movement for this purpose. He had his own work to do at Mount Vernon, and the only part he foresaw for himself in public affairs was that of an adviser who would use his great personal influence on the side of the right. But when the Federalists were ready to make their attempt at a peaceful revolution, they needed Washington's active support if they were to have any chance to succeed. So Washington was drawn into politics, the activity for which he was temperamentally least fitted.

When Washington described himself as a man who inherited 'inferior endowments from nature,' he was not indulging in false

modesty, but telling what seemed to him to be the truth. His
talents, as he compared himself to the men with whom he had
worked, seemed distressingly few. He had no power to move
crowds, like Patrick Henry; no hard, intellectual brilliance, like
Hamilton; no speculative ability, like Jefferson; no erudition, like
John Adams. And whatever others might say, he was too realistic
to picture himself as a great general; he knew better than any
other man how much of his success he owed to Germain, and
Clinton, and the brothers Howe. In his own eyes, therefore,
Washington appeared a very simple man — direct, and unyielding, and with a tendency to think things through, but with few
natural advantages. His humility was genuine; and along with
it there went shyness, which explains his reserve of manner. Because of this humility and this shyness, Washington found it
unusually hard to face public abuse and misrepresentation. Yet
he was too wise to think that any man could take part in public
life without incurring such abuse. So it was with a sad mind that
he left Mount Vernon to become President of the United States.
'About ten o'clock,' he wrote in his diary, 'I bade adieu to Mount
Vernon, to private life and to domestic felicity, and with a mind
oppressed with more anxiety and painful sensations than I have
words to express, set out for New York.' As he travelled north,
he was met everywhere by crowds that gave way to a delirium of
hero-worship. Washington's comment on these outbursts was
that they 'filled my mind with sensations as painful (considering
the reverse of this scene, which may be the case after all my labour
to do good) as they were pleasing.'

The work that Washington had to leave unfinished at Mount
Vernon, each time that he was called away by public affairs, was
not simply that of a country gentleman administering a large
estate. Washington was aiming, by experiment and example, at
the reform of American husbandry. He had learned that in the
implements used, in the size of crops, and particularly in the size
of farm-animals, the United States was far behind England.
Washington studied the new books, corresponded with men like

Arthur Young in England, imported implements, and tried out new methods. This work seemed to him as important as any he could do for the welfare of the agricultural empire that he foresaw in North America; and it was work that he knew himself fitted for by training, taste, and character.

At Mount Vernon, Washington could carry out his experiments on a scale to make them informative. By the time of Washington's death the place contained eight thousand acres and stretched ten miles along the Potomac. Thirty-five hundred acres were in cultivation; there were more than two hundred slaves. Mount Vernon had its own carpenters, bricklayers, blacksmiths; its own distillery, where whiskey was made for sale as well as for consumption; its own cider-press; its own mill; its own schooner to take the flour to market; its own fisheries in the Potomac; and its own looms which wove textiles from its own wool and flax. The future America of which Washington dreamed would profit more, he felt, by what he could teach it from his researches at Mount Vernon than by anything he could do, with his inconspicuous gifts, in the alien world of politics. And yet in order that such an America should have the chance to come into being at all, he had to quit his little kingdom and take up a new profession at the age of fifty-seven.

Would Washington have made this painful sacrifice if he could have foreseen the America that would result from the work he was about to begin? Gloomy as were his forebodings when he travelled to New York through cheering villages, he was spared the suspicion of what a century of progress would bring. His dream was of an agricultural world. In 1788, the year before he became President, he wrote to Jefferson, 'I perfectly agree with you that... the introduction of anything which will divert our attention from agriculture must be extremely prejudicial if not ruinous to us.' Property, to Washington, meant land, which is why he was always zealous to defend it. Such cities as he foresaw in his dream of America were to be the complements, and not the antitheses, of the countryside — cities like the Casterbridge of Hardy's description, where 'bees and butterflies in the cornfields at the top of the town, who desired to get to the meads at the bottom, took no circuitous course, but flew straight down High Street without any apparent consciousness that they were traversing strange latitudes.' It is not pleasant to compare Washington's vision with the United States of today. The fork of the Allegheny and Monongahela Rivers, whence the young Washington and his frontiersmen planned to drive the French, was then the center of a fertile unravished West that made him feel Providence had designed this country for a new, benign experiment in human life. Today it is Pittsburgh, the center of a smoke-defiled kingdom of coal and steel, where Huns and Bulgars and Poles and Sicilians are finding a new depth of hardship and of lost hope.

6

If Washington were still dreaming of a purely agricultural United States, the men who had secured the adoption of the new Constitution, and the man who was to determine the economic policies of Washington's administration, had no such illusions. These men understood the economic forces at work under the surface of American life. They saw that the issue between the friends of a strong central government and the supporters of the old loose confederacy was not one of political theory, but of financial interest. The creditor, commercial, financial classes wanted a strong government that could compel the payment of debts, that could suppress paper money, that could pay off the Revolutionary bonded debt (most of which was by now in the hands of speculators), that could remove commercial restrictions between the States and make commercial treaties with foreign powers. The farmer and mechanic classes, however, wanted none of this. Their grievance against England had been that the British Government adopted precisely this policy, and having broken free from England they now expected cheap money, light taxation, and a liberal extension of mortgages. John Marshall, when the struggle for the adoption of the Constitution was at its height, described the friends and foes of the new form of government in terms which, though exaggerated, show how clearly the economic cleavage was seen by the leaders of the Federalist Party. He described the friends of the Constitution as people who believed that the distresses of individuals were 'to be alleviated only by industry and frugality, not by a relaxation of the laws or by a sacrifice of the rights of others.' Of those who wished to continue under the Articles of Confederation, he said, 'To exact a faithful compliance with contracts was, in their opinion, a harsh measure which the people would not bear.'

None of the radical leaders were present at the Philadelphia Convention that made the new Constitution. Jefferson was in Paris, as American Minister; Patrick Henry refused to attend; Samuel Adams was not chosen. The Convention consisted of the friends of property and business — merchants, lawyers, speculators in public lands and public securities. The Constitution that these men drew up had, in their opinion, two great merits: it provided for as strong a central government as the people could be persuaded to accept, and it made a bulwark against simple majority rule. The House of Representatives was to be elected by those who voted for the lower houses in the legislatures of the several States — which meant, for the most part, those who owned property. The Senate was to be appointed by the State Legislatures, by whatever method they saw fit. The President was to be chosen indirectly: each State was to appoint, or to elect (as it saw fit), a number of presidential electors (the number to be in proportion to its population); the electors were then to meet and choose whatever American seemed to them best fitted for the presidency. The anti-democratic tendencies of the Constitution may be summed up as follows: States (not citizens) were given equal representation in the Senate; the Southerners were given representation in the House of Representatives for three-fifths of their slaves; the President, in addition to being indirectly elected, had a veto over any act of the legislature not backed by a two-thirds majority; and a Supreme Court (with

members appointed for life) was given power [1] to nullify unconstitutional acts of the legislature.

Even after the adoption of this strong, conservative Constitution, the financial interests of the country did not feel themselves safe. Most Americans, after all, were still poor farmers,
and these farmers had shown themselves susceptible to radical,
inflationist propaganda. There was danger that the new government might be captured by the agrarians. Security could only
come, the counter-revolution could only be stabilized, if a large
capitalist class were quickly formed and if an economic policy
were adopted which would make as many people as possible feel
that their interests were identified with those of the capitalist
class. It was this which Alexander Hamilton, whom Washington
appointed Secretary of the Treasury, set himself to do. His chief
measures were the following: (a) he funded the entire national
debt, principal and interest, at its face value, and to this he added
all the State debts, which he induced the National Government
to assume; (b) he created a National Bank, with stock three-fourths
of which consisted of subscriptions in the recently funded six
per cent securities, and one-fourth in specie; (c) he adopted a
system of protective tariffs in the interests of American industry;
(d) he created a sinking fund to enable the Government to sustain the value of the public stock by purchasing securities when
necessary; (e) he adopted a policy of selling public lands in large
lots, as well as small, and accepting six per cent public securities
in payment. 'The upshot of the whole procedure,' writes Professor
Beard in *The Economic Origins of Jeffersonian Democracy*, 'from an
economic point of view, was the transformation of well-nigh
worthless public paper into substantial fluid capital to be employed in commerce, manufacturing, and the development of
Western lands. It was not merely the payment of the debt that
Hamilton had in mind; on the contrary, the sharp stimulation of
capital — banking, commerce, and manufactures —was an equally
fundamental part of his system.'

[1] Or possibly merely seized the power.

The beneficiaries of the Hamiltonian policies were: directly, the security-holding capitalists; indirectly, traders, commercial men, and industrialists in need of capital; and incidentally, land-owners who held unmortgaged property. These three groups made up what Hamilton described as the class who 'considered maxims of public credit as of the essence of good government, as intimately connected by the analogy and sympathy of principles with the security of property in general, and as forming an in-separable portion of the great system of public order.' It was a large and active class, and Hamilton, by making it feel that its interests were identified with the success of the new government, gave that government a stability, in the course of four years, such as few new states acquire in a generation. By his penetration to the economic realities of the situation, and his intelligent ex-ploitation of class interest, he showed himself one of the most effective statesmen of modern times. But the middle-class, capi-talist state that he founded with such startling speed was not cal-culated to forward Washington's dream of an agricultural empire.

Shortly after Washington's Administration got under way, Jefferson returned from France, whereupon Washington asked him to become Secretary of State. The agrarian, egalitarian Jefferson, full of the newest French ideas, was opposed to Hamil-ton in theory and in temperament. They disagreed with increas-ing bitterness at Cabinet meetings, until Jefferson, finding that Washington supported Hamilton on every important point, re-signed his office and set himself to create a party of opposition, a party that would seek to undo the centralizing, authoritarian, capitalistic, oligarchic counter-revolution of the Federalists.

It has been the custom to picture Washington as outside, or above, this Hamilton-Jefferson quarrel — a quarrel from which arose the two main parties of American political history. But Washington was not outside the quarrel; he was a firm supporter of Hamilton, and of all Hamilton's major policies. Even if he had understood the full economic consequences of Hamilton's statecraft, even if he had seen that his Secretary of the Treasury was fastening large-scale capitalism upon the country of which he himself had written that 'the introduction of anything which will divert our attention from agriculture must be extremely prejudicial if not ruinous to us,' Washington would probably have sided with Hamilton notwithstanding. For there was a temperamental affinity between Washington and Hamilton: both men were realistic and logical; both were authoritarian; both distrusted the political capacities of the common people; both had a strong love of property and a strong tendency to acquire more and more of it. The great division between them was that for the Virginia gentleman property meant land; for the self-made New York lawyer property meant paper. It was the difference between the old world and the new, and on this one point Washington and Jefferson saw eye to eye. But Jefferson's agrarianism was bound up with theories of equality and the rights of man; Washington's agrarianism was more that of a feudal landlord, or the owner of a Roman *latifundium*. He believed that Jefferson, by stirring up the people to agitate for their 'rights,' was endangering the life of the country. Of the 'Democratic Societies,' organized to protest against the conservative tenor of his administration, Washington wrote, 'If these self-created societies cannot be discontinued, they will destroy the government of the country.' And again, 'My opinion is that you could as soon scrub the blackamoor white as to change the principles of a professed Democrat, and that he will leave nothing unattempted to overturn the government of the country.' Also, Washington had no great opinion of Jefferson's abilities. For example, in a letter to Robert Livingston, in January, 1783, Washington wrote: 'What office is Mr. Jefferson appointed to that he has, you say, lately accepted? If it is that of commissioner of peace, I hope he will arrive too late to have any hand in it.' So Washington sided with Hamilton, feeling that the paramount need was for a strong and financially stable government. The geography of the country, he believed, would ensure that the United States remained agricultural.

After four years in office, Washington hoped to return to Mount

Vernon; but Hamilton insisted that he accept a second term as President. The repercussions of the French Revolution were beginning to be felt in America by 1792, when the Presidential elections were held. The Jeffersonian group was becoming more and more extreme in its demands for legislation in the interests of the poor, instead of in the interests of Hamilton's moneyed class. If Washington stepped down now, said Hamilton, the Jeffersonians might come to power and all the good work that had been accomplished might be undone. After another four years, however, capitalism and sound business principles would be safely entrenched. So, reluctantly, Washington stayed on in Philadelphia, where the Government was now seated pending the building of the new capital city on the Potomac. In addition to lending his support to the Hamiltonian fiscal measures, Washington wished, during the next four years, to keep his hands on foreign policy. He knew his country would be destroyed if it allowed itself to be dragged into the turmoil that was brewing in Europe. But the Jeffersonians were rabidly anti-English, and his own party was anti-French, and no one except himself seemed to know how weak the United States was and how quickly it would go under in a serious war. So he felt that at any cost he must remain in office and preserve neutrality. The cost proved to be a mad outburst of public hostility against himself. In 1794, John Jay was sent to England to negotiate a treaty settling various matters of dispute which had arisen from the treaty of 1783, and arranging for more favourable commercial relations between the two countries. The resulting treaty contained one offensive article, which the United States Senate struck out — the excision being accepted by England. For the rest, the treaty was as favourable as should have been expected by an unimportant little power negotiating with the mercantilist British Empire of those days. But it was made the excuse, among the American radicals, for an explosion of anti-English rage. Jay was burned in effigy; Washington was abused with a violence that would have seemed excessive had he been found to be in the pay of King George. Probably the agrarian radicals were working off against England the rage that they really felt against their own conservative government, whose financial policy was producing effects — so far as the farmers and labourers were concerned — similar to those of the pre-Revolutionary British policy. At any rate, Washington learned the full truth of his forebodings as to the fickleness and cruelty of the lunatic mob. Naturally, this did not incline him toward the party of democracy. In the last year of his life — the year before the elections in which Jefferson came to power — Washington, in a letter to Patrick Henry, described the growth of the Jeffersonian party as a crisis 'when everything dear and valuable to us is assailed, when this party hangs upon the wheels of government as a dead weight.' And in the same year he expressed similar anti-Republican feeling in a letter to his nephew. In the light of such evidence, it is foolish to describe Washington as a non-party man, or as holding the balance evenly between Hamilton and Jefferson. Washington was not so flaccid in the face of a fundamental issue.

On March 4, 1797, Washington attended the inauguration of John Adams as President, and five days later he left Philadelphia for Mount Vernon. The following year, when war with France threatened, Washington accepted the appointment as Commander-in-Chief of the American army. But the war did not come, so Washington had no further military duties. He devoted the last two years of his life to restoring order on his estates. In a letter written at this time he states 'that I begin my diurnal course with the sun, that if my hirelings are not in their places at that time I send them messages expressive of my sorrow for their indisposition, that, having put these wheels in motion, I examine the state of things further; and the more they are probed, the deeper I find the wounds are which my buildings have sustained by the absence and neglect of eight years.'

All his life, ever since his first expedition across the Blue Ridge Mountains, Washington had been subject to attacks of dysentery and malaria. These wasting sicknesses, combined with the excessive physical activity of campaigning, made him feel his years to the full. In December, 1799, at the age of sixty-seven, he developed an inflammation of the throat, following on a bad cold. Within two days he was dead.

CHAPTER II

JOHN ADAMS AND JEFFERSON

I

WHEN, in 1797, John Adams was inaugurated President of the United States, the retiring President was the center of public interest. Adams felt hurt and neglected. He was a vain man, and for years he had resented the pre-eminence of Washington in the regard of the people. Adams was one of the half-dozen men who had made the War of Independence. He had worked for colonial liberty for twelve years before Washington took a hand; and, when the time came for military action, it was Adams who caused Washington to be named Commander-in-Chief. No king-maker has ever lived gracefully in his second place.

> Thou shalt think,
> Though he divide the realm and give thee half,
> It is too little, helping him to all.

The contrast in personal appearance between the two men added to the cruel effect of the inauguration upon Adams's mind. Washington was tall and lean, Adams short and pudgy; Washington was dignified, Adams pompous; Washington looked like a great man, Adams like a fussy, short-tempered professor. As we know from his embarrassingly self-critical diary, Adams had ever since boyhood been awkwardly self-conscious about his appearance. And here he was, in the center of the stage, at what should have been one of the great rewarding moments of his career, and the public ignored him in favour of his more handsome and more famous rival.... Only by remembering that John Adams, for all his greatness, could be deeply hurt by such a situation, can the tragedy of the next four years be understood. If Adams felt abused and slighted on March 4, 1797, this was nothing to the fierce bitterness that drove him from Washington at dawn on March 4, 1801, to avoid attending the inauguration of his erstwhile friend, Thomas Jefferson.

The contrast in physical appearance between Washington and Adams was no greater than the contrast between the worlds the two men represented. It was Virginia planter society at its best, facing the best of Massachusetts Puritanism; and it is proper that the Virginian should have had a large dignity and the man from Massachusetts a worried, somewhat priggish air. The cantankerous self-criticism of the Puritan (whose life, unalleviated by ritual or ceremony, was lived forever in the Great Taskmaster's eye) led to a habit of suspicion and anxiety, lest he be overlooking some of his own faults, or some of his neighbours'. The best people in Massachusetts went in for the law, commerce, or the Calvinist Church — contentious callings that did not induce serenity; in Virginia, such people were landowners, or else lawyers who took their tone and their view of life from the planter aristocracy. The planters' lives were almost self-sufficient, economically. Once a year they would send tobacco to England, and order luxuries from their London agents. For the rest, they supplied their needs from their own estates. A result of this was that they thought in terms of the simple realities of existence, rather than in terms of money — hence their hospitality, a virtue that always tends to diminish in a money-society. The Boston merchant, if tempted to ask a visitor to linger for a week, would think of what this would cost him in shillings, and he could not help being aware that these shillings, if they were not lavished on a guest, could be invested, and would soon become even more shillings. But the Southerner, if he thought of what a visitor would cost him, would think in terms of potatoes, corn, butter, rum, and chickens. It would be unnatural to grudge such things as these, whereas money is made to be clutched and hoarded. And Puritanism is made for people who live by money, rather than by things. It came after the commercial and financial revolutions, the growth of cities, the joint-stock company, the legalization of usury. Its birth marks the end of those dark centuries during which feudalism and Christianity hampered business. It is the creed of the middle class. In the words of Mr. Santayana, 'contemplation

seems to it idleness, solitude selfishness, and poverty a sort of dis-
honourable punishment.' By contrast, the pagan Anglicanism
of the eighteenth century suited the earthbound, unbusinesslike
life of the South. Even the New-Englander could be charmed
by the tempo of that life. In 1799–1800, William Ellery Channing, with all Massachusetts on his conscience, spent twenty-one
months in Virginia. 'I blush for my own people,' he wrote home
from Richmond, 'when I compare the selfish prudence of a
Yankee with the generous confidence of a Virginian. Here I
find great vice, but greater virtues than I left behind me. There
is one single trait that attaches me to the people I live with more
than all the virtues of New England — they *love money less* than
we do; they are more disinterested.' Then his sense of responsibility reasserted itself, and he added, 'Could I but take from the
Virginians their sensuality and their slaves, I should think them
the greatest people in the world.'

In moral courage and in strength of character, there was
nothing to choose between the best of the two worlds. Washington and John Adams were equal there. And if grace and charm
were all on the side of the South, in intellectual power Adams was
the superior. He was the most learned man in American public
life until his own son surpassed him. His political philosophy was
as realistic — as well founded in economics and in a disillusioning
knowledge of history — as Hamilton's; and it was superior to
Hamilton's in that it was based on a conception of justice, and not
merely of expediency and of property rights. Adams knew his
superiority in these respects, and his desire to assert himself was
by no means merely selfish. But he was thwarted — partly by
Hamilton, partly by his own querulous pride. The tragedy was
as much his country's as his own.

2

John Adams belonged to the fourth generation of his family
to be born in Massachusetts, where a certain Henry Adams had
been granted land in 1636. The family had risen from poverty

to the possession of a small estate; but they had never gained a position of importance either in learning or in trade. Then, in October, 1735, John Adams was born. By some strange muta-tion, the yeoman family had become a nursery of greatness. Two of America's chief statesmen, her leading diplomat and her lead-ing historian: that is the Adams contribution, in direct descent, for the next four generations. More astonishing still has been the continuity of character throughout the family's history. From John Adams to his great-grandson they are all alike: sarcastic, self-critical, learned, tireless in work, confident, stubborn, sus-picious, regarding disinterested public service as the natural life of man, convinced that the Adamses know what God intends or earth and that whoever opposes an Adams is the ally of hell.

John Adams, as the eldest son, was given a college education. He graduated from Harvard in 1755. In those days, the students were ranked according to their social position, and Adams was fourteenth in a class of twenty-four — even that somewhat humble position being his by virtue of his mother's family, the Boylstons. He was intended for the ministry, but disappointed his elders by choosing the law instead. His temperament was wholly secular; and in addition, there was a Miltonic self-sufficiency about his mind that would have made him a recalcitrant member of any ministry.... There are some amusing entries in his diary for this period, which show that the life of a serious Massachusetts Puritan was not all work and no play. On one occasion, he writes: 'Friday, Saturday, Sunday, Monday. All spent in absolute idleness, or, which is worse, gallanting the girls.' And again, 'On a Sunday. I will read the Enquiry into the Nature of the Human Soul, and for amusement, I will sometimes read Ovid's Art of Love to Mrs. Savil.'

A few years after beginning his law practice, Adams married Abigail (Quincy) Smith — a woman of wide, humane learning, with all his own elevation of character, though quite without his vanity and ungraciousness. She is one of the great characters in her country's history; her letters are among its literary treasures, and her personal influence may account in part for the continued eminence of the Adams family. In addition to all this, she brought her husband a group of influential connections. His law-practice began at once to prosper. He would soon have been a man of wealth — something that no Adams, for the next three genera- tions, had time to become — had his marriage not coincided with the first rumblings of the quarrel with England.

From the moment he heard of England's new commercial pol- icy, and especially of the Stamp Act, Adams never hesitated as to the side he would take in the impending fight. He foresaw a long, unhappy struggle; he was one of the first to realize that if the colonies resisted, there was no logical end save war and in- dependence — and yet he never considered an alternative to resistance. In all sincerity he felt that a great wrong was being done, that tyranny was threatening a free people. He expressed this feeling so persuasively that to this day it is hard for Americans to realize that nothing more world-shaking was involved than local economic interest. No nation has ever solved the problem of administering an empire so that all its parts feel equally bene- fitted. Twentieth-century America has failed, in this task, as conspicuously as eighteenth-century England. 'In Alaska,' writes Mr. James Truslow Adams, 'we are, to a great extent, repeating the story of eighteenth-century misgovernment by England, to say nothing of the anomalies of our situation in Hawaii, the Philip- pines, Porto Rico, and our other overseas "possessions."' The Americans, nevertheless, would be surprised if an Alaskan leader arose to denounce them as tyrants and sworn enemies to the rights of man. What is it that explains the moral fervour in John Adams's resistance to the English trade laws?

In part, the explanation is to be found in one of the most per- sistent traits in the Adams family character: a suspicious, hostile attitude toward the outer world, a readiness to believe that all men's hands are, for some evil reason, turned against an Adams. In John Adams this trait was so strongly developed that at times it amounted almost to a persecution mania. In 1765, when the courts were closed as a result of the protest against the Stamp Act and the consequent refusal to buy stamps, Adams wrote in his diary: 'I was but just getting... under sail, and an embargo is laid upon the ship. Thirty years of my life are passed in preparation for business; I have had poverty to struggle with, envy and jealousy and malice of enemies to encounter, no friends, or but few, to assist me, so that I have groped in dark obscurity, till of late, and had but just become known and gained a small degree of reputation, when this execrable project was set on foot for my ruin as well as that of America in general, and of Great Britain.' If this outburst be compared with the facts, it is seen to be ludicrous in its inaccuracy. Adams had received, at his father's expense, the best education Massachusetts could offer. He had the love and support of the most remarkable woman in North America, and through her he had acquired rich friends and patrons. England, before embarking on her 'execrable project,' had pointed out to the colonies that she was burdened with a debt of £140,-000,000 — much of it acquired in their defence — and had asked them to suggest a scheme of voluntary co-operation in bearing a fraction of the burden. This they could not do. Yet, when a Stamp Tax was imposed, John Adams felt it was a plot on the part of King and Parliament to frustrate his young career, already hideously handicapped by 'envy and jealousy and malice of enemies.' Such ingenuity in discovering a grievance, and such rancour in nursing it, is a prerequisite for the successful leader of a revolution.

A second factor in Adams's decision was his apparent lack of feeling for the British Empire. The rich merchants of Boston knew the meaning of imperial patriotism; but Adams came from a family of poor farmers who never had contact with a larger world than Massachusetts. Years later, in explaining his conduct at the time of the Revolution, Adams wrote: 'I very deliberately, and indeed, solemnly, determined at all events to adhere to my principles in favour of my native country, which, indeed, was all the country I knew, or which had been known by my father, grandfather or great-grandfather.' He had, therefore, no problem of a divided allegiance. The British Empire was a harmless abstraction so long as it did not interfere with the career of John Adams. When it did interfere, its 'execrable project' was clearly the work of Satan. In opposing British 'tyranny,' however, Adams had no intention of forwarding a social revolution in the colonies. The passage just quoted, about his 'native country,' continues as follows: 'But, on the other hand, I never would deceive the people, nor conceal from them any essential truth, nor, especially, make myself subservient to any of their crimes, follies, or eccentricities.' Adams was disgusted with the rioting of the 'Sons of Liberty.' His idea of resistance was to draw up resolutions presenting the legal case for the colonies, to refuse obedience to the new regulations, and to prepare for the conflict that he saw was coming.

Adams's statesmanship is shown by the fact that from the first he saw that a war for independence was the necessary outcome of the course he and his fellow-patriots were following. For many years, while almost every other colonial leader preached compromise and reconciliation, Adams knew that no compromise was possible. He described the situation to himself with simple logic: there could be no government without taxation; taxation without representation was intolerable; effective colonial representation in the English Parliament was not possible. If these three propositions were admitted, there was but one conclusion: the colonies must govern themselves. There were many leaders who asserted the propositions daily, yet closed their minds to the conclusion.

3

In 1770, there came a dramatic test of Adams's vow not to bow before the people's 'crimes, follies, or eccentricities.' A mob of Boston patriots had attacked an English soldier on sentry duty with sticks and stones and verbal abuse. He called for aid, and was reinforced by a Captain Preston with six more soldiers. The mob increased in size and violence, finally frightening the soldiers into firing a volley, with the result that five men were killed. The officer and soldiers were arrested and tried for murder. Adams was asked to take charge of their defence. He accepted, in the face of violent mob hostility; and he secured his clients' acquittal. He was accused of having sold his 'country' for money, and the foolish charge was revived from time to time throughout his life. Actually, he had received £19–19–0, and had given the first of many proofs that no clamour and no threats could turn him from what he considered the service of right.

In 1774, Adams attended the First Continental Congress, meeting at Philadelphia to establish a common policy against England. By this time, freedom had become for him not merely the logical result of the policy of resistance, but a glorious end in itself. Submission, therefore had become ignominy. 'Should the opposition be suppressed,' he writes, 'should this country submit, what infamy and ruin! God forbid! Death in any form is less terrible.' And in a letter to his wife, he says: 'Frugality, economy, parsimony must be our refuge.... Let us eat potatoes and drink water. Let us wear canvas and undressed sheepskins, rather than submit to the unrighteous and ignominious domination that is prepared for us.' Surveying the issues with the detachment of today, it is hard to understand the violence of such language. Part of it, at least, must come from the Adams tendency to identify personal desires with the will of God, feeling that the moral law trembles when an Adams is thwarted.

In spite of the strength of his emotions, Adams had to refrain from advocating independence at the First Congress. The other colonial leaders were neither so logical nor so deeply moved as himself, and he feared he might scare them off if he kept reminding them of where they were heading. For the first and last time in his life, he managed to be somewhat diplomatic and restrained, reserving his real opinion of the shuffling, dilatory Congress for his letters to his wife. He had his reward the following year, at the Second Continental Congress; for by that time events were marching so fast that not even the leaders could refrain from noticing them. An avowed party of independence appeared in Congress, with John Adams at its head. His first aim was to induce Congress to adopt the unofficial army that was already besieging the British in Boston, and to appoint Washington Commander-in-Chief. By boldness of attack and characteristic willingness to accept full responsibility, he got his way; but it was not until more than a year later that his long effort to commit the colonies to independence was successful. The Declaration was written by Jefferson, and the motion of 'certain resolutions respecting independency' was made by Richard Henry Lee of Virginia; but the direction and organization of the campaign was Adams's, and in the debate on the Declaration, Adams was the whole strength of his side. Normally, he had no great merit as a public speaker; but when thoroughly aroused he lost all self-consciousness, and then his sincerity and learning and passion made him a true orator.

Immediately after the adoption of his programme of independence, Adams, with wise and characteristic pessimism, wrote as follows: 'If you imagine that I expect this Declaration will ward off calamities from this country, you are much mistaken. A bloody conflict we are destined to endure.... If you imagine that I flatter myself with happiness and halcyon days after a separation from Great Britain, you are mistaken again. I do not expect that our new government will be so quiet as I could wish, nor that happy harmony, confidence and affection between the colonies, that every good American ought to study and pray for, for a long time. But freedom is a counter-balance for poverty, discord, and war, and more.' Here again his statesmanship is shown by his power to see truly into the future. Knowing nothing of military affairs, he probably overestimated the colonies' chances of winning the war. But he had no rosy picture of the conditions that would then arise. He had watched the riotings of the Sons of Liberty; he had experienced the mob's fickleness when he defended Captain Preston; he believed that if the country he was calling into being was to prosper, it must have a strong, anti-democratic government, and he understood that with the destruction of the conservative English influence such a government would not be easy to establish. As early as 1773, he had criticized a statement sent by the Massachusetts legislature to the Royal Governor, saying that the report 'was full of very popular talk and of those democratical principles that have done so much mischief to this country.' On another occasion, he described democracy as 'the most ignoble, unjust and detestable form of government.' His most important published work, the *Discourse of Davilla*, is an onslaught on democracy; and as late as 1815. long after the triumph of Jeffersonianism, he wrote to John Taylor, 'Democracy has never been and never can be so desirable as aristocracy or monarchy, but while it lasts, is more bloody than either. Remember, democracy never lasts long. It soon wastes, exhausts, and murders itself. There never was a democracy that did not commit suicide.'

By most of the leaders of America in the late eighteenth century, these views were regarded as simple common sense. Hamilton's brief protest against democracy is well known: 'Your people, sir — your people is a great *beast!*' Gouverneur Morris made the same point more realistically: 'Give the votes to the people who have no property and they will sell them to the rich.' (New York's most distinguished cynic could not foresee the day when it would not even be necessary to pay for a man's vote, when the mere promise of future plunder would suffice.) Fisher Ames, three years after the triumph of Jefferson, wrote: 'Our country is too big for union, too sordid for patriotism, too democratic for liberty.... Its vice will govern it, by practicing upon its folly. This is ordained for democracies.' And once, feeling more than usually mournful, Ames remarked that democracy, like death, is 'only the dismal passport to a more dismal hereafter.' Another disgruntled New England worthy, George Cabot, stated, 'I hold democracy in its natural operation to be the government of the worst.' And again, 'If no man in New England could vote for legislators who was not possessed in his own right of $2000 value *in iand,* we could do something better.' Even among the Jeffersonians, there was surprising agreement on this point. Charles Pinckney of South Carolina advocated a property qualification of $100,000 for the President, of $50,000 for Justices of the Supreme Court, and of a proportionate sum for Members of Congress. And he said that the election of Representatives by popular vote was theoretical nonsense that would bring the councils of the United States into contempt. More surprising still, James Madison, Jefferson's close friend and follower, the man whom Jefferson chose to succeed him in the Presidency, held views as anti-democratic as those of John Adams, expressing them with clarity and concision — albeit anonymously — in the famous tenth number of the *Federalist.* In the Constitutional Convention, discussing the problem of suffrage, Madison stated: 'The Freeholders of the country would be the safest depositories of Republican liberty. In future times a great majority of the people will not only be without landed, but any other sort of property. These will either combine under the influence of their common situation; in which case, the rights of property and the public liberty will not be secure in their hands, or, which is more probable, they will become the tools of opulence and ambition; in which case there will be equal danger on another side.'

That a country whose leaders foresaw so clearly the dangers of democracy should have drifted helplessly and quickly into the worst abuses of that creed can only be explained on two counts: first, that the storm of the French Revolution gave an impetus (and also the sanction of great names and spectacular deeds) to the egalitarianism that would naturally be strong in a country with so large a frontier population as the United States; second, that the fathomless riches of North America offered a temptation for plunder such as no society could resist unless it were restrained by a unifying and powerful religion; but in order to embark on the plunder it was necessary to get the government out of the hands of men with a tradition of disinterestedness and responsibility.

4

Adams remained in Congress for more than a year after he had secured the recognition of independence as the colonial aim; but after July 4, 1776, the center of interest had shifted from Congress to the battlefields and to Europe, where the colonies were trying to raise money and allies. Late in 1777, Adams was ordered to Paris to join Franklin and Arthur Lee. On arriving in Paris, he quickly decided that three envoys were too many, so he secured Lee's transfer to Madrid, he himself returning home. There he took an active part in the Massachusetts Constitutional Convention which made the property qualification for voting double what it had been in the days of English rule. During his stay in Paris, Adams had made one important discovery, namely, that the French interest in America was not the romantic, disinterested emotion that his compatriots thought it. This knowledge stood him in good stead when, at the end of 1779, he was sent back to France, to be on hand in case peace negotiations were suggested by the English. Hope of such negotiations proving premature, Adams went to Amsterdam, where, after a long struggle, he succeeded in getting himself recognized as Minister from the United States. Finally, in 1783, came the peace conference, and Adams returned to Paris. There he was head of the American mission, which was supposed to consist of five members. But one member — Jefferson — never arrived, and another member — Laurens — came only at the very end. The work, therefore, was done by three men: Adams, Franklin, and John Jay. Their instructions were to undertake nothing without the knowledge and consent of the French, and to be guided by French advice and opinion. It was obvious at once that if this were done the United States would make a very poor peace — for the French did not wish to create too flourishing a nation across the Atlantic. Adams summed up their policy as follows, 'to deprive us of the grand fishery, the Mississippi river, the Western lands, and to saddle us with the Tories.' Unhesitatingly, Adams took the responsibility of disregarding instructions, he and Jay overruling Franklin on this point. By ignoring the French, and then presenting them with the *fait accompli* of a detailed agreement with England, the Americans secured a most favourable settlement, including the Western lands as far as the Mississippi, the right of navigation on that river, and the right to make use of the Newfoundland fisheries. For the latter point Adams fought alone and bitterly — which is one reason why, even when his fortunes were at their worst, New England never deserted him.

By securing these peace terms — in violation of his instructions and at the risk of disgrace if he had failed — Adams accomplished the last of the unclouded triumphs of his career. He had been one of the chief makers of the War of Independence; he had secured the appointment of Washington to command it; he had won recognition, and money, from Holland; he had made, in September, 1783, a peace as satisfying as could have been dreamed by any patriot. Thenceforward his life was to be a tangle of bitterness and increasing failure. One of his greatest achievements was still to come; but it was to be greeted, not with gratitude, but with hatred.

Before returning to take part in national politics, Adams spent another five years in Europe. Ordered to stay on to make a commercial treaty with England, he was later — in 1785 — appointed the first American Minister to Great Britain. At the court of George III he was treated with marked coldness, and he had the misfortune of representing a government which — under the Articles of Confederation — was manifestly and steadily ridiculous. It was also bankrupt — a fact which added to the contempt in which it was held by England. Adams was outraged by England's attitude toward her late colonies and toward himself; it is a mark of his political high-mindedness that he was soon to earn the hostility of his own countrymen by his Anglophile attitude on the issues raised by the French Revolution. In 1788, at the age of fifty-three, he resigned his post and returned home — too late to take part in the creation of the new Constitution, or in the battle for its adoption, but in time to be chosen Vice-President in the first election held under that Constitution.

5

At the beginning of this new period in Adams's career, he came into conflict with the schemes of Alexander Hamilton — an ugly forecast of the future. Circumstances had doomed these two men to enmity. There was nothing Adams could do to avoid it — or Hamilton either, unless he were willing to relinquish his claim to second place in America. Such an act, for all his greatness, was beyond him.... A West Indian, and of illegitimate birth, Hamilton was sent to America for his education, by friends who recognized his precocious power. Attending Kings College (now Columbia) in New York City, he was only nineteen when the War of Independence began. But already his mind was mature, his opinions fixed, and he had shown in controversy his deadly combination of clarity and ferocity. In the war he served on Washington's staff — thwarted of his desire for more active service by his indispensability to the Commander-in-Chief, who used him as secretary and diplomatic agent. Later, he was one of the first to forward the movement for a new Constitution, and by far the most important leader in the fight for its adoption. By 1788, when Adams returned to the United States, Hamilton was Washington's chief adviser; he was accepted by the rich throughout the North as America's political genius; he was expecting to enter Washington's Cabinet and there to build the new country according to his heart's desire, stepping into first place on Washington's retirement. His well-known contempt for the people and his West Indian birth made it doubtful if he could ever be President; but he intended to dominate the politics of the nation, and to rule her Presidents if he could not rule her directly himself. John Adams stood in the way of all these schemes. Hamilton, with his brilliance, his good looks, his courtly manners, his romantic youth, might be the favourite of wealth and society; but there was no question that in the gratitude and respect of the American public Adams stood next to Washington. And Adams would take orders from no man — least of all from Hamilton, whom he was, with his customary charity, to describe as 'the bastard brat of a Scotch pedlar.' Lastly, Hamilton could not hope to best Adams by the power of intellect, for in learning and in statesmanship Adams was at least his equal. Lacking the younger man's fire and persuasiveness, Adams was his superior in political wisdom. His politics were as realistic, as practical, as Hamilton's, and they were more humane and moral. The two men agreed on the need for a strong state and on the evil of democracy; but whereas Hamilton did not regard the capitalistic class, which it was his purpose to strengthen, as in any sense a danger to the state, Adams feared the aggression of the rich as much as the 'crimes, follies, or eccentricities' of the poor. He wrote, 'As to usurping other's rights, they are all three (i.e., the democratical, aristocratical, and monarchical portions of society) equally guilty when unlimited in power.' He agreed with Hamilton in admitting that society must be divided into the rich and the poor; but he went on to posit the need of preventing either class from exploiting the other, and all his political works are a discussion of schemes for accomplishing this end. His politics, in other words, were related to a moral concept ot justice. Hamilton s were not.

As the new government came into being, therefore, Hamilton was faced with the following state of affairs: Adams, as Vice-President, would have four years (perhaps eight years) of honourable obscurity; at the end of that time, he would expect to step into Washington's place; if he did so, he would go his own way, conceitedly unaware of the superior merits of Hamilton, and all Hamilton's fine work in creating the new government — all he hoped to do, in Washington's Cabinet, by way of stabilizing it — would merely go to increase John Adams's power. If this were allowed to happen, it might be sixteen years before Washington and Adams were both done with the Presidency — and that was too far ahead to look, even for a young man just past thirty. So Adams must be thwarted. With his usual efficiency, Hamilton began at once.

As the first election approached, it was felt that Washington would be the unanimous choice for President. It occurred to Hamilton that if the second votes of the electors were scattered among a number of candidates, so that Adams won the Vice-Presidency by as small a majority as possible, the gulf that separated him from Washington in the people's regard would be dramatically shown, and Adams would be brought down to earth, where he could safely be rivalled by ordinary men. Hamilton was able to accomplish this, and it had just the effect he had wished — both on Adams's self-conceit and on other men's opinion of him. It also called Adams's attention to Hamilton's hostility. Already ungracious about having to take second place to Washington, Adams was outraged at the thought of this upstart lawyer seeking to thwart him. At once there began an open war that led both men into folly and malignancy, tarnishing two otherwise splendid careers — a war that has been refought by three generations of American historians.

In spite of the quarrel, however, Adams preserved his sense of duty in public affairs. During his first term as Vice-President, the Senate was evenly divided between the supporters and the enemies of Hamilton's policies; therefore John Adams, as presiding officer, cast the deciding vote. On twenty separate occasions, he cast his vote for Hamilton's measures — and this in spite of his knowledge that the unpopularity of these measures would all come back upon his own head, since Washington had not yet been dragged into the mire of political abuse and men were afraid to attack Hamilton — both because of his own ferocious rejoinders and because he had a devoted personal following among the most powerful men in the country. Jefferson once described Adams, as 'disinterested as the Being who made him'; and so far as his public acts are concerned, this proud tribute from his political enemy is deserved.

At the end of Washington's second term, when the new President was to be chosen, Hamilton schemed among the electors to have Thomas Pinckney of South Carolina chosen instead of Adams. He could not come out openly for Pinckney, but tried to have

Pinckney's election appear an accident — a chance result of the constitutional provision that the electors were to vote for two candidates without specifying which was intended for which office, the candidate with the greatest number of votes becoming President, and the one with the next greatest number, Vice-President. Hamilton's plot failed; but it led to Adams being elected by a very few votes, and, as a result of the double-dealings within the Federalist Party, Thomas Jefferson, leader of the opposition party, became Vice-President. So on the day of Adams's inauguration, in addition to feeling wounded because the people ignored him in favour of Washington, Adams was full of rancour against the chief figure in his own party. The new Administration was beginning badly, and it had stormy problems to face.

6

During Adams's second term in the Vice-Presidency, Jefferson had been building up a party of opposition to the Hamiltonian, Federalist policies. The new party was agrarian, representing the protest of the landowner against the use of all the powers of government for fostering the banking and manufacturing class. Had Jefferson possessed as clear a mind as Hamilton, had he been able to keep steadily before him the economic issue, he might have led history's first successful stand of the farmer against the business man and the banker. The people were on his side; he had a genius for political management; but he never understood the implications of his own thoughts, and therefore he never had an integrated policy to oppose to the sharp, clear plans of Hamilton.

In his lifetime, Jefferson was worshipped and hated with even more violence than is usually lavished on a political leader. Since his death, historians have continued to show him either as saint or demagogue. There is material in his life, and in his writing, to suit either picture; yet clearly the historian's task is to combine these contradictions into a possible human figure.

Versatility is the chief quality of Jefferson's mind. He had an eager curiosity about every branch of human knowledge — except ethics and metaphysics — and his quickness of mind, his capacity for hard work, made it possible for him to explore all fields. He was an amateur of literature, with a fair knowledge of the classics, of English literature, and of French and Italian; natural philosophy and mathematics were his favourite subjects, and in the latter he had more than the talented amateur's knowledge. He possessed the fashionable eighteenth-century smattering of science, and in agriculture he was an acknowledged expert. In architecture, his æsthetic and his practical talents could work together, and some of his designs for buildings — notably at the University of Virginia — show eighteenth-century grace and dignity at their best. And Jefferson mirrors the eighteenth century in his religious beliefs. He was brought up, of course, in the Anglican faith. He retained belief in a Supreme Being, and the habit of occasional attendance at church, but defined his adult attitude to Christianity as follows: 'I am a Christian in the only sense in which Jesus wished anyone to be; sincerely attached to his doctrines in preference to all others, ascribing to him every *human* excellence; and believing he never claimed any other.'

With so much learning and so much practical knowledge, and with a speculative mind that delighted in generalities, it is no wonder Jefferson was a success in Parisian society. In addition to his versatility of mind, he had a delicacy that was almost feminine. All his life he shrank from personal unpleasantness, from direct contest. There was a gentleness about him, a need for friendship, a desire for sympathy, that probably accounts for a large part of his charm — the only good quality that his enemies have granted him. Jefferson's career would be incomprehensible if it were not for his charm. The strangest of political leaders, he wielded his autocratic power almost entirely by indirection. He had a group of devoted disciples — men of great ability, like Madison, or of fiery devotion, like John Randolph of Roanoke — and his dealings with the American people were almost entirely through the mediation of such men. He was a bad public speaker; except in an intimate group he had no magnetism of voice or person. Henry Adams says of him: 'As reserved as President Washington in the face of popular familiarities, he never showed himself in crowds. During the last thirty years of his life he was not seen in a Northern city, even during his Presidency; nor indeed was he seen at all except on horseback, or by his friends and visitors in his own house.' And yet Jefferson became a popular hero. He received utter confidence and trust, both from the people and from the politicians of his own party. For twelve years he ruled this party like an autocrat; his mild and indirect orders were obeyed with more precision than Napoleon could command. His enemies explained this by saying that he never ordered anything unless the majority was already in favour of it. This is partly true, for it is impossible to imagine Jefferson combatting a popular movement. If the people seemed to be deserting him, he would stand aside tranquilly and hold his peace, waiting for them to return. And they always did return. Somehow, through his endless letters or through his effect on personal friends, he had impressed his charm and benevolence upon the public. The people felt he was a delightful man who sincerely wished them well. In this they were quite right, and it is natural that their hearts should have gone out to him.

Exaggerated charm, however, is usually associated with softness of character, and in Jefferson's case the association held true. It is his lack of character that explains his seeming shiftiness and the contradictions of his conduct. A man of genuine good feeling, with the habit of treating his enemies generously, Jefferson committed one of the meanest acts in history: he made a collection of all the nasty rumours, the idle, malicious slander, that he could find — even at second or third hand — about Hamilton; and he left this unclean testament to be published after his death, when all the people who could disprove it were in their graves and he himself could no longer be called to account. A sincere hater of slavery, Jefferson answered a request to join the French Society for the Abolition of the Slave Trade by first painting a fearful picture of the horrors of the institution and then refusing to join the Society on the grounds that 'the influence and information of the friends of this proposition in France will be far above the need of my association.' In other words, it was one thing to dislike slavery, it was another thing to be committed to a practical stand on the matter.

Men like Washington and John Adams were all of a piece. In a moment of passion they might behave in a way they would afterward deplore; but they would not stoop to planned, deliberate malice; they would not cautiously refrain from taking too active a stand in favour of something in which they believed. Hamilton, perhaps, had no more of this bedrock of strength than Jefferson; but his dominating mind at least imposed consistency upon his career. Jefferson was as far from Hamilton's clarity as from Adams's character, so there was sad confusion to much that he said and did. Yet under it all there was a ground-tone of kindness, sympathy, cultivation, and a sustained desire to benefit his fellow-men. In his relations with his wife and children, his friends, and his slaves (who had a heart-lifting affection for him), this noble side of Jefferson's nature is uncontradicted.

7

The philosophy of Jefferson's party finds purest expression in the writings of John Taylor of Caroline County, Virginia. In opposition to Adams's thesis that an aristocracy of wealth must exist in every society, Taylor published *An Inquiry into the Principles and Policy of the Government of the United States*. In this, he contended that a true democracy — safe against both communism and capitalistic exploitation — could be founded on the basis of the landed interest. But no such democracy, he said, could exist side by side with a capitalistic aristocracy of 'paper and patronage, more numerous, more burdensome, unexposed to public jealousy by the badge of title, and not too honourable or high-spirited to use and serve executive power for the sake of

pillaging the people.' He described this group as 'without rank
or title; regardless of honour; of insatiable avarice.... After an
invasion, suspended rights may be resumed, ruined cities rebuilt,
and past cruelties forgotten; but in the oppression of an aristocracy of paper and patronage, there can be no respite; so long as
there is anything to get, it cannot be glutted with wealth; so
long as there is anything to fear, it cannot be glutted with power;
other tyrants die; this is immortal.'

The War of Independence had left practically all landholders
in debt; hence they tended to draw together in opposition to
Hamilton's creditor-class finance. It was the good fortune of the
agrarians that they possessed, in the Southern landowners, a group
with the cultural equipment for leadership. It was their misfortune that the political genius of this group should have been
Thomas Jefferson, a man who combined the philosophy of agrarianism with a deep distaste for authority and with an alarming
woolly-mindedness. Such a man could create a party capable of
ousting the party of Hamilton at the polls, but incapable of reorganizing society according to any plan or purpose.

Jefferson's theory of democracy, like John Taylor's, presupposed a system of landowning farmers, for Jefferson knew that
the growth of a large proletarian class would make equality and
democracy impossible. 'Generally speaking,' he wrote, 'the proportion which the aggregate of the other classes of citizens bears
in any state to that of its husbandmen, is the proportion of its
unsound to its healthy parts, and is a good enough barometer
whereby to measure its degree of corruption.' And again: 'For
the general operations of manufacture, let our workshops remain
in Europe. It is better to carry provisions and materials to workmen there, than to bring them to the provisions and materials,
and with them their manners and principles.... The mobs of
great cities add just so much to the support of pure government,
as sores do to the strength of the human body.... Were I to in-
dulge my own theory, I should wish them [the States] to practice
neither commerce nor navigation, but to stand with respect to

Europe precisely on the footing of China.' Elsewhere, he says that when the time comes that farming can no longer support the whole population of the United States, he would turn the surplus to the sea in preference to manufacture, adding, 'I consider the class of artificers [i.e., artisans] as the panders of vice, and the instruments by which the liberties of a country are generally over-turned.' The strength of this belief in Jefferson's mind is shown by his comment during a yellow-fever epidemic. 'Most evils,' he said, 'are the means of producing some good. The yellow fever will discourage the growth of great cities in our nation, and I view great cities as pestilential to the morals, the health, and the liberties of man.'

A community of small-scale farmers, such as Jefferson desired, might have governed themselves in the simple, *laissez-faire* state of Jefferson's dream. If his premises be granted, it is easy to sympathize with his plea for 'a wise and frugal government, which shall restrain men from injuring one another, which shall leave them otherwise free to regulate their own pursuits of industry and improvement, and shall not take from the mouth of labour the bread it has earned.' And it is easy to sympathize with his desire for political democracy, granted a world of independent landowners and a government whose activities were so simple that they could be grasped by the ordinary, untrained citizen.[1] It is less easy to sympathize with him for building his new party, not on the single foundation of agrarianism, but on a farmer-labour basis, appeal-ing for votes (in the name of egalitarianism) to the mechanic as well as to the landowner. When Jefferson was elected President, in 1800, he owed his victory to the fact that the State of New York turned its back on New England and voted with the agrarian South. And New York did this for no imaginable principle, but simply because Jefferson had allied himself with the Clinton-Burr-Livingston machine: a group of irresponsible careerists who were

[1] Jefferson wrote that 'good government springs from a common interest in public affairs, and that such common interest is possible only when the field of activities is circumscribed.'

delighted to join the new party of frugal government, convinced
that once they got into office they could interpret *laissez-faire* to
mean that they might do whatever they pleased.

Meanwhile, many years before his election as President, Jefferson had carried through a series of reforms in Virginia (such as
the abolition of entails and primogeniture, and the disestablishment of the Church), the net result of which had been to impover-
ish the gentry without increasing the welfare of the poorer farmers.
In other words, he had, so far as he was able, diminished the
power and prestige of the class from which the agrarians should
draw their leaders, and he then gave a vested interest in the
agrarian party to the carefree demagogues of New York City.
And yet Jefferson did all this with honest intent. He was led
astray by confusing the principles of agrarianism with a vague, abstract affection for humanity. Believing that city mobs were 'the
panders of vice,' and as useful to humanity as sores to the human
body, he formed a political party to prevent the growth of such a
class; but then, unhappily, he remembered some of his own
phrases anent the rights and the nobility of man — so he invited
the city mobs, with their demagogic bosses, to join his new party.

This same confusion of mind is shown in Jefferson's comments
on his own political career, years after his retirement. 'The cherishment of the people,' he writes, 'was our principle, the fear and
distrust of them, that of the other party.' And again: 'the sickly
weakly, timid man fears the people and is a Tory by nature. The
healthy, strong and bold, cherishes them and is formed a Whig
by nature.' But if Nature's Whigs confine their efforts to 'cherishing' the people, and do nothing toward creating the institutions
that might protect the rural society of their desire, it is only to
be expected that they will find themselves the slaves of Nature's
Business Men. To this planlessness, this substitution of good-will
for an economic programme, Jefferson added an unusual inco-
herence of thought. In his first inaugural message, for example,
he spoke of placing 'absolute acquiescence in the decision of the
majority.' And yet, in the same message there occurs the follow-

ing passage: 'All too will bear in mind this sacred principle, that though the will of the majority is in all cases to prevail, that will, to be rightful, must be reasonable; that the minority possess their equal rights, which equal laws must protect, and to violate which would be oppression.' The man who could write such sentences was capable, in good faith, of seeking to implement the conceptions of John Taylor of Caroline by means of political alliance with De Witt Clinton and Aaron Burr.

Shorn of its sentimental contaminations, Jeffersonian democracy simply meant 'the possession of the Federal Government by the agrarian masses led by an aristocracy of slave-owning planters, and the theoretical repudiation of the right to use the Government for the benefit of any capitalistic groups, fiscal, banking, or manufacturing.' [1] This theory was opposed, in the late seventeen-nineties, by two rival theories: first, by the Hamiltonian theory that stability and prosperity could only be assured by identifying government with the interests of the capitalistic class; and second, by the Adams theory that an aristocratic republic, administered by a governing class with traditions of disinterested public service, could preserve a balance, securing the welfare both of a moderately rich capitalist group and a moderately poor farmer-labour class. Hamilton's scheming prevented Adams from winning a trial for his system. Jefferson, by his failure to define his own intentions, prevented himself from winning a trial for his system. And the lamentable end of it all was that democratic, egalitarian principles suitable to the rural world of Jefferson's dream were grafted on to a greedy, middle-class Hamiltonian capitalism — but not until after another Adams had been defeated in the effort to build a true republic.

8

When Jefferson became Vice-President under Adams, he hoped to exploit the Adams-Hamilton quarrel, thus winning the President to a more sympathetic attitude toward his own plans. The

[1] Charles Beard, *The Economic Origins of Jeffersonian Democracy*, 467.

two men had been friends in the past, having worked together enthusiastically in the cause of independence. But their beliefs were now sharply opposed, and personal feeling could not obscure the fact to Adams. He went his own way, and soon became the most friendless figure in public life. The leaders of the Federalist Party — the men of money throughout the Union — idolized Hamilton, whose whole policy had been directed toward buying the country and presenting it to them. Adams, with his conceptions of justice and public service, made small appeal to their imaginations and less to their self-interest. They came to regard him through the eyes of Hamilton, as a tiresome old man, a legacy from Revolutionary days, who could not be pushed aside because of the sentimental hold he had on the voters of New England. But though they recognized that Adams had to be given his day, they felt that he should be kept from working mischief and that the real leadership of the party should remain with Hamilton, who had now retired to his law practice in New York.

Adams decided to retain Washington's Cabinet, as it had been reconstructed after the resignations of Hamilton and Jefferson. It was difficult, with the salaries that were then paid, to get good men to serve in the Cabinet; and Adams thought it better to keep men who had learned their jobs rather than experiment with untried friends of his own. It was a fatal mistake. The three effective members of the Cabinet — Pickering, Wolcott, and McHenry — were devoted followers of Hamilton. They began at once to betray Adams to the unofficial leader of his party, to frustrate him, to reveal Cabinet secrets, to take their orders from New York. The same attitude was adopted by the Federalist leaders in the Senate.

It was soon evident that, as a result of the French Revolution, foreign affairs were to become the major issue of Adams's Administration. Jefferson's new Democratic-Republican Party was naturally pro-revolutionary, and for political purposes the egalitarian elements in Jefferson's thought came to be emphasized more and more and the economic agrarianism less and less. As a result, the Federalists stressed the anti-democratic element in their creed. The Jeffersonians became violently pro-French, the Federalists pro-English. These passions were increased by the measures against American commerce that were adopted by both France and England; and among the rank and file of the two parties there grew up an insane desire to enter the European struggle. John Adams knew how fatal this would be to the weak and divided United States; but Hamilton — who had always believed that his true sphere was military leadership — was keen for war against the French, using his influence to force the Government in that direction. In the midst of this struggle there came news that made war seem inevitable.

Just before the close of Washington's Administration, Monroe, the American Minister in France, had been recalled on account of his too great friendliness for the Jacobins. General C. C. Pinckney had been sent in his place. Shortly after Adams's inauguration, news came that the French Directory (annoyed at the recall of their friend, Monroe) had refused to see Pinckney. Adams decided to send two other envoys to join Pinckney and to negotiate, as a commission, for the reopening of diplomatic relations. He chose Elbridge Gerry and John Marshall, who sailed for France in the summer of 1797. Arriving in Paris, the American Commissioners were asked to pay large bribes to Talleyrand and to certain members of the Directory. They were told that if this were done the French Government might be willing to treat with them. They rejected the proposal, whereupon a new decree was issued against American commerce. By the spring of 1798, Adams had full information of what had happened; he sent word to Congress that hope of accommodation with France was temporarily at an end. At once there came a party battle between Federalists and Jeffersonians in Congress, on the question of war with France. In the course of the battle, Congress demanded copies of all the dispatches, and when the President had supplied these, and Congress and the country learned how the American envoys had been treated, the war-fever became acute. A large

number of Jeffersonians deserted their party and joined with the
anti-French Federalists. Hitherto Adams, in seeking to restrain
his party, had been able to use the argument that the country
was not only weak but divided; but now it had become very
nearly united in begging Adams to go to war. He knew what an
outburst of cheap popularity would greet him if he did as he was
asked. His own party would accept his leadership; the feud with
Hamilton would be buried; at last he would be playing second to
no man. Years before, in his diary, Adams had written harshly
of himself, 'Vanity, I am sensible, is my cardinal vice and cardinal
folly.' But his cardinal virtue of disinterestedness was now to
prove stronger than his vice. He knew that his country might
be destroyed if it entered the European war; therefore, there
could be no excuse for entering, except on a matter of high prin
ciple. It was France who had been dishonoured by the presen
transaction; and the fact that France's temporary rulers wert
venal cynics was no reason for gambling with the life of the
United States. So Adams stood out against the storm, and instead
ot a war-President's popularity he won the angry contempt of
the people. Not even the pro-French Jeffersonians became more
friendly toward Adams, for during the time of war-frenzy he signed
two repressive measures fathered by the Federalists in the Senate
– an alien law and a sedition act. Both of these measures roused
the Jeffersonians to fury and led to resolutions by the States of
Kentucky and Virginia that contained the first sketch of the
famous States'-rights and nullification platform on which the
South was later to unite.

Another by-product of the war-scare was a fierce quarrel between Adams and Hamilton over who was to be the senior of the
three major-generals appointed as part of the preparation for
war. As he approached the end of his term, therefore, Adams's
feud with Hamilton was more bitter than ever; his entire party
was alienated; he had accomplished nothing in the way of establishing his own views of government in the place of Hamilton's.
The greatest act of his Administration had been received with

hatred. He had only one hope left: if he were re-elected, he might, in his second term, redeem the negative record of his first. By this time he had at last come to realize the perfidy of his Cabinet, and had rid himself of its two least harmful members — retaining Wolcott, who (as a more naturally dishonest man than either of the others) had betrayed Adams with such a smiling face that he was still regarded as a friend.

As the elections approached, Hamilton made a tour of New England, to discover whether it was necessary to let Adams be a candidate for a second time. To his disgust, he found that it was. The rich and powerful were willing to accept any man of Hamilton's choosing; but the lesser leaders, and the New England electorate as a whole, could not be trusted to stay in the Federalist Party if Adams were abandoned. So Adams was given his second chance; but Hamilton saw to it that it was a hopeless one. He wrote a long arraignment of the Adams Administration — making use of much confidential material supplied him by the genial Wolcott — the conclusion of which was that Adams was unfit for public office, but that Federalists had better vote for him anyhow, since he was the best they could get. Ostensibly, this was printed for private circulation; but a copy soon fell into Aaron Burr's hands, and was at once made public. The document cost Adams the election. Seventy-three electors voted for Jefferson and Burr, sixty-five for Adams, and sixty-four for Pinckney. That Adams should have done so well, in spite of Hamilton's fantastic contribution to the campaign, is a sign that the Adams character and conception of public service still made an appeal to the American people.

No such reflection, however, softened the bitterness of Adams's feelings. His last chance had gone from him, and he had accomplished nothing. His anger at Hamilton was terrible. And his anger at Jefferson was almost as great — for during the campaign Adams had been made a figure of fun — a pompous, pro-British tyrant, a monarchist at heart, whose only interest in public service was in the accumulation of honours. Unaccustomed to the savageness of democratic politics, Adams took all this to heart, and in his bitterness he felt that Jefferson had betrayed an old friendship. Adams's tendency to persecution-mania returned with dangerous force. Washington, Hamilton, Jefferson — they all had done evil to him; the people hated him; he had no friends. In his humiliation he could not face the triumph of his enemies. He sat working until the last hour of his last day as President, and then drove out of Washington at dawn, to avoid attending Jefferson's inauguration.[1]

Among the final acts of Adams's Administration, however, was one of the most important that he ever performed. After his dismissal of Pickering from the post of Secretary of State, he had appointed John Marshall to that office; then, toward the end of his Presidency, he raised Marshall to the Chief Justiceship of the United States. There were to be no more Federalist Presidents; but for the next generation an arch-Federalist was to interpret the Constitution. Mr. James Truslow Adams writes: 'By his nomination of Washington as Commander-in-Chief, Adams had made a nation possible. By his nomination of Marshall he gave, for centuries following, the fundamental law to that nation.'

9

By the time of the election of 1800, the constitutional plan for a free choice on the part of the presidential electors had been abandoned. The organization of parties made an end of that, and the electors became figureheads, registering the choice of the party leaders. The Jeffersonian electors, therefore, all voted for their party's two candidates, with the result that Jefferson and Burr were tied for first place. Under the original plan (altered by constitutional amendment as a result of this election) the electors did not specify which candidate they intended for President, and in the event of a tie the House of Representatives

[1] In November, 1800, the Government had settled in the emptiness and mud of this unfinished capital city: "This famed metropolis," as Tom Moore called it, "where fancy sees squares in morasses, obelisks in trees."

was to choose between the two leading candidates. But the Federalists still had enough power in the House to obstruct the election of either candidate; so it naturally occurred to them that it would be a pleasant political manœuvre to put Aaron Burr, whom nobody wanted, in the Presidency, and to send Jefferson, the creator of the party, back to the obscurity of the Vice-President's office. Hamilton, however, was still capable of large-mindedness on a question that did not concern Adams, so he used his influence to secure Jefferson's election. While so engaged, he gave a description of Jefferson's mind and character that remains an illuminating comment on that obscure subject. 'I admit,' he wrote, 'that his politics are tinctured with fanaticism; that he is too much in earnest with his democracy;... that he is crafty and persevering in his objects; that he is not scrupulous about the means of success, nor very mindful of truth, and that he is a contemptible hypocrite. But it is not true, as is alleged, that he is an enemy to the power of the Executive.... While we were in the Administration together, he was generally for a large construction of the executive authority and not backward to act upon it in cases which coincided with his views.... I have more than once made the reflection that, viewing himself as the reversioner, he was solicitous to come into the possession of a good estate. Nor is it true that Jefferson is zealot enough to do anything in pursuance of his principles which will contravene his popularity or his interest. He is as likely as any man I know to temporize — to calculate what will be likely to promote his own reputation and advantage; and the probable result of such a temper is the preservation of systems, though originally opposed, which, being once established, could not be overturned without danger to the person who did it.... Add to this that there is no fair reason to suppose him capable of being corrupted.'

These are the judgments of Jefferson's fiercest political enemy. And when Hamilton describes Jefferson as a 'contemptible hypocrite,' he is led astray by his inability to imagine a murky and illogical mind. But after allowing for all this, the Hamiltonian analysis — supplemented by a recognition of the many amiable qualities that Hamilton did not feel called upon to mention — provides a key to Jefferson's career as President.

10

According to tradition, the Jefferson family came from Snowden, in Wales. Although they were among the first settlers in Virginia, they remained obscure and unsuccessful until the time of Thomas Jefferson's father — a physical giant of a man who acquired nineteen hundred acres of land in the wilderness at the foot of the Blue Ridge Mountains, and who also married Jane Randolph, thus allying himself to one of the leading families of the colony. Thomas Jefferson, the eldest son of this marriage, was born in 1743. He spent his boyhood in what was, for those days, the wild West — only a hundred miles from the coast, yet inhabited by backwoodsmen to whom the democracy of the frontier seemed the one possible form of society. It was not until he entered William and Mary College, at the age of seventeen, that the boy had experience of the civilized life of tidewater Virginia. The college was at Williamsburg, the capital of the colony, where the great landowners came for the winter session of the legislature. Here Jefferson's Randolph blood made him free of the best houses. He quickly acquired the manners and tastes of society; but his politics and his social philosophy remained those of the frontier where he had passed his childhood.

In personal appearance, Jefferson was an interesting blend of the frontier and the planter types. He was over six feet tall, slender, loose-jointed, and ungraceful. He had a high forehead and high cheekbones, mild blue eyes, sandy hair verging on reddish, and a large, sensitive mouth. The first impression he made was one of awkwardness — a quality that was accentuated by his lounging way of sitting with one shoulder hunched higher than the other. Nevertheless, there was a dignity to Jefferson's bearing, and a cold reserve when among strangers, that was more in keeping with the Randolph than with the egalitarian.

At college, Jefferson acquired a classical education; but this did not rid his mind of vagueness and sentimentality. John Adams represents the Johnsonian eighteenth century, with its gruff common sense and pessimism; Jefferson represents the eighteenth century of dilettantism and sensibility, of the Noble Savage, and of Ossian — a poet who, for some years, was one of Jefferson's favourites.[1] After graduating from college, Jefferson studied law, beginning to practice in 1767. A successful lawyer, he was soon earning a good income at the bar and also making an unusual profit from his farms — having increased his land-holdings to five thousand acres and become the master of fifty-two slaves. In 1772, he married Martha Wayles Skelton, a young widow whose father shortly died and left a considerable fortune. By this time, Jefferson was moderately wealthy; but money had no more effect than society upon his deep-seated egalitarianism.

Soon after beginning his career at the bar, Jefferson became a member of the House of Burgesses. By this time the quarrel with England was well under way, and Jefferson joined the extremists on the side of resistance. Opposition to authority was a matter of temperament with Jefferson (years later he was to write that it would be well for his country to have some sort of rebellion every twenty years); the British Government was the upholder of a system of rank and privilege that offended his frontiersman instincts; and since living in Williamsburg he had come much under the influence of Patrick Henry.

As one of the most gifted among the radicals, Jefferson was sent, in 1775, to the Second Continental Congress. Lacking the logical mind of John Adams, he did not yet perceive that the course he was following must lead to independence. 'I would rather,' he wrote to his relative, John Randolph, the Loyalist Attorney-General of Virginia, 'be in dependence on Great Britain, properly limited, than on any other nation on earth, or than on no nation.' The words, 'properly limited,' make this

---

[1] He wrote to Macpherson for the Gaelic manuscript — planning to learn that language and make a translation of his own!

statement meaningless; for if England was to have no power of taxation, she could have no control over the colonies. By 'limited' dependence, Jefferson meant independence; but he was slow in reaching this conclusion. He reached it, however, in time to be nominated to draft the Declaration of Independence. As he was a bad public speaker, he had to leave the defence of his Declaration to John Adams, who secured its adoption almost unchanged. Congress did, however, strike out a passage in which Jefferson had denounced George III for encouraging the slave trade — a fortunate excision, since the trade was carried on by New England shipowners and supported by Southern purchasers.

The Declaration accepted, Jefferson refused re-election to Congress, returning to Virginia and the House of Burgesses. In this decision he gave proof for the first time of his political acumen — of that craftiness which Hamilton ascribed to him. He knew that now, during the first revolutionary excitement, was the time to strike if he was to remould the government of Virginia according to his frontier ideals. Everything conservative, everything authoritarian, could now be identified with the hated English. So Jefferson and his friends (including Madison) went ardently to work, the result of their efforts being the destruction of the basis of Virginia society. The only one of their reforms with which, for the time being, they could make no headway was the provision of educational facilities.

In 1780, after his work in the Virginia legislature, Jefferson became Governor of the State. It became his task to find men, arms, money, and provisions, and to counter the English invasions of the State. Ruthlessness and quick decision were required; Jefferson, having neither of these qualities, made a poor war-governor, and at the completion of his term the legislature showed its nice knowledge of the English tongue by thanking him for an 'impartial... and attentive administration.'

After this disillusioning term of office, Jefferson withdrew to his estate, in the administration of which he had always found his chief pleasure. Like Washington, he was an agricultural reformer, feeling that no more useful work could be performed than the improvement of a nation's husbandry. In making a list of his major achievements, he included the disestablishment of the Church in Virginia, the ending of entails, the drafting of the Declaration of Independence, and the importing of olive plants from Marseilles and of heavy upland rice from Africa.... His retirement to the land, however, was not to be happy on this occasion; for his wife, after giving birth to her sixth child, became seriously ill, dying after a four-months-long decline. This was a deep grief to Jefferson, whose marriage had been happy, although his home was sadly familiar with death — only two of his six children having survived infancy.

In 1783, Jefferson returned to public life, serving first as a member of the United States Congress and then, in the summer of 1784, going as American Minister to Paris. There he witnessed the gathering and the early stages of the French Revolution. His intellectual and social graces and his natural radicalism made him popular with Lafayette and his friends. By the time Jefferson left France, in 1789, his belief in liberty and equality had been confirmed. It seemed to him that the political principles he had learned from the backwoodsmen of Virginia were on the point of triumphing throughout the white man's world.

Returning home on what he hoped would be only a visit, Jefferson was induced, sharply against his will, to become Secretary of State in Washington's Cabinet. On first seeing a copy of the new Constitution, Jefferson had been inclined to disapprove of it as creating too strong a state; but the arguments of Madison had helped to bring him round, and in 1788 he wrote, 'I look forward to the general adoption of the new Constitution with anxiety, as necessary for us under present circumstances.' After a short time in Washington's Cabinet, where Hamilton was laying the foundations of a powerful capitalist state, his fears began to return — but before he clearly understood what Hamilton was up to he had been made use of by that astute young man. Jefferson joined the Cabinet just as the question of the Government's assumption of the States' war debts was dividing Congress. The capitalist North and East were in favour of Hamilton's measure; the agrarian South was opposed, and succeeded in defeating the bill. Meanwhile, the same groups were at odds on the question of the location of the new national capital. Hamilton proposed to Jefferson that he urge his Southern friends to accept a compromise, whereby the Northerners would vote for a capital on the Potomac River, and the Southerners, in return, for the assumption of State debts. As a result of Jefferson's influence, this was effected; but later he began to see that assumption was not a simple matter of paying honest debts, but an essential part of the Hamiltonian plan for making a federal league into a strong national government, and an agrarian into a capitalist state. As soon as this was clear to Jefferson, he was horrified at having helped the scheme along, and began complaining that he had been tricked by Hamilton — 'most ignorantly and innocently made to hold the candle.' Thenceforward he examined Hamilton's schemes with a more critical eye. But it was too late for caution; the work had been done. Jefferson made a bitter fight against the national bank through which Hamilton was to put the final touch to his system; but in spite of Jefferson's efforts, and those of his followers in Congress, the Bank Bill was passed; and in spite of his attempts to persuade Washington that it was unconstitutional, it was signed by the President.

As a result of the struggle over Hamilton's fiscal measures, and of the division of the whole nation into French and English sympathizers on the question of the French Revolution, Jefferson emerged, even while he was still Secretary of State, as the leader of an opposition party. When, in 1793, he resigned from the Cabinet and retired to his plantation, he had more free time to give to political organizing — chiefly at long distance, by means of letters. When he returned to public life in 1797, as Vice-President under John Adams, he was the head of a disciplined party. For the next four years Jefferson was the pleased spectator of the great quarrel between Adams and Hamilton. When the anti-French excitement was at its height, he watched his followers deserting to the pro-British Federalist camp; but he made no comment. When the war-mania had blown over, his followers returned, and the party prepared for the election of 1800. One important feature in this election was the opposition of Jefferson's party to the repressive Alien and Sedition Acts. Jefferson drafted a resolution declaring that these acts were a violation of the Constitution, and therefore null and void. The State Legislature of Kentucky passed this resolution, with its fateful implication that a State could review the acts of Congress and nullify any measure that it thought unconstitutional. Nothing came of this doctrine for many years; yet, in writing the Kentucky Resolution, Jefferson struck one of his few effective blows against the growing power of Hamilton's capitalist state. A manner in which that power could be challenged had been suggested. A bolder and a more logical man than Jefferson was to profit by the suggestion.

It has been the fashion, among admirers of Jefferson, to refer to the election of 1800 as a revolution, implying that some great reversal of policy followed on Jefferson's election. In fact, there was no important change. Hamilton's prediction that Jefferson would temporize, thus preserving a system of which he disapproved, was fulfilled. The Democratic-Republicans made no attempt to strike at the foundations of Federalist policy, i.e., at Hamilton's fiscal measures.[1] Accepting those, they accepted everything; for with a Federalist Chief Justice of the United States, and a Federalist system of finance, it was only a question of time before the business community would dominate America and the agrarians would have to choose between meek surrender and war.

Jefferson's Administration made a parade of simplicity. Rigid economy was practised at the expense of the army and navy, with the result that in the War of 1812 the United States was

[1] This abstention was so marked that Jefferson was accused of having bargained with the Federalists, when the election was before the House of Representatives, and of having promised not to interfere with the foundations of Federalist policy. The evidence is clear, however, that he did not commit himself in an improper way.

nearly helpless. The British Minister was scandalized and officially insulted by the carpet-slippers and unkempt clothes in which the President received him for his first audience. All this was doubtless popular, but it did not better the position of the land-owner *vis-à-vis* the business man, or of the poor man *vis-à-vis* the rich. Neither did it give anyone the vote. There were three main ideas for which the Democratic-Republican voters believed their party stood: political democracy, the cherishment of the people, agrarianism. On none of these points did Jefferson reverse the policy of the preceding Administrations.

Another of Hamilton's predictions was that Jefferson would not show himself averse to a large construction of executive authority. Here again Hamilton was right. Jefferson's most important act as President was done by an unconstitutional extension of executive power. If he had been the pedantic jurist that he had sometimes appeared to be, when opposing some act of which he disapproved, he could not have made the Louisiana Purchase.

So long as the infirm empire of Spain was the only neighbour of the United States to the west and south, Americans had no great fear either of being attacked or of being hampered in their use of the Mississippi. In 1795 a treaty with Spain had given the United States the right to trade through New Orleans. All seemed well, when suddenly — in 1802 — the port of New Orleans was closed, and at the same time it was learned that two years previously Spain had promised to cede to France the territory of Louisiana — i.e., all the land between Mexico and the Canadian border, and between the Mississippi River and the Rocky Mountains. Instantly the West was aroused to fight for its life, for if New Orleans were closed to Americans, the Western farmers would be ruined. And with Napoleon to confront, instead of the tired Spaniards, the prospects were not encouraging. Jefferson, with his frontier training, saw the importance of the issue. 'There is on the globe one single spot,' he wrote, 'the possessor of which is our natural and habitual enemy. It is New Orleans.... The day that France takes possession of New Orleans,... from that mo-

ment we must marry ourselves to the British fleet and nation.'
He undertook to buy the town, and sent Monroe to Paris to join
Livingston, the American Minister, in treating with Napoleon.
Congress made a special appropriation of $2,000,000. But before
Monroe arrived, Napoleon had decided to renew the European
war. Knowing that he must lose Louisiana to the superior English
fleet, and being, as always, in need of money, he astounded the
American Minister by offering to sell the whole of Louisiana for
about $15,000,000. The Americans accepted; but when the news
reached the United States, Jefferson was abashed. At first he
thought of taking no action until he had secured an amendment
to the Constitution authorizing this acquisition of territory; but
then his 'large construction of executive authority' asserted itself
and he decided to take Louisiana while the offer was good, and to
let the wisdom of the act be its constitutionality. Instructing his
followers in the legislature, Jefferson wrote, 'Whatever Congress
shall think it necessary to do should be done with as little debate
as possible, and particularly so as regards the constitutional
difficulty.'

At the election of 1804, Jefferson was the only serious candidate.
The Federalist Party had never recovered from the Adams-Hamilton fight; and the very fact that the 'Revolution of 1800' had
resulted in no important changes of policy discouraged the opposition. Jefferson won 162 votes in the Electoral College, and his
Federalist opponent won 14. But the second term, so easily obtained by Jefferson, was to prove a crown of thorns.

The one serious revolt within his party, during all his years of
leadership, occurred at the end of 1805, when John Randolph of
Roanoke — a wild, intransigent purist in politics — turned against
Jefferson on the ground that he was just another politician who
lived up to none of his professions. Randolph took eight or ten
men with him into opposition — their defection having no political, but some moral, significance. This revolt was soon overshadowed by foreign affairs, for the Napoleonic struggle in
Europe was reaching its critical stage, with the result that the

English and French were ruthless in suppressing neutral trade. The English, having a paramount navy, were more effective than the French, and it was against their depredations that American feelings were strongest. Jefferson attempted to coerce the English Government with an embargo act. Against the protest of the New England commercial interest, Jefferson's docile followers passed the act; but the English Government, so far from being coerced, was pleased to see American commerce committing suicide.... During the last year of his Presidency, Jefferson knew that the embargo had failed and that it should be repealed. But he could not bring himself to permit repeal, for if the failure of the embargo were admitted, the alternative policy of war might be demanded. And Jefferson's horror of violence and of authority made him unable to face the thought of war. He preferred doing nothing, leaving Madison, his successor, to deal with the dilemma.

On retiring for the last time to Monticello — the splendid house he had built himself on a hilltop near Charlottesville, Virginia — Jefferson did not withdraw from the public eye. His life for the next fifteen years was a perpetual popular levee. Uncommonly hospitable even for a Virginian,[1] he entertained relatives, friends, acquaintances, and mere travellers, on a magnificent scale. Often he had fifty people staying at his house. Captain Bacon, the steward of Monticello, described the scene with some bitterness: 'They... came in gangs, the whole family with carriage and riding horses and servants. We had thirty-six stalls for horses and only used about ten of them for the stock we kept there. Very often all of the rest were full, and I had to send horses off to another place. I have often sent a wagon-load of hay up to the stable, and the next morning there would not be enough left to make a bird's nest.' This way of living rapidly impoverished him, and in the last year of his life there was danger of all his estates, and of the house itself, being sold for debts. A popular subscription

---

[1] As a youth, he spent a romantic hour designing 'a small gothic temple of antique appearance' to be used as a burying-place for his family — one half of this unusual tomb to be appropriated for the family itself, the other half for the use of 'strangers,' etc.!

was started, and the house at least would undoubtedly have been saved had not Jefferson's death cut the movement short.

The most important work of his declining years was the founding of the University of Virginia. Jefferson induced the State Legislature to create and support this University, he himself selecting the best teachers he could find in the United States or Europe to occupy the first professorships, and being largely responsible for the design and the location of one of the finest and most appropriate groups of buildings in North America. The University was opened in 1825.

During the last years of his life, Jefferson had renewed relations with his old friend, John Adams. Except in the unhappy case of Hamilton, Jefferson was never given to nursing a grudge, and on hearing that Adams had made kindly remarks about him, Jefferson opened a correspondence that gave both men great pleasure during their declining days. Adams, since 1801, had been living in comparative obscurity on his farm at Quincy. On returning there immediately after his Presidency, he wrote to a friend: 'I found about 100 loads of sea-weed in my barnyard, and, recollecting Horace's

Et genus et virtus, nisi cum re, vilior alga est,

I thought I had made a good exchange, if Ulysses is an orthodox authority in this case, which I do not believe, of honours and virtues for manure.' For the most part, he maintained this philosophical temper through the quarter of a century that still remained to him. He did some controversial writing in defence of his Administration, attended the Massachusetts Convention for making a new constitution, and took great pleasure in watching the career of his son. Abigail Adams lived until 1818; John Adams until July 4, 1826. He was ninety-one when he died, and the old days must have been in his mind at the end, for the last words he spoke were, 'Thomas Jefferson still survives.' But he was wrong; a few hours earlier on that same fourth of July, Thomas Jefferson had died at Monticello.

CHAPTER III

MADISON, MONROE, AND JOHN QUINCY ADAMS

I

WHEN Jefferson made it clear that he had selected James Madison as his successor in the Presidency,[1] John Randolph of Roanoke made, on behalf of his small insurgent group, a bitter protest. The protest had no effect; but it contained an interesting comment on Madison's career. 'We ask for energy,' wrote Randolph, 'and we are told of his moderation; we ask for talent, and the reply is his unassuming merit; we ask what were his services in the cause of Public Liberty, and we are directed to the pages of the *Federalist*.' This is not so harsh an indictment as Randolph took it to be, for the pages contributed by Madison to the *Federalist* are an achievement of uncommon worth. They show Madison as a clear, far-sighted political thinker, with as firm a grasp as Hamilton on economic realities and with a wider awareness of the realities of American life. As a Virginian who had lived long in the North, Madison saw that the welfare of the two sections could never be served by a single system, and he predicted the ugly struggle that was to come.

In the days of the Articles of Confederation, Madison was one of the leaders of the movement for a more powerful form of national government. At the Philadelphia Convention, he was largely responsible for the Virginia Plan, which was the basis for the Constitution as finally adopted. And in the struggle for ratification, it was he who won a reluctant assent from the State of Virginia; it was he who induced Jefferson to give the new project

[1] When Washington retired from the Presidency at the end of his second term, he did so on the grounds of health and personal inclination; but when Jefferson retired, also after two terms, he did so on the ground that he thought no President should serve for more than eight years. He established a custom that has not yet been broken.

his blessing from Paris; and as a result of his contributions to the *Federalist*, his influence in the North was second only to that of Hamilton. Until Washington's first Administration got under way, Hamilton and Madison agreed on all major points of policy. They agreed that a Federal Government with power to operate directly on the people — instead of merely to treat with the sovereign States — was a necessity; they agreed in an economic interpretation of politics, in distrust of majority rule, and in zeal to frustrate the attacks of the masses upon the rights of property. Nevertheless, as soon as the Hamiltonian policy of Washington's Administration was defined, Madison, in the House of Representatives, went into opposition. He was one of the first to see the real meaning of Hamilton's plans, and he knew that with a strong central government administered in the interests of the capitalist class, his own section of the country must be sacrificed to the Northern business man. It was the ruthless capitalism of the Federalists that drove Madison into opposition — not their hatred of democracy, or their exaltation of private property. On the last two points Madison was in accord with them — only, as a Virginia gentleman, he thought of property in terms of land and animals, and not in terms of mortgages on the same. The true nature of Jeffersonian democracy — i.e., the fact that it stood for agrarianism rather than for modern political democracy — is shown by Jefferson's choice of Madison to carry on his work.

Although 'the pages of the *Federalist*' are, therefore, a more substantial claim to fame than John Randolph would have admitted, the rest of his jibe at Madison was fair enough. Moderation rather than energy, unassuming merit rather than talent, are displayed throughout his career. His great days were at the Philadelphia Convention; his feeblest days were at the White House. In 1811, Washington Irving attended a Presidential reception, and then wrote the following impressions of the Madisons in a letter to a friend: 'Mrs. Madison is a fine, portly, buxom dame, who has a smile and a pleasant word for everybody. Her sisters, Mrs. Cutts and Mrs. Washington, are like the two Merry

Wives of Windsor; but as to Jemmy Madison — Ah! poor Jemmy!
— he is but a withered little apple-John.' The phrase is uncom-
fortably true. Madison was small, quiet, precise, dressed neatly
and inconspicuously: black breeches, black silk stockings, pow-
dered hair. There was always something demure and meek
about his looks. In print he had authority and effectiveness; but
he had neither of these qualities as chief executive of the nation
during three years of war-scare and two years of misdirected war.

2

Madison's family, though not one of the most distinguished in
Virginia, was well-to-do and was reputed to be descended from
one of the colonists of 1623. Madison's father owned large estates
in Orange County, Virginia. In 1769, at the age of eighteen,
Madison went North to the College of New Jersey (later Princeton
University). After graduating he stayed on for a year, studying
for the ministry — a strange pursuit for this practical-minded
young man whose chief interest in religion appears to have been
a desire to deprive the Church in Virginia of its political support.
After this Northern interlude, Madison returned home, where he
continued his studies in theology and Hebrew.

In 1775, the first year of the war, Madison became chairman of
the Committee of Public Safety for Orange County; and the
next year he began his important public work, as delegate to
the State Convention to make a new constitution. It was in order
to attend this convention that Jefferson had refused re-election to
the Continental Congress, and here for the first time the two men
worked together. Their co-operation and their friendship were
to be lifelong. They made a strange pair. The matter-of-fact,
dispassionate, safe-minded Madison was an unlikely companion
for the visionary Jefferson, the versatile, unsteady genius with
his flair for a little knowledge and a large assumption. The
'withered little apple-John' must sometimes have been astonished at the wild and whirling mind of his political leader; yet
the two men seem never to have disagreed seriously. It is sig-

nificant, however, that the greatest deeds of Madison's life — his work in creating, and winning ratification for, the Constitution — were performed while Jefferson was out of the country, and for a cause of which Jefferson originally disapproved. As soon as Jefferson began to form his Democratic-Republican Party, Madison became the faithful lieutenant. In that office he did useful and distinguished work; but he never again approached greatness. And when he succeeded to Jefferson's position as President, he approached the reverse of greatness.

Between the close of the State Convention in Virginia, and the close of the War of Independence, Madison's career was undistinguished. In 1777, he failed — because of his prosaic refusal to distribute rum and punch — of election to the State Legislature. But he became a member of the Privy Council of State, and later was sent as a delegate to the Continental Congress. Immediately after the war, he entered the Virginia Legislature, where he opposed the paper-money inflationism of the radicals and the attempt to confiscate all the British debts. Then came the constitutional struggle, followed by his opposition, in the first Congress of the new government, to Hamilton's uncompromising aggrandizement of business interests.

In 1798, when Jefferson composed the famous Kentucky Resolution, in protest against the Alien and Sedition Acts, Madison composed a similar resolution for the Virginia Legislature. Madison's resolution was less extreme than Jefferson's.

Meanwhile, in 1794, Madison had married Dorothy Payne Todd, the widow of a Philadelphia lawyer. This was the 'fine, portly, buxom dame' of Washington Irving's description — a woman of charm and unusual social grace, who long outlived her husband, becoming an almost legendary figure in the Washington of the forties.

During the eight years of Jefferson's Presidency, Madison held the office of Secretary of State. The ill-fated embargo plan, which was finally left for him to liquidate, was largely of his devising; and it is fair to suppose that he encouraged Jefferson — or at least refrained from discouraging him — in allowing the army and navy to go completely to seed. The army was used as a place of retirement for politicians to whom some debt was due, but who were clearly too incompetent to be put in charge of a custom house, or even of a tollgate. As a result, when Madison succeeded to the Presidency in 1809, he found himself in charge of a country which, though obviously drifting toward war, had a contemptible army and the merest remnants of a navy. The situation demanded one of two decisions — either there should be a firm stand against war, with notice served on the 'War-Hawks' in Congress that the Administration would have none of their mischief, or else war should have been accepted as a probability and an attempt made to resuscitate the fighting forces. Madison made neither decision, with the result that in the end he found himself at war, but with no army.

The traditional view of the War of 1812 is that it was fought for the freedom of the seas, as a protest against the searches, captures, and impressments of American sailors by the British navy. Actually, all this was a pretext used by men who were bent on having war for reasons that had nothing to do with the sea. American shipowners, whose trade was hampered by the British depredations, were so averse to war that they undertook to prove that the Government's statements as to impressment outrages were much exaggerated. The men who demanded war came, not from the seacoast, but from the Western frontier, and their true motives were the desire to suppress the Indians who were under British protection, to corner the fur trade, and to acquire the farming lands of Canada. A more happy way of putting this latter point was the desire to implement the manifest purpose of God. 'The waters of the St. Lawrence and the Mississippi,' said one member of the House of Representatives, 'interlock in a number of places; and the great Disposer of Human Events intended those two rivers should belong to the same people.' To many of the Southern planters, it was equally clear that the Disposer of Human Events intended East and West Florida to belong to the United States, instead of to Spain, and it seemed probable that a war might hasten this arrangement.

So, in spite of the hostility of the seafaring sections of America, and in spite of Madison's pacific intentions, the young War-Hawks in Congress forced the conflict. Representatives of the mercantile and financial interests voted solidly against the war; representatives of the agricultural frontier voted solidly for it. Josiah Quincy, of Massachusetts, stated the facts in Congress: 'This war,' he declared, 'the measures which preceded it, and the mode of carrying it on, are all undeniably Southern and Western policy, and not the policy of the commercial States.' And on another occasion, he described the invasion of Canada as 'a cruel, wanton and wicked attack... upon an unoffending people, bound to the Americans by ties of blood and good neighbourhood.' Throughout New England, the contest was referred to as 'Mr. Madison's war.' And yet Jefferson was able to write, in good faith, to an English friend: 'Surely the world will acquit our Government from having sought it. Never before has there been an instance of a nation bearing so much as we have borne.'

Wanton and wicked the invasion of Canada may have been; but to describe it as cruel was needlessly flattering. The British resistance was organized and led by the Loyalists who had settled in Canada after being driven from their homes in the United States. But for their strenuous efforts, the scheme to annex Canada must have succeeded, since England was occupied with Napoleon. Naturally, however, the Loyalists had their hearts in the task of defence, whereas the war party in America was divided in purpose, the Southerners being only avid for Florida, and the Northwesterners for Canada. The result was a disgraceful series of defeats for the United States. 'In the conduct of this strange contest,' writes Professor Beard, 'the United States called out about fifty thousand regulars, ten thousand volunteers, and four hundred and fifty thousand militiamen [1] to cope with the British forces which at the moment of greatest strength did not exceed

[1] For a country with eight million inhabitants, this was a large army.

seventeen thousand disciplined soldiers.' Nevertheless, the British army was not destroyed, and no part of Canada was ever conquered. The only gratifying victory was won in the South, by Andrew Jackson against the British at New Orleans — but the practical, if not the moral, value of this victory was diminished by the fact that before it took place peace had already been signed.

On the sea, the tiny American navy and the numerous American privateers rendered a good account of themselves. But the only result was to wake the British Admiralty to the realization that a war was taking place; thereupon, the English made devastating use of their sea power, blockading the Atlantic Coast with complete effectiveness. And it is worth noting that until 1814 Massachusetts was exempted from this blockade — the feeling being that New-Englanders were more friends than foes, and that if gently treated they might return to their British allegiance. The meaningless contest was finally brought to an end, in December, 1814, by a peace treaty which made no mention of any of the alleged causes of the war. Madison's Government, however, which was well on its way toward bankruptcy, was delighted to be out of the struggle on terms which were not humiliating. When news of the peace reached the United States, the people indulged in an hilarious celebration, and from that day to this the American nation has been convinced that it defeated the English for a second time.

A few months after the declaration of war, Madison was reelected President. Since 1811, James Monroe had been Secretary of State. He had proved himself the one man of real merit in the Cabinet, and when the War Department had become the most important feature of the Government, Monroe added that department to his own, winning, by contrast with the generals and with his colleagues in the Cabinet, a reputation for efficiency and force. When, therefore, it became time for Madison to retire, at the end of his second term, Monroe was the obvious candidate of his party. And the candidate of the Democratic-Republican Party was the only candidate who counted, for the Federalist

Party, sickening ever since the Hamilton-Adams quarrel, had almost died of its opposition to the War of 1812. For that war, as soon as it ended, was taken to the hearts of the people and made into a glorious episode. A new, brash nationalism seized upon the country, and the Federalist stand against 'Mr. Madison's War' made the party look unpatriotic. James Monroe, therefore, was elected with little opposition.

Madison, who had found his executive post a harsh, thankless experience, and who must have felt that the peace of 1814 (and the public reception thereof) had rescued him from disaster almost by a miracle, retired gratefully to Montpelier, his estate in Orange County, Virginia. Except for the fact that he was not the centre of quite such embarrassing and expensive public enthusiasm, his remaining years were similar to those of his old friend, Jefferson. The Madisons, at Montpelier, entertained with Virginian liberality. In 1820, Mrs. Madison wrote to her sister: 'Yesterday we had ninety persons to dine with us at one table, fixed on the lawn, under a large arbour.' And the Madisons also indulged in agricultural experiments — the result, as in the case of Jefferson, being financial difficulties. These were aggravated, in Madison's case, by the extravagances of his stepson; yet he managed to avoid the complete collapse that overtook Jefferson's fortunes and to live undisturbed among his books and his farm problems until his death in 1836.

Except for attendance at the State Constitutional Convention of 1829, Madison took no part in public affairs after his release from the Presidency. By temperament he was a scholar and a country gentleman. Stirring events had dragged him into active life, and his association with Jefferson had kept him there; but never, except in the intellectual work of constitution-making, had he been at home in the world of politics.

3

The twelve years following Madison's retirement from public life, during which Monroe was President for two terms and

J. Q. Adams for one, are among the most momentous years of American history. The first two-thirds of the period did not express, in political terms, the revolution that was taking place in America; but during the last four years the issues began to be fought out savagely in the open. With the defeat of Adams, in 1828, the America of the founding fathers died; the America of the Civil War was born. Two new and mighty forces produced the transformation of the United States after the War of 1812: the Industrial Revolution and the rise of the new West. There was a brief, fierce struggle to determine whether the inevitable changes should be directed and controlled by statesmanship, or whether they were to grow haphazard. The triumph of Jacksonian democracy meant that the country was committed to the latter course.

The South changed more dramatically, during these twelve years, than any other section of the country.[1] The Industrial Revolution in England had created a vast textile industry, demanding hitherto unimagined quantities of cotton. And the cotton-gin, invented in 1793, was making it possible for the South to supply this demand. Also, the gin was opening up a new empire for the cotton-grower. Before the invention of the gin, the only cotton that could be grown in the upland districts (the short-staple cotton) was economically useless, since the labour of picking the seeds from it by hand made the cost prohibitive. The gin, however, made short-staple cotton marketable, enabling the Southern planter to move west from the exhausted soil of the tidewater region. The figures are impressive: in 1791, tidewater South Carolina and Georgia produced practically the whole American cotton crop of 2,000,000 pounds. By 1826, the old South was producing 180,000,000 pounds, and the new Southwest 150,000-000; a few years later, the old South produced 160,000,000, and the Southwest 297,000,000 pounds.

[1] The classic description of the economic revolution in the United States during these years is to be found in F. J. Turner's *The Rise of the New West*, from which come many of the facts that are here presented.

One result of all this was that slavery changed from a dying to a vigorous institution, and that Southerners stopped regarding slavery as the transitional status of the Negro and came to look upon it as his permanent lot. With the exhaustion of the land in tidewater Virginia, slavery had begun to be a burden on the masters. The old Virginia planter was being ruined — witness the financial difficulties of Jefferson and Madison and the still greater disaster that overtook Monroe. Things were reaching such a pass that John Randolph prophesied the time was coming when masters would be running away from their slaves and the slaves be advertising for them in the newspaper. But with the sudden rise to power of King Cotton, the Virginians, who lived too far north to grow this crop, had a chance to recoup their fortunes by breeding slaves and selling them to the prosperous planters of the Gulf States. And when economic leadership had passed to the deep South, political leadership soon followed. The Virginia group — Washington, Jefferson, Madison, Marshall, John Randolph, Monroe — were succeeded by such men as Calhoun and Hayne and Crawford, from South Carolina and Georgia.

Still another result of the spread of cotton-growing was the unification — economic and political — of the entire South. Hitherto, the tidewater planters, with their staple crops and slaves, had been at odds with the frontier settlers in the uplands, who raised livestock, wheat, and corn. The seaboard counties had kept political control of their States by refusing to allow the frontiersmen representation in proportion to their numbers. But as cotton-growing, and hence slavery, spread into the uplands, this political friction lessened. The backwoodsmen of mixed stock — English, French-Huguenot, Scotch-Irish, and German — were assimilated by the old South, and the farmer-type gave way to the planter. John Calhoun, the greatest Southern leader between the War of 1812 and the Civil War, the idol of his whole section and the creator of the new Southern political philosophy, was the grandson of a Scotch-Irish settler of the eighteenth century.

This unified, staple-producing, slave-holding South depended
for its prosperity upon trade with England. Meanwhile, the new
industrialism in the North was producing a revolution which
would soon leave New England and the Middle States dependent
for their prosperity upon a high tariff. The Jefferson-Madison
Embargo Act and the War of 1812 had stimulated manufacturing
in the North,[1] and at the same time had struck at the prosperity
of New England's shipping. By the eighteen-twenties, the mercantile interest was waning, and by the end of that decade New
England was solid for a protective tariff, at just the time when the
South had come to realize that its salvation lay in free trade.
And at the same time, to the west of the Appalachian Mountains
an even more far-reaching change was under way. In 1811, the
first steamboat had been launched in the Western waters; and by
1825 the Erie Canal was completed, connecting the East, via
the Hudson River, with the West, via the Great Lakes. Immediately the flow of population into the Ohio Valley increased, for
the mountains no longer isolated that huge district from the outside world.

South of the Ohio River, the States of Kentucky and Tennessee
had entered the Union while Washington was still President; and
along the Gulf of Mexico, where the mountains were not a barrier,
westward expansion followed immediately on the rise of King
Cotton; but north of the Ohio an improvement in communications was necessary before the country could attract heavy settlement. However, the same industrial revolution that gave the
South its cotton kingdom also provided these improved communications; so between Jefferson's Presidency and the end of
Monroe's first term six States were added to the Union: Alabama,
Mississippi, and Louisiana along the Gulf of Mexico; Ohio,
Indiana, and Illinois north of the Ohio River. With this beginning of large-scale westward expansion, three vital issues were
forced upon the country.

[1] In 1807, there were 8000 cotton spindles in the United States; in 1815, there were
500,000.

The first issue was democracy. The simpler conditions of life in the new country made for social and political equality. All the new States in the North, and most of those in the South, adopted constitutions providing for white manhood suffrage. This created a demand for similar concessions in the older States, and it was clear that the demand would not be resisted. As more and more democratically governed Western States joined the Union, the little group of seaboard republics, with their ruling-class traditions, would have to give way. Geographic conditions had committed the United States to the democratic experiment, in spite of a contempt for that form of government on the part of almost all the statesmen who founded the new country. It only remained to see whether the forebodings of those states-men were justified, whether, as the country became a political democracy, it would prove impossible to keep government in the hands of such trained and comparatively disinterested men as had dominated American politics during the first gener-ation.

The second issue created by the rise of the new West was that of slavery. The original thirteen States could have lived side by side, half slave and half free, indefinitely. They were divided by economic interests, but this division was not aggravated by the slave question. However, as soon as westward expansion became a formidable movement, two new problems arose in regard to slavery. The first had to do with the control of the National Gov-ernment. Hitherto, the agrarian, slave-holding South and the capitalistic North, with its more customary wage-slavery, had been almost evenly balanced in the Senate — with the result that each section felt it could block, in that upper chamber, such laws as were wholly hostile to its interests. But as new States entered the Union, this balance was continually threatened. For the new free States, although agricultural, were not staple-pro-ducing, and were therefore not dependent for their prosperity upon foreign trade. Hence they were quite as likely to side with the Northern financial interests as with the free-trade South....

And the second new slavery problem produced by westward expansion arose from the impossibility of the slave-worked plantation system existing in the same State with a system of small independent farmers. This meant that there was keen rivalry between the Southern planters and the Northern farmers for possession of the new lands. They could not share them, side by side; they had to divide them, State by State.

These problems were presented in an acute form in 1819, when Missouri applied for admission to the Union with a constitution favouring slavery. Missouri lay almost wholly north of the then dividing line between slave and free States, and the Northerners feared that if the slave system were introduced there, it would menace both the balance of power in the Senate and the future westward expansion of Northern settlers.[1] An attempt was made to provide for the liberation of Missouri's slaves, and at once passion rose high on both sides. The country was shocked to realize how dangerous the issue was. 'This momentous question,' wrote the ageing Jefferson, 'like a fire-bell in the night, awakened and filled me with terror. I considered it at once as the knell of the Union.' For the time being, a compromise was effected. Missouri was admitted as a slave-holding State, but in the remaining land belonging to the United States, slavery was prohibited north of latitude 36° 30′ — i.e., north of the southern boundary of Missouri.

In addition to democracy and slavery, the rise of the West forced upon the country still a third vital issue, namely, the method of disposing of the vast public domain. Was this great empire simply to be handed over to 'the people' — a course which, as the statesmen of the day were aware, would mean that the public property would for the most part be exploited by a rapacious few; or was this property to be fostered and developed according to some system, so that the new wealth that must accrue from it would go, not to the private speculator, but into the

---

[1] The issue, in other words, was wholly economic and had nothing to do with the morality of slavery.

public treasury, where it could be used for education and social betterment? In the language of the demagogues of the day, this latter course meant that the public land was to be guarded as if it were a King's Forest. As it turned out, the public-land question was settled by the triumph of democracy. The new type of politician who then rose to power could not keep his hands off such imperial plunder.

4

The eight years of Monroe's Presidency, 1817–1825, while these far-reaching issues were shaping themselves, were for the most part years of superficial tranquillity. The sudden flame-up of the Missouri issue was a sign that all was not quiet beneath the surface; but aside from that, foreign affairs, which were in the capable hands of J. Q. Adams, provided the only obviously dramatic issues of Monroe's Administration. For such a period of readjustment and realignment of forces, Monroe made an ideal President.

The last of the 'Virginia Dynasty,' James Monroe was born at Monroe's Creek, Westmoreland County, in 1758. He appears to have been descended from an Andrew Monroe, a major in the royal army, who settled in Westmoreland County in 1660. His mother was of Welsh descent. At the age of sixteen, Monroe entered William and Mary College; but two years later he left college to take part in the War of Independence, becoming a lieutenant in a Virginia regiment. In 1780, lack of troops made his services as officer superfluous and he retired to the study of law, under the direction of Jefferson, who was then Governor of Virginia. Monroe never lost the friendship and support of Jefferson, and his actions and opinions were always much influenced by those of his older and more brilliant friend.

At the age of twenty-four, Monroe entered the Virginia House of Delegates. When the war ended, he was sent to the Confederate Congress, and while attending Congress in New York he married Miss Eliza Kortright, a young lady of property and social position.[1] After three years in Congress, he began a law practice in Fredericksburg, Virginia, but was soon returned to public life, being sent to the United States Senate during Washington's first Administration. He quickly became one of the leading opponents of the Hamiltonian policies, and was therefore surprised when, in 1794, Washington appointed him United States Minister to France. In Paris he was very popular, with his Jeffersonian ideas and his undiplomatic tendency to explain away the unpopular acts of his Government on the ground that the faction in power did not represent the real (and ardently pro-French) feelings of the country. In 1796 he was recalled, in something like disgrace, and the following year he published his defence: *A View of the Conduct of the Executive in the Foreign Affairs of the United States.* Washington, who by that time had retired, took no public notice of this work — which is as well for Monroe's reputation, judging from the cold acidity of the marginal notes in Washington's copy of the book.

The State of Virginia, which by this time was predominantly Jeffersonian, compensated Monroe for his discomfiture by electing him Governor for three successive terms. In 1803, Jefferson sent him to France to help Livingston negotiate for the purchase of New Orleans, and after the unexpected success of the Louisiana Purchase, Monroe was transferred to London, where he was expected to negotiate a treaty with England on the question of impressments and the seizure of American boats. The treaty that he arranged was so unsatisfactory that Jefferson did not even show it to the Senate, and it has been assumed that this was another example of Monroe's diplomatic incapacity. This is unjust, for Monroe had secured all that could be got from the English Government at that moment, and Lord Holland, with whom he negotiated, was of the opinion that if the treaty had been accepted, the War of 1812 would not have occurred. Lord Holland's opinion of Monroe was that 'he was plain in his man-

---

[1] Monroe was the first of the famous Virginia Presidents not to have married a widow.

ners and somewhat slow in his apprehension; but he was a diligent, earnest, sensible, and even profound man.' This is very different from the impression of flightiness which Monroe had made ten years before in Paris; but it seems probable that Lord Holland made a just judgment, and that Monroe, having in the interim experienced almost every form of public service, had slowly developed into a cautious and balanced man. Many years later, J. Q. Adams, who had worked under Monroe for eight years, described him as 'of a mind, anxious and unwearied in the pursuit of truth and right, patient of inquiry, patient of contradiction, courteous even in the collision of sentiment, sound in its ultimate judgment, and firm in its final conclusions.' This is startling praise from John Quincy Adams, whose misanthropic comments on all his contemporaries are famous. Monroe possessed neither the imagination and originality of Jefferson, nor the knowledge and intellectual power of Madison. But by the time experience had ripened him he developed into a diligent and reliable public servant. This unsensational competence was mirrored in his appearance; he was tall, but inclined to stoop, a little ungainly, with mild blue eyes and a worried air.

In 1807, Monroe returned to the United States. He served again in the House of Delegates of Virginia, and then became Governor of the State for a fourth term. In 1811, he resigned the Governorship to become Madison's Secretary of State, and during the fiasco of the war he was the ablest man in the Cabinet, finally inducing Madison to get rid of the inept Secretary of War, and undertaking, for a few months, to run that department as well as his own. In 1816, Monroe was elected President by 183 electoral votes to 34 for his Federalist opponent. Four years later, he was given every electoral vote but one.

Needless to say, this extinction of the Opposition did not mean that strife had departed from American politics. It merely meant that with the startling changes that were then coming over American life, no man quite knew where he stood; and while the leaders were looking about them and trying to understand what was happening, they all gave formal allegiance to the group that was in power. Jefferson's Democratic-Republican Party appeared to have destroyed all opposition; actually, it was as moribund as the Federalist Party which it seemed to have driven from public life. Founded to resist the economic doctrines of Hamilton — to protect the common man by preserving America for agrarianism, and by resisting too great an aggrandizement of the National Government — Jefferson's party had failed at every point. Hamilton's interpretation of the Constitution had triumphed, and was now personified in John Marshall, the Chief Justice of the United States; Hamilton's economic principles had triumphed, and by the time of Monroe the Democratic-Republicans had given up the struggle against aggressive capitalism — so much so that when, in 1816, John C. Calhoun of South Carolina introduced a bill chartering a second Bank of the United States to replace Hamilton's bank, the charter of which had lapsed, he announced that to discuss its constitutionality would be a waste of time! Having lost the constitutional and the economic battle, the Jeffersonians had no power with which to fight for agrarianism. But the agrarians were not defeated. New leaders, with a clearer and more realistic political philosophy than Jefferson's, were to rise in their support — and in the end the issue had to be settled by Grant's guns above Vicksburg.... J. Q. Adams served as Secretary of State in Monroe's Cabinet, Calhoun as Secretary of War. In this perplexing 'Era of Good Feeling,' these two men worked side by side in what appeared to be a united party and a united country. Before Monroe's eight years were out, however, they had begun to realize that the Industrial Revolution had destroyed that unity, and that they themselves represented two irreconcilable factions which could never again meet on common ground.

After two highly successful terms as President — the most notable achievements of which are in the field of foreign relations, and therefore come into the story of J. Q. Adams — Monroe retired, in 1825, to Oak Hill, his place in Loudon County, Virginia. There he suffered the usual financial collapse that was overtaking Virginia gentlemen in this period, his troubles being mitigated by a grant of $30,000 from a grateful Congress. In 1826, he became a regent of the University of Virginia, in the affairs of which he and Madison and Jefferson had again collaborated — the three old friends and ex-Presidents who were the last of the Virginia leaders of America.

In 1831, while visiting his daughter in New York City, James Monroe died. He, too, like Adams and Jefferson, died on the fourth of July.

5

The election of 1824 was the first expression of the revolution in American life that had been taking place during Monroe's two terms. At the close of the War of 1812, the country had become suddenly nationalistic. But before the new feeling had a chance to grow deep into the nation's consciousness, before any genuine unity could be achieved, the Industrial Revolution divided the United States into three self-conscious sections: a united South, a partially united North, and a crazily expanding West. The 'United States' had become a geographical expression. An illustration of how, and why, this tentative nationalism quickly changed into sectionalism can be seen in the tariff legislation of these years. In 1816, Calhoun and Clay — nationalist leaders in Congress — undertook to bind the nation together by an economic program which Clay named the 'American System.' This was to combine protective tariffs for the manufacturer, a National Bank for the protection of capitalism, and a great system of national roads and canals to enlarge the market for the farmers. The ardent nationalism of the moment overcame Southern scruples against protection; even Jefferson was temporarily converted. So the tariff of 1816 was passed, the New England shipping interests being the only important dissenters. Four years later, the manufacturers' appetite for protection having been whetted, a bill was introduced to raise the rates. But by this time the nationalism of the South was cooling; the advantages of free trade to a staple-producing region overweighed sentimental attachment to an 'American System,' and the South opposed the bill. Nevertheless, the bill passed. New England was equally divided for and against it — a sign that the manufacturing interests were overtaking the commercial in that section; and the industrial Middle States, and the grain- and wool-producing Ohio Valley, were strong for increased protection. Four years later, in 1824, the rates were again raised, and by this time the opposition of the South was violent. 'If,' threatened Randolph of Roanoke, 'under the power to regulate trade, you prevent exportation;... if, *secundum artem*, you draw the last shilling from our pockets, what are the checks of the Constitution to us? A fig for the Constitution!... There is no magic in this word *union*.' In 1828 the rates went up again. By this time New England was solidly pro-tariff and the Southern leaders were talking of violent resistance — Representative McDuffie of South Carolina asserting that forty out of every hundred bales of Southern cotton were in effect being plundered by Northern manufacturers, and drawing the suggestive comparison between the wrongs of the South and the wrongs on account of which the colonists had revolted from Great Britain.   In protest against these mounting tariff-burdens, Calhoun composed his famous South Carolina Exposition, in which the ideas suggested by Jefferson in the Kentucky Resolution were logically developed to form the basis of the coming Southern revolt. The Constitution, declared Calhoun, was a compact between sovereign States, each of which was entitled to determine for itself whether the central government was usurping powers that had never been granted it. Thus, one of the parents of the 'American System' of 1816 became the leader of Southern sectionalism and the exponent of the extreme anti-national view of the Constitution.

With such forces as this at work, it was natural that the election of 1824 became a sectional quarrel. The chief candidates were Adams of New England, Crawford of the South, and Jackson and Clay of the West. The new parties which were to dominate American politics until the Civil War were not yet formed, and all four candidates were nominally Democratic-Republicans. Jackson received ninety-nine electoral votes, Adams eighty-four, and the other two were not in the running. No candidate, however, received a majority of the electoral votes; therefore, according to the Constitution, the election devolved upon the House of Representatives. Clay, who was very powerful in the House, asked his followers to support Adams, and Adams was thereupon elected. Although, in the election, Adams had been the choice of a section — his eighty-four electoral votes coming almost entirely from New England and New York — he was the one candidate with a broadly nationalistic programme. Caring nothing at all for the prejudices or selfish desires of his supporters, Adams had a far-sighted and practical plan for the development and welfare of the country. The frustration of this plan was a turning-point in American history.

6

John Quincy Adams, the eldest son of John and Abigail Adams, was born in 1767, two years after his father had come forward as one of the leaders in the quarrel with England. He was eight years old when the War of Independence began, so his entire childhood was passed in an atmosphere of patriotic work and hope. His father was one of the first men in North America to desire independence. His mother, in mind, manners, and religion, represented all that was best in rebel New England. With two such examples of devotion to the colonial cause, it is no wonder that the boy grew up a patriot. And his patriotism was made national rather than local, enlightened rather than narrow, by the extraordinary circumstances of his education.

At the age of eleven, and again when he was thirteen, he accompanied his father to Europe, where he was first put to school in Paris and later in Holland. Already the Adams capacity for hard work, combined with the Adams belief in being the elect of God with a calling to important public service, had made John Quincy one of the most precocious children in history, both in learning and in maturity of mind. In Holland he perfected his knowledge of Latin and Greek, meanwhile learning to speak Dutch and French. And the Adams trait of self-analysis (combined with sarcastic depreciation of all about them) was shown when the child began his famous diary, which he continued until his death in 1848 and which is one of the most absorbing historical source-books and revelations of mind and character ever left behind him by a great man.

In 1781, at the age of fourteen, John Quincy left Holland to go as secretary to Francis Dana, the American Minister to Russia. He remained at St. Petersburg for a year, studying German with a tutor and continuing with his Latin and Greek. Then he decided to return to his studies at Leyden, making his way back to Holland via Sweden. During the peace negotiations he joined his father in Paris, and about this time John Adams wrote that he had been studying with his son in the evenings, and had taught him 'geometry, trigonometry, conic sections, and the differential calculus.' Subsequently, John Quincy decided, on his own initiative, that it would be unwise to remain longer in Europe, and that since he was fitting himself for American public life he would do better to return home and attend Harvard College. It is interesting to notice the liberty of choice which the domineering, self-confident father allowed this astonishing son. It has been the characteristic attitude of Adams parents to Adams children for four generations. Sadly lacking in trust of the world at large, the Adamses have had thorough confidence in one another.

On graduating from Harvard, John Quincy studied law, and in 1790 was admitted to the Massachusetts bar. The following year he published a series of articles, over the signature *Publicola*, in refutation of Paine's *The Rights of Man* — and in this early effort the main outlines of Adams's political philosophy are clear. Paine had asserted the complete sovereignty of the majority will, as expressed at any given moment: 'that which a whole nation

chuses to do, it has a right to do.' Against this dictum John
Quincy erected the dictum of the ethical absolute as final law,
thus attacking the fundamental tenet of democracy. For if there
is an authority superior to that of the sovereign people, then the
will of the people has no final validity. To Adams, it was the task
of the enlightened statesman to interpret and implement this
higher authority; therefore, no such statesman could consider
himself responsible to the whims of the people who elected him.
'The eternal and immutable laws of justice and morality,' wrote
Publicola 'are paramount to all human legislation. The violation
of those laws is certainly within the power, but is not among the
rights of nations.' Holding such views, Adams could make no
concession to the extreme claims of democracy; and his career
was determined by that fact.

The *Publicola* papers attracted the attention of Washington, and
when J. Q. Adams was twenty-seven he was sent as American
Minister to The Hague. There he found little work to do, but
spent the leisure hours completing his linguistic education by
learning Italian. In the summer of 1797 he was in London on
diplomatic business, and there he married Louisa Catherine
Johnson, whose father (belonging to a prominent Maryland
family) was United States Consul in London, and who had spent
all her early life in France. This cosmopolitan training — which
caused Abigail Adams to wonder anxiously whether her daughter-
in-law would find life in Boston congenial — admirably fitted
Mrs. John Quincy Adams to share the far-wandering life that
her husband was to lead for the next twenty years.

Shortly before his marriage, Adams had been appointed Minister to Portugal; but before he set out for that country, his father,
who had just become President, changed the appointment to
Berlin. Both father and son had been worried about John Quincy's
remaining in the public service during his father's Presidency;
but their scruples had been lessened by a letter from Washington
to John Adams, expressing 'a *strong hope* that you will not with-
hold merited promotion from Mr. John [Quincy] Adams because

he is your son. For without intending to compliment the father or the mother, or to censure others, I give it as my decided opinion that Mr. Adams is the most valuable public character we have abroad, and that there remains no doubt in my mind that he will prove himself to be the ablest of our diplomatic corps.'

On arriving at Berlin, Adams was detained at the gate of the city by a lieutenant who had never heard of the United States — a state of ignorance that was very nearly reciprocated across the Atlantic, for in 1814 George Ticknor complained that he could not find a German teacher or dictionary in Boston, or a German book in the Harvard Library.

On hearing of John Adams's defeat in the election of 1800, John Quincy wrote a characteristically frigid and formal letter to his brother, in which he remarked, 'Were I not therefore acquainted with the genuine energy of your father's character, and the pure magnanimity of his soul, my keenest feelings at this time would arise from concern at what the effect of this event would be upon his mind.' And he then tells his brother to consider 'all and every part of my property in your hands, whether of principal or interest, as subject at all times to his disposal for his own use.' This inability to express warm feelings with warmth interfered with John Quincy's relations, both public and private. Outside of his own immediate family he never had devoted followers or warm friends; so when his bad hour came he stood alone, as his father had done. The two men were strong enough to stand this, but their cause was not. It would have been well for America had personal magnetism been among the Adams family traits. 'I am,' wrote John Quincy Adams, 'a man of reserved, cold, austere, and forbidding manners.' In this there is the exaggeration with which he always stated his own faults and the faults of others; but the statement is close to the truth. And Adams's personal appearance did nothing to counteract the effect of his forbidding manners: he was short and stocky, with piercing eyes and a disapproving set to his mouth. By the time he became President his very large head was almost completely bald. His voice was high, with a tendency to break sharply when he was excited; nevertheless, when he was deeply moved, he had the passionate eloquence of his father, and those who heard him in Congress, in his old age, found his voice impressive. At no time, however, were any of his personal characteristics found ingratiating.

In January, 1801, Adams was called home by his father. The next year he entered the State Senate of Massachusetts, and shortly afterward was sent to Washington as United States Senator. At once he began to put into practice his theory that the statesman should follow only the dictates of his mind and conscience. To the anger of the Federalists who had put him in office, he sided with Jefferson's Administration on several important issues — notably the Louisiana Purchase and the Embargo Bill. It was the increasing sectionalism of the Federalist Party that drove Adams toward the Democratic-Republican camp. In 1808, the Massachusetts Legislature retaliated by electing Adams's successor nine months ahead of time, and adopting resolutions against the Embargo, resolutions which were intended as instructions to Adams in regard to his vote. Adams immediately resigned. 'As to holding my seat in the Senate of the United States,' he wrote, 'without exercising the most perfect freedom of agency, under the sole and exclusive control of my own sense of right, that was out of the question.' 'Two theories of government had come into collision,' writes Mr. James Truslow Adams. 'The rising tide of democracy had rushed for a moment up over the rock of intellectual integrity. Adams's resignation was inevitable.'

A year after Adams resigned from the Senate, President Madison appointed him Minister to Russia. He remained at St. Petersburg until 1814, when he was ordered to Ghent to preside over the American peace commission. The United States was powerfully represented at Ghent, as was recognized by the Marquis of Wellesley, who stated in the House of Lords that the Americans 'had shown a most astonishing superiority over the British during the whole of the negotiations.' Within the American Commission,

however, there was violent discord. Next in ability to Adams
stood Henry Clay, the romantic young man from Kentucky, who
had done more than anyone else to create the war, and who was
eager to go on with it indefinitely rather than make an inglorious
peace, since the latter might ruin his own promising career. The
more realistic Adams knew that if the United States could make
a peace that left her no worse off than she had been before the
war, she would have accomplished wonders. However, like his
father in 1783, Adams would have wrecked the negotiations at
any moment rather than relinquish New England's fishing claims
— whereas to Clay, the Westerner, these claims seemed unimportant. Also, Clay's flamboyant social life and his continual
gambling met with Adams's disapproval; so the tactful and conciliatory Albert Gallatin had to work almost as hard at keeping
peace between his fellow-commissioners as at making it with
England. The final result, however, was gratifying. The United
States, having lost almost every land battle and suffered a complete blockade of her coasts, secured a peace in which she lost
nothing at all. To be sure, she gained nothing; and no word was
said of the British abuses which were alleged to have driven
America to war. But the peace was a triumph of diplomacy —
though the American people chose to receive it as if it were a
triumph of arms.

Still following in his father's footsteps, John Quincy Adams
became the first American Minister to Great Britain after the
conclusion of the peace. Meanwhile, in February, 1815, Adams
had sent word to his wife to wind up their affairs in St. Petersburg
and join him in Paris. So Mrs. Adams set out in midwinter, with
her son Charles Francis, on a two-thousand-mile journey across
a war-disordered Europe, reaching Paris a few days before
Napoleon arrived on his return from Elba. It is fortunate that
John Quincy had not chosen a wife, as his mother seemed to have
desired him to do, with an eye to whether she would enjoy living
in Boston.

In London, Adams met with the hostility that three generations of his family were destined to incur, since they chose unfortunate moments to represent their country in that capital. In 1817 he was called home to become Secretary of State in Monroe's Cabinet. Adams was now fifty years old, and the first period of his eventful career was closed. For the past thirty-nine years he had spent half his life in the capitals of Europe. Throughout that period he had made rich use of his opportunities, and he now returned home a man of learning and broad culture, with a deep and mature mind, with an ardent and truly national patriotism, and with a conception of public service which not only surpassed that of his contemporaries, but which has been tragically rare in America since his death. After his term as President, when the Plymouth District in Massachusetts asked him to be a candidate for Congress, his friends urged that this was beneath his dignity. Adams replied that no public office could be beneath the dignity of any man. Added to his zeal and his experience, Adams had an integrated creed by which he directed his life. His son, Charles Francis, paid tribute to this side of John Quincy's nature in a letter to Henry Adams. 'In my opinion,' he wrote, 'no man who has ever lived in America has so thoroughly constructed a foundation for his public life as your grandfather. His action was always deducible from certain maxims deeply graven on his mind. This it was that made him fail so much as a party man. No person can be a thorough partisan for a long period without sacrifice of his moral identity. The skill consists in knowing exactly where to draw the line, and it is precisely here that it seems to me appears the remarkable superiority of your grandfather over every man of his time. He derives support from everything he can seize. But if circumstances force it out of his hands, he is still found standing firm and alone.' 'Firm and alone' — it was Adams's fate to spend the last twenty-four years of his life in that position; but before that fate overtook him he was to have eight years of striking success as Monroe's Secretary of State.

With his knowledge of European affairs, his power of mind and character, and his patriotism, Adams was well fitted for the office of Secretary of State during the troublesome period of foreign affairs that followed the War of 1812. The aggressiveness and sarcasm of some of his diplomatic correspondence make surprising reading; but at a time when young lieutenants in Europe had never heard of the United States, and when most Foreign Offices preferred to pretend that they, too, had never done so, Adams's methods were beneficial. Had his policy not been well-founded, his lofty tone would have made his country ridiculous; but under the circumstances, it made his country respected. 'If we are not taken for Romans we shall be taken for Jews,' he exclaimed to someone who was shocked at his bold language.

Ever since the Louisiana Purchase, the United States had been trying unsuccessfully to buy the Floridas from Spain. In 1818, Andrew Jackson was sent to Georgia to avenge some Indian outrages. Finding that the Indians were raiding Georgia from Spanish territory, he crossed the Florida line, captured a Spanish fort, seized the town of Pensacola, and executed two British citizens whom he accused of complicity in the Indian raids. Most of Monroe's Cabinet was horrified, and there was talk of sacrificing Jackson to appease the foreign storm. But Adams would have none of this. To the indignant Spanish Minister he declared that it was Spain alone who was to blame, since she had refused either to govern Florida herself or to sell it to the country that was prepared to govern it. And when the Spanish Minister, in a long, inconsequential note, happened to remark that 'Truth is of all time,' Adams coldly replied: 'The observation that truth is of all time, and that reason and justice are founded upon immutable principles, has never been contested by the United States. But neither truth, reason nor justice consists in stubbornness of assertion, nor in the multiplied repetitions of error.' In the end, there was trouble neither with England nor Spain, and in 1819 Adams secured a treaty buying the Floridas from Spain and adjusting the boundary between Louisiana and the Spanish territory of Texas.

Meanwhile, the revolt of the Spanish colonies in South America presented Adams with problems of recognition, and also with the critical question of European intervention to restore the lost territories to Spain. It was as a result of this last threat that the Monroe Doctrine was evolved. This was rightly named after the President who sponsored it and who accepted the responsibility for it; but in conception, and in most of its details, it was the work of John Quincy Adams.

The simplest account of the meaning and implications of the Monroe Doctrine is that given by President Polk, in 1845: 'The people of this continent,' he wrote, 'alone have the right to decide their own destiny. Should any portion of them, constituting an independent state, propose to unite with our Confederacy, this will be a question for them and us to determine, without any foreign interposition. We can never consent that European powers shall interfere to prevent such a union because it might disturb the "balance of power" which they may desire to maintain on this continent.... Existing rights of every European nation should be respected; but... no future European colony or dominion shall with our consent be planted or established on any part of the North American continent.' And, three years later, Polk affirmed what had merely been implicit in Monroe's original message, that the transfer of American territory to a non-American power would not be permitted by the United States. Except for a slight extension of its application under Roosevelt, this is what the Monroe Doctrine has always been taken to mean. It represents the one fixed dogma in the foreign policy of the United States.

When Adams was elected President, in 1824, he chose Henry Clay for his Secretary of State. His reasons were clear: with the exception of Jackson, whom Adams thought an ignorant demagogue, Clay was the most important man in public life who shared Adams's nationalism. There were other men who professed it, but their actions proclaimed them sectionalists, whereas Clay was willing to sacrifice local interests to the national cause. In addition to this qualification, Clay represented the West and to some extent the South — hence he was a desirable choice for the chief position under a New England President. And finally, the two men had worked and quarreled together at Ghent and had respect for each other's ability. No sooner was the announcement of Clay's appointment made, however, than Jackson and his friends raised the cry of 'corrupt bargain,' claiming that Clay had sold the votes of his followers in the House of Representatives in return for the office of Secretary of State. Clay asked for an investigation, but it was never granted — the Jackson forces preferring to let the charges fester. The only satisfaction that Clay could get was in fighting a duel with Randolph of Roanoke, who had referred in the Senate to the alleged Adams-Clay bargain as 'the combination, unheard of until then, of Blifil and Black George — the Puritan and the blackleg.'

Adams's Administration, therefore, got off to a bad start. A new party was rapidly forming about General Jackson. It had no programme, but it had a grievance — namely, that 'the people' had been deprived, by the alleged corrupt bargain, of their true choice as President. With this grievance as excuse, and with the spoils of office as incentive, the Jackson party was coming together. Its managers made clear that there would be no nonsense about 'merit' when it came to making the many appointments that the President controlled. There would be a clean sweep of every office-holder who had not been a Jackson man, and 'the faithful' would come into their own. So the first fruits of the new democracy, the first contribution of the new West to politics, was the destruction of the tradition that appointments and removals in the public service were to be made for merit or demerit only. When it became clear that Adams would not yield to the new method, would not build a party of his own by the judicious use of patronage — would not even dismiss men, such as his Postmaster-General, who were using their power to help Jackson for the next campaign — the politicians knew that he was lost. He could neither be re-elected nor get support from Congress for his policies.

Adams was lost, but to understand American history it is necessary to know what was lost with him. He had a vision of the possibilities of America that recalls the vision of Washington. An intensely religious man, Adams believed that God intended to produce a new and happy civilization when He endowed one nation with the riches that had been lavished upon the United States. This seemingly endless store of land, timber, minerals, water-power, could be developed in such a way as to make America the wisest as well as the richest of the nations — and this was the end and meaning of Adams's ambition. By keeping the Western land in the hands of the National Government, by securing its gradual and economic development, and by using the wealth derived from the careful disposal of this land for public improvements and public education, Adams wished to create a United States that would be free from poverty and ignorance and from all temptation to the grosser forms of greed. In a message to Congress he announced that 'the great object of the institution of civil government is the improvement of those who are partners to the social ompact.' It was his plan to begin with a system of roads and canals, and then to take advantage of the increased price of public lands that would follow on such improved communications to endow education and science on a scale that had never previously been dreamed by man. He foresaw a republic of informed men and women, administered by trained and conscientious servants such as himself; and though his Adams pessimism must have kept him from believing in this vision too completely, he felt that he could lead the nation toward an approximation of it. But to do this he would have to induce Congress to take steps that would not be immediately popular with the electorate. In other words, he would have to combat the new, triumphant democracy, and establish his old thesis that the will of the majority must not prevail over reason and morality. 'Are we to slumber in indolence,' he demanded, 'or fold our arms and proclaim to the world that we are *palsied by the will of our constituents?*' And the answer was 'yes.' The answer might have been different but for the fact that the unyielding and unconciliatory Adams was opposed by wily politicians (trained to flatter and mislead the new democracy) who looked upon the public lands with a very different eye from that of the President. 'Ages upon ages of continual progressive improvement, physical, moral, political, in the condition of the whole people of this Union, were stored up in the possession and disposal of these lands,' said Adams years afterward, when the battle had been lost forever. But the Jackson men saw something more attractive in these lands than ages upon ages of physical, moral, and political welfare: they saw plunder. They saw a vast gamble, in which a lucky few could profit unimaginably, and which could be described to the electorate as the simple process of throwing open to 'the people' that which rightfully belonged to them. And some of them saw a plan more devious still: the Southerners, who were constantly afraid that the new West might join with the East to oppress them with tariffs and to interfere with slavery, saw the chance to make a bargain that might keep control of the Government in their hands. Senator Benton of Missouri was one of the originators of this scheme, and his tactics in recommending it to the public are shown by the following sentence from one of his speeches in 1826: 'I speak... to an assembly of legislators, and not to a keeper of the King's forests. I speak to Senators who know this to be a Republic, not a Monarchy; who know that the public lands belong to the People and not to the Federal Government.' Even Jackson — who for all his faults was an honest man — was taken in by this argument and was induced to recommend that all public lands should be given away to individual adventurers and to the States in which the lands were situated. The whole scramble tor plunder was described by Adams, in Congress, in 1838: 'The thirst of a tiger for blood is the fittest emblem of the rapacity with which the members of all the new States fly at the public lands. The constituents upon whom they depend are all settlers, or tame and careless spectators of the pillage. It were vain to attempt to resist them there.'

In 1828, therefore, when Adams was overwhelmingly defeated by Jackson, it meant that democracy had laughed at his belief in an honest and able civil service, and laughed at his ambition to administer the public property for the public good. The Jackson men were promising the spoils of a continent, and the people could hardly wait to get them into power. 'Alike from Mr. Adams's point of view or from ours,' writes Brooks Adams, 'the test had been crucial. Democracy had failed to justify itself. Man alone, unaided by a supernatural power, could not resist the pressure of self-interest and of greed.'

The campaign of 1828 was another sign that with the triumph of democracy the United States had entered upon a new era. A new level of scurrility and irrelevance was attained, the press on both sides ignoring the vital issues that were at stake. Adams was accused of dissipation and thievery and corruption. Because, at his own expense, he had provided the White House with a billiard table and a set of chessmen, he was said to have spent the public's money on gambling machines. Also, it was said that while he was at St. Petersburg he had procured a beautiful American girl for a Russian nobleman. Adams himself took no part in the campaign, it being his fixed principle never to solicit public office; but the newspapers that supported him — chiefly in New England — showed their readiness to learn the new tricks by calling General Jackson a murderer (because he had killed a man in a duel), a drunkard, an illiterate and a debauchee.

When the returns were in, Adams felt despairing. He knew his friends believed he had ruined them by refusing to adopt, even on a small scale, the new methods in the use of patronage; he knew the decision that had just been made was irrevocable, and that America's chance to use her riches wisely was gone forever; and he probably knew that he could have made a better fight if he had possessed more personal charm, if he had been less 'reserved cold, austere, and forbidding.' There is a surprising passage in his diary, where he recalls the impression made on him by the opera, *Cœur-de-Lion* (which he had heard forty-five years before in Paris), and especially by the song,

> *O Richard! O mon Roi!*
> *L'Univers t'abandonne,*

adding that 'in the year 1829 scarce a day passed that did not
bring it to my thoughts.'

One of the experiences that led him to feel betrayed, at this
time, was his treatment by a group of leading Bostonians. During
the election, it had been asserted on the alleged authority of
Jefferson that in 1808 Adams had accused some of the chief Federalists in Boston of planning secession. These men now demanded
an explanation. Adams, with unusual patience and politeness,
explained exactly what he had said. But the Bostonians — among
whom were such men as Harrison Gray Otis, Henry Cabot, and
John Lowell — still felt that their honour was unsatisfied. They
continued to attack Adams both in public and private. Thereupon he prepared a four hundred-page book, in which his controversial powers are shown at their best, vindicating himself
completely from charges of unfairness, and making the great men
of Boston look absurd for claiming that their honour had been
wounded. And then, having written this damaging and final
answer, Adams, with scornful magnanimity, refrained from publishing it. But in 1877 his grandson published it, and Boston
learned that this stern old man had thought it beneath him to
defend himself from the political and social insults of its leading
citizens. The blow, though delayed, was deadly.

It looked, in 1829, as though Adams was to parallel his father's
career to the end, and to close his life with a long period of inac-
tivity. This he could not have borne with the fortitude that his
father had shown, for he was endowed with an energy, a delight
in exhaustingly hard work, such as few men have known. When
President, he rose at five, and worked steadily, except for meal
hours, until four-thirty in the afternoon, at which time he took
a walk for about an hour and a half. He would dine at about six-
thirty, and then work until eleven. In summer he allowed himself the additional pleasure of an early morning swim in the
Potomac; but finding that he was pressed for time, he began rising
at four-fifteen instead of five. These hours explain how he was
able to find time for such extra work as his report on weights and

measures, prepared at the request of Congress while he was Secretary of State, and embodying so much historical research that in 1906 Sir Sandford Flemming, in a report to the Royal Society of Canada, said that it 'is still a classic, and shows an almost incredible amount of investigation.'

Adams was preparing to try and turn this energy into the writing of history; but he was spared the effort, for in 1830 the voters of the Plymouth District asked him to be a candidate for the House of Representatives. He answered that he would be glad to do so on two conditions: first, that he should never be expected to ask for their votes, and second, that if elected he would do and say exactly what he chose and would not feel himself under obligation to follow the whims of the men who elected him. On these terms he was chosen by a great majority, and on these terms he was kept in Congress until the day of his death. This was a deep satisfaction to Adams — and rightly, for it showed that some stand could still be made against the worst evils of democracy which were then sweeping the country, against demagogic vote-catching on the one hand and frightened submission to the mass mind on the other.

Adams's free-lance career in Congress was more picturesque than influential. When the Southern members forced through a 'gag rule' that petitions against slavery should be laid on the table without being printed, or referred, or acted upon in any way, Adams led a long fight against the restriction; and in 1845, when he was seventy-eight years old, he had the rule repealed. As a result of this battle for the freedom of petition, Adams, who was not an abolitionist,[1] received anti-slavery petitions from all over the country, and his attempts to present them kept him continually at odds with the Southern members.

---

[1] His position was that which conservative opinion in the North increasingly adopted, namely, that slavery should be kept out of the new Territories so far as possible, but should not be interfered with where it already existed. He had, therefore, favoured the Missouri Compromise, as better than dividing the Union; but he had no illusions that such a compromise was permanent. 'The President,' he wrote in his diary in January, 1820, 'thinks this question will be winked away by a compromise. But so do not I. Much am I mistaken if it is not destined to survive his political and individual life and mine.'

One of the plans that President Adams had urged in his first message to Congress was the erection of an astronomical observatory. The idea filled the Jackson men with special glee, and they used it to symbolize the visionary madness of their enemy. It was with great pleasure, then, that Adams accepted the invitation, in 1843, to visit Cincinnati and dedicate the first observatory in the United States. It was a difficult journey for a man of seventy-six, and the public demonstrations in his honour, with their attendant hand-shaking and speech-making, very nearly wore him out. His diary-comment on the demonstrations is characteristic: 'The only comfort I have,' he wrote, 'is that they are intended to manifest respect, and not hatred.' When he returned East from this trip, his health and vitality were impaired, and though he lived five years longer he was never again the tireless, robust man that he had been. His grandson, Henry Adams, described the old man at this period: 'He seemed always to be writing — as, indeed, he was... a very old-looking gentleman, with a bald head and a white fringe of hair — writing, writing — with a perpetual inkstain on the forefinger and thumb of the right hand.' And when he was not writing, he was wandering about the grounds, always alone, 'hatchet and saw in hand, pruning and watching his seedlings.' His wife, to the grandson, was now a 'vision of silver-gray, presiding over her old President, and her Queen Anne mahogany, an exotic like her Sèvres china; an object of deference to everyone and of great affection to her son Charles.'

It was only when Congress was not in session, however, that Adams had time for his books and his seedlings. Neither age nor weariness could keep him from Washington, where he still fought alone for the principles of a vanished America. One day in February, 1848, he fell insensible while trying to rise from his seat in the House of Representatives. He was carried into the Speaker's room, where two days later he died.

PART TWO
DEMOCRACY

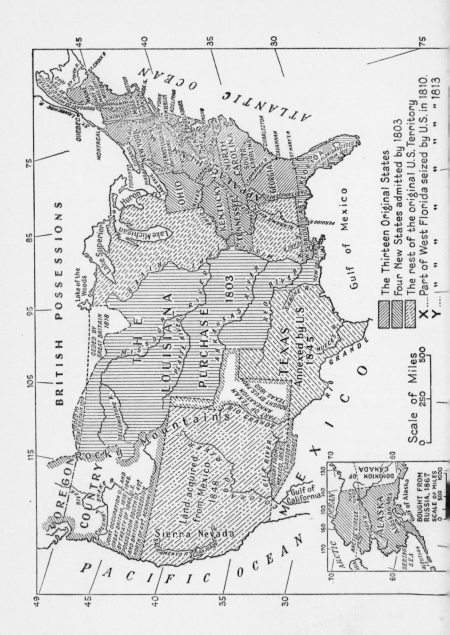

INTRODUCTION TO PART TWO

THE first attempt to create a planned society in America had ended in failure. The Adamses' ideal of an ordered state, which would take advantage of its lucky ownership of vast resources to ensure comfort and real instruction to its citizens — this ideal had been rejected, in the name of 'the people.' The problem for the leaders in the second period of American History was to find something to put in its place.

In the new States (roughly described as 'the West') the leaders did not see that anything was needed in its place. Once the tyrannous, interfering notions of Adams had been put down, democracy would ensue — and democracy was felt to be the perfect government. This point of view was natural, but unimaginative. For in the frontier States democracy was not an ideal; it was an inescapable condition, like the weather. It had not been striven for; it had been thrust upon these States. It was praised sentimentally, but nothing was done to protect it. Had the Westerners really cherished their democracy, they would have clung to a Jeffersonian simple life, they would have defended themselves against the wealth, the inequalities, that industrial progress offered them. In fact, it was the wealth and inequalities they wanted. So their democracy was not a chosen way, but a transition — made as brief as possible — between an anarchic backwoods life and an anarchic plutocracy. The West was a period; it was never a plan.

The industrial East — growing in wealth and beginning to tap the cheap labour supply of Europe — had what it considered a plan; but this was merely the desire to establish the Hamiltonian economic programme as quickly as possible. It was a business plan, not a political one. The State was never considered; the relations of the parts to the whole were never thought out; even the simple question of what would happen to the existing democratic

forms of government, in a booming world of rich men and poor
foreign labourers — even that question was not faced. Hamilton
had seen well enough what would happen, and had made it clear
that in his ideal state democracy was impossible. But the new
Eastern leaders were content to take Hamilton's economics and
combine them with the politics of the frontier West. The unpleasantness of the result was long concealed, because so rich and
vital a country as young America can survive political anarchy —
for a time.

Only in the South, during this second period, was there an attempt at a planned society. The Southerners, under the leadership of Calhoun, saw that if they were to preserve their way of
life (which they felt to be good) they must protect it by planning
their politics as a whole, by creating a public pride in the institutions of the South (a pride which would lead the best men to
serve the State), and by preparing to defend their institutions
against the growing power of the business world. Their effort to
do this, their temporary success, their final destruction in the
Civil War, is the chief feature of the second period of American
history.

During these years, between 1829 and 1865, the population of
the country grew from 12,000,000 to 34,000,000, and for the first
time foreign immigration became an important factor in the
growth. From 1789 to 1830, the total immigration was under
400,000; but in the next decade there were 599,000 immigrants;
between 1840 and 1850, there were 1,713,251; and between 1850
and 1860 over two and a half million. These immigrants settled
in the North and West, avoiding the slave States in the South.

CHAPTER IV

JACKSON AND VAN BUREN

I

WHEN Andrew Jackson arrived at the White House after his in-auguration, he held a reception for 'the people,' who behaved even worse than their most hostile critics could have hoped. Punchbowls were spilled, glasses broken, chairs ruined by muddy boots. Thousands of rough Westerners had made the trip to see 'their' President installed in 'their' White House, and it is probable that the worse they behaved the better they pleased Jackson, who was proud to dramatize his contempt for the ways of the upper classes. Jackson himself was too much of a man to be lacking in all restraint and dignity; but he had been embittered by the campaign, and by the recent death of his wife (which he sentimentally attributed to the harsh things that had been written about her by the pro-Adams newspapers), and it amused him to watch the horror of official Washington. The unpleasant display had real significance, however, for it not only marked the triumph of democracy in national politics, but it gave a hint as to how the masses would respond to their new responsibility. The ruined upholstery and broken glassware of the White House were a symbol of what was to happen, in the long run, to the country with the greatest natural riches in the world.

Nothing so disastrous was to take place, however, while Andrew Jackson was in the White House. He was no newspaper-made hero, but a genuine leader of the people. He really possessed the qualities for which his followers loved him, and he did the best for his country that was possible to an honest, ignorant, untrained, undisciplined man. If democracy had been able to find more Andrew Jacksons to lead it, it might not be discredited today. But once it had been proved that with the new democratic West (and with the rapid extension of the suffrage in the older States) it was possible to elect a man with no public record, no positive programme, and no knowledge, the politicians took the hint. In the future that was to be the norm for American Presidents — with the added requirement of no strength of will, so that they would do what they were told, as Jackson never did.

2

Jackson was born on the frontier in 1767, just at the dividing line between North and South Carolina. His parents were Scotch-Irish immigrants, who had only recently arrived in the colony. His father had died a few months before Jackson was born, and his mother was left with no money and the care of three children. Living with relatives, in extreme poverty, the boy was bred to backwoods conditions at their worst.

Toward the end of the War of Independence, Jackson was involved in some local skirmishes and was taken prisoner by the English. The harsh treatment he received at their hands was never forgotten — for vindictiveness was one of Andrew Jackson's chief traits. When the war was over, he was able to study law in Salisbury, North Carolina, being admitted to the bar in 1787, the year of the Constitutional Convention at Philadelphia. In 1788 he was appointed prosecuting attorney of the western district of North Carolina, and moved across the mountains to the land that was soon to become the State of Tennessee. This move was probably the chief determining event of Jackson's life. Had he remained east of the mountains (as did Calhoun, his great enemy of later days, whose Scotch-Irish parents were frontiersmen in South Carolina) he would have grown into a Southerner and been assimilated, along with his backwoods neighbours, into the new prosperous planting system of that district. Nothing could have altered Jackson's strange, fierce character; but his views, in so far as he had any, were the obvious product of his environment; so it is probable that the decision to cross the mountains had an important effect on American history.

Along the new frontier in Tennessee, Jackson quickly acquired renown. He had all the qualities that would attract attention in such a district. He was impetuous, quarrelsome, honest, brave, bitter, revengeful, and violently indiscreet. These are the traits of the barbaric hero, as found in all the primitive epics of the race, and Jackson's Tennessee neighbours responded to them with such love and hatred that he was soon a man of note. His appearance was in keeping with his nature. Tall and very thin; a long, stern face and lantern jaw; deep-set, wild blue eyes that all observers agreed were terrifying in anger; high cheek-bones and a strong mouth; the whole face crowned by a great shock of intractable hair, soon to turn grey — he was not a man who could be overlooked. Strength of passion and resolve were expressed in his body, but not great physical strength, for Jackson was flat-chested and had a slight stoop. Throughout his life he suffered from indigestion, and from the effect of serious gunshot wounds picked up in the duels and brawls of his youth.

In 1792, Jackson married Mrs. Rachel Robarbs, née Donelson. She appears to have been an estimable and pious female, and Jackson loved her all his life; but the unfortunate circumstances of this marriage were of permanent importance both to Jackson and to his country. Mrs. Robarbs's first marriage had been a failure, and after various attempts at improving matters she and her husband separated. Some time later it was reported in Tennessee that Robarbs had secured a divorce via the Virginia legislature. Thankfully accepting this report, Jackson proposed to Mrs. Robarbs, and soon after married her. Two years later it became known that no divorce had been granted, the Virginia legislature having merely authorized proceedings. Robarbs now sued for divorce, and obtained it, on the grounds of his wife's adultery with Jackson. Thereupon Jackson and Mrs. Robarbs were married. The importance of the story is in the fact that, although Jackson undoubtedly acted in good faith on the occasion of his first marriage, he must later have been uneasily conscious that in spite of his legal training he had accepted an unplausible story

Furthermore, he must have felt guilty over the whole affair. There is no other way of explaining the insane passion that was always roused in him by the suggestion that he or his wife could possibly be accused of sin. He killed one man for making this accusation, and fought many others; and thirty-six years later, he refused to behave with formal politeness toward John Quincy Adams, the President of the United States and the man who had saved Jackson's reputation and career after the Florida episode, because he had been told that Adams countenanced the mean-spirited references to the Robarbs incident which had appeared in the anti-Jackson press.

The story of the duel in which Jackson killed his adversary shows the cold-blooded rage that this issue always roused in him. The immediate cause was a quarrel over the payment of a forfeit in a horse-race; but Jackson's lethal fury came from the fact that Dickinson, his opponent, had referred while drunk to the Jackson 'adultery.' They fought with pistols at eight paces. Dickinson was one of the famous shots of the West, far quicker on the trigger than Jackson; so Jackson decided to let him fire first. He shot Jackson through the breast, missing the heart. Jackson took careful aim and pulled the trigger; but the hammer of his pistol caught at half-cock. After consultation, the seconds decided that Jackson had the right to another try, if he demanded it. Jackson did demand it, and this time the pistol went off and Dickinson was killed. Jackson's subsequent comment was, 'I snould have hit him if he had shot me through the brain.' This was in 1806, when Jackson was almost forty years old, and had served in the House of Representatives and the United States Senate and had been a judge of the Tennessee Supreme Court. A few years later he got into a brawl, in a Nashville tavern, with the Benton brothers — one of whom was later the famous Senator from Missouri. They fought with pistols and knives, and it was only the bystanders that kept them from exterminating one another. Jackson was seriously wounded, and this injury, added to the wound he received from Dickinson, plagued him all the rest of his life.

In 1813–14, Jackson led Western militiamen against the Creek Indians of Georgia and Alabama. Successful in this, he became, in 1814, a major-general in the regular army, and was entrusted with the defence of New Orleans. On January 8, 1815, General Sir Edward Pakenham led one of the most foolhardy attacks in British history — a frontal attack in close columns against earthworks protected both by artillery and by the Western riflemen. Over two thousand Englishmen were killed, and thirteen Americans. The war was already over when this battle was fought; but if General Pakenham had known that fact, and had been seeking to do the most harm possible to his late enemies, he could not have found anything more ingenious than making Jackson into a military hero.

From the battle of New Orleans until his inauguration as President in 1829, Jackson's career was a series of rash, erratic acts. He began by ruling New Orleans as if it were a conquered ship at sea; and as a result of his treatment of a judge who resisted this autocracy, Jackson was fined one thousand dollars on the re-establishment of civil law — a fine which a grateful country repaid him with interest in 1844.... In 1818 came the Florida exploit, which almost provoked war with both England and Spain. And again in 1821, when Jackson was military Governor of Florida (which by that time belonged to the United States), he came into collision with the civil authority. Once more he was extricated from his difficulties by J. Q. Adams.

By 1824, as the time for the Presidential elections approached, Jackson was established as the hero of the Western democracy, and, to a great extent, of 'the people' everywhere. Violent, brave, successful, honest, and foolish, there was much about him to stir the enthusiasm of simple men. He was a moderately successful farmer and the owner of a few slaves; he had an intuitive feeling that the very rich were knaves; aside from that his politics consisted of patriotism, a dislike of direct taxes, and a belief that the government should be economical. To the ruling classes of the day, his candidacy seemed absurd, for he was almost totally ignorant, spoke inaccurately, wrote worse, had little experience with government and none with foreign affairs.

Ever since the formation of parties in the United States, Presidential candidates had been nominated by a caucus of their party's representatives in Congress. The State Legislature of Tennessee, in 1822, had put Jackson before the country as a candidate; but the Congressional Caucus in 1824 did not nominate him. This was made into a grievance by the new democratic politicians who were beginning to cluster about Jackson; in 1828, therefore, the Congressional Caucus System was abandoned, and nominations were made by State legislatures. In 1832 the present system of nominating candidates was devised — namely, an extra-legal party conference, the delegates to which are chosen by the party machine in various localities. This is alleged to be a highly democratic device; at any rate, it puts the choice of candidates in the hands of professional politicians.

Just at the time that this evolution was taking place, there came the final breaking-down of the constitutional provisions for ensuring that the President should not be elected by the people. The electors had for some time been virtual figureheads who registered the party's choice; and now the State legislatures were even relinquishing their privilege of appointing the electors, and were arranging for them to be chosen by popular vote. By 1824 only six States preserved the older method; by 1832 only one — South Carolina. Therefore, just when the electorate was being extended to include all adult males, the choice of President was being handed over to the electorate, and the choice of presidential candidates to a convention of hack politicians. It is interesting to notice that from the time this process was complete, the American Presidents (who had previously been men of stature even by world-standards) became for the most part a feeble and meritless tribe. At the same time the House of Representatives — also chosen by the new electorate — began declining toward its present ignominious position both in attainment and in public respect. Only in the Senate were the old standards upheld. Webster, Clay,

Hayne, Calhoun, Jefferson Davis, Douglas, Benton, Sumner, Seward — those are the men who dominated American public life in the middle period between Jackson and the Civil War. And the Senators were not elected to office; they were appointed by their State Legislatures.

The House of Representatives had no sooner elected J. Q. Adams to the Presidency than the professional politicians began to rally to the standard of Jackson. From all sides they scrambled aboard the floating ship. They knew that their hero, who stood for nothing more precise than the rights of 'the people,' could be elected if he had a little expert handling; and they had not yet seen that, once elected, he might prove hard to manage. Foremost among these new allies was Martin Van Buren, the 'red fox' from New York. In the disorderly, sordid politics of that State, Van Buren had come to the top. He was a suave and imperturbable careerist, always glad to be as honest, as kindly, and as useful as was compatible with keeping himself in high office. It was he and his fellows who had first developed the 'spoils system' to perfection, and having found how useful the system was for building and maintaining a machine in State politics, he had long been looking hungrily toward Washington. In 1822, he wrote that 'the Post Office Department is one of the most interesting departments of the Government, and instead of spending our time in small matters, I am for taking the bull by the horns at once.' But Monroe was President in 1822, and he would not help Van Buren strengthen his local machine with Federal patronage. And when J. Q. Adams was inaugurated, it quickly became clear that he, too, had no intention of helping Van Buren escape from 'small matters.' So Van Buren became a Jackson man; for although the General was honest, and did not propose to debauch the public service, he was inexperienced and easy to persuade, once his confidence had been gained. The 'spoils system' could be presented to him under the flattering title of 'rotation in office.' It was undemocratic, his new friends explained to him, for one little group of public servants to hold the Federal jobs year after year. It was more just, more American, to hand them about among the people, so that as many citizens as possible could do their share in the running of the country. The argument was so convincing to Jackson, who saw himself as above all else a demo-crat, that more civil servants were ousted during the first month of his office than during the previous forty years of American history. And when John McLean, the Postmaster-General who had de-served well of Jackson by betraying Adams, refused to remove postmasters solely on political grounds, Jackson appointed him to the Supreme Court and found a Postmaster-General who was more pliable.

In this question of appointments, just as in the case of his marriage, Jackson must have had an uneasy conscience. When Elbridge Gerry, whom Jackson had promised to leave in his job as Surveyor of the Port of Boston, travelled to Washington to protest against his removal, Jackson raged at him and ordered him out of the White House — presumably for mentioning this broken promise. And when a delegate from the Florida Territory pro-tested to Jackson that twelve good officials had been turned out to make way for worthless men, Jackson angrily answered that no man had been turned out except for oppression or defalcation. The delegate took this story to Van Buren, asking what crime the twelve men had committed. Van Buren blandly replied, 'The President's recollection must be at fault. We give no reasons for our removals.'

One of the first results of Jackson's election was the formation of two new parties. Under Monroe and J. Q. Adams the country had been changing so rapidly that the politicians and their or-ganizations had not been able to keep pace. But the affection and hatred inspired by Jackson were themselves enough to create parties; the issues came later. The rank and file of Jackson's fol-lowers were the farmer-labour group throughout the country — yeomen and petty planters in the South, pioneer farmers in the West, labourers and German and Irish immigrants in the East-ern cities. Jefferson's old party had been called Democratic-

Republican. The Jackson men dropped the word Republican, and became the Democratic Party. In the eighteen-thirties it was a class party, strong only because it had a dynamic leader and crafty organizers, but internally weak because 'the people' in the three parts of the country did not have similar eonomic interests.

The opposition party, after trying the cumbersome name of National Republican, adopted the title of Whig Party.[1] This was one of the most incongruous groups that ever tried to hold together. Created by the dominant personalities of Clay and Webster, it consisted, first, of the old Federalists; second, of all who favoured Clay's 'American System' of high tariffs, a National Bank, and internal improvements at national expense; third, of the special beneficiaries of the National Bank, which Jackson was destroying; fourth, of the opponents of the new democracy and of Jackson's 'executive tyranny.' Obviously, the Whigs also tended to be a class party — a party of the rich as opposed to the Jackson rabble. But the rich in the South had no common interest with the rich in the manufacturing North. And the Westerners who followed Clay into the party were not rich at all, but merely wished a strong capitalist Government which would build roads, canals, and railways for their benefit. Both the new party groupings, therefore, were based on personalities and compromises. As a result they were unstable. Only one man saw the realities of the situation, and slowly forced the new, realistic grouping — the grouping which, because it cleared the issues, led straight to the Civil War. But this work could not be begun until the overpowering personality of Jackson was out of the way.

3

Shortly before his inauguration, Jackson was consulted by his friend and supporter, Senator Eaton of Tennessee. Eaton wanted to marry the beautiful, notorious Peggy O'Neil, and suspecting

[1] The original Whigs, in America, professed to protest against the autocracy or King George. The new Whig Party professed to be outraged at the autocratic methods of 'King Andrew.'

that Jackson was planning to offer him a Cabinet position he wished to discover whether the marriage would stand in his way. Naturally, he pictured Peggy O'Neil to Jackson as a misunderstood and maligned woman. Jackson's long-loved Rachel had recently suffered from a scurrilous newspaper campaign during which the irregularity of her first marriage with Jackson had been grossly featured; so Jackson immediately attached all his fierce loyalty to Peggy O'Neil, and all his rage to those who were 'wronging' her. He told Eaton that of course he must marry her, if he loved her; and Eaton cheerfully acted on the advice. Mrs. Eaton was received by Mrs. Jackson, which in Jackson's eyes put the final mark of approbation on her. Then Mrs. Jackson died, and her husband's wrath against gossip-mongerers grew bitterer still, for he ascribed her death to the abuse she had received during the campaign. Immediately after his inauguration, he appointed Senator Eaton Secretary of War.

Peggy O'Neil had served as a combination of barmaid and decoy duck in her father's tavern in Washington. She had been married to a man called Timberlake, a drunken purser in the navy, who cut his throat, in 1828, while on duty in the Mediterranean. Senator Eaton, who had boarded at the tavern since 1818, was said to have been Peggy's lover both before and after the suicide. Whether or not this was true, there was no denying that the girl was socially unsuitable, and that it was unusual to pass from even the most moderate fondling of men at a Washington tavern to the position of wife of a Cabinet officer. All this meant nothing to Jackson; but it meant something to Mrs. Calhoun, the wife of the Vice-President and a member of one of the best families of South Carolina. She refused to meet Mrs. Eaton; the wives of the other Cabinet members followed her lead; and a political crisis resulted. Jackson — who by now felt he was championing his departed angel — would not hear of Eaton's resigning, and undertook to force the unwanted Peggy upon Washington society. The high-handed methods that had made his reputation in Indian warfare and frontier brawls proved ineffective in social combat, and

Jackson made no headway. The only Cabinet member who was kind to Mrs. Eaton was Van Buren, the Secretary of State, who, being a widower, had no social responsibilities, and who quickly saw that this farcical affair was likely to win him the Presidency. Calhoun had been the chief figure in the Administration and the obvious heir to Jackson's position; but Calhoun and Jackson were now at odds, and Van Buren was in the General's good graces.

The seriousness with which Jackson took the affair is shown by his threat to demand the recall of the Minister from Holland if that gentleman's wife gave an official ball and refrained from inviting Mrs. Eaton. Van Buren, however, had no intention of allowing matters to go so far as to wreck the party. He restrained the General's more fiery impulses; and after getting himself accepted in the position of heir-apparent, he persuaded Jackson to solve the social difficulty by reorganizing his Cabinet. He himself prepared the way by resigning; Eaton resigned next, and Jackson forced the remaining Cabinet members to do the same. Van Buren was sent as Minister to England; but the Senate, out of spite, refused to confirm the appointment. So he returned home to run for Vice-President on Jackson's ticket, in 1832, and to be made President in 1836.[1]

No sooner had the Eaton scandal quieted than Jackson plunged into the bitterest fight of his life — the 'War on the Bank.' The new Bank of the United States, which had been chartered in 1816 for twenty years, was as much disliked by the debtor class as was the original Bank of 1791. After the panic of 1819, which resulted from an orgy of speculation following the War of 1812, the National Bank foreclosed many hundreds of mortgages, thus coming to own large parts of many Western cities. The West began to call the Bank 'the Monster.' Senator Benton expressed this feeling when he spoke of 'the great cities of the Northeast, which

---

[1] Peggy Eaton lived until 1879. She left behind her a passionate defence of her honour and morals, in the form of an autobiography. This was published in 1932, and gives an interesting, if biased, picture of Washington in Jackson's days.

have been for forty years, and that by force of Federal legislation,
the lion's den of Southern and Western money — that den into
which all tracks point inward; from which the returning track of
a solitary dollar has never yet been seen.' Since most of the
Jacksonian democrats were poor, an attack on this rapacious
'Monster' was good politics, and Jackson's 'kitchen cabinet' of unofficial advisers persuaded him that the Bank was nothing but the
tool of the people's enemies, of the rich Easterners who sneered at
Jackson's motley following and whose newspapers had accused
Rachel of adultery. Jackson attacked the Bank (gently, for him)
in his first three messages to Congress; but it was not until 1832,
when Congress, under the leadership of Clay, passed a bill renew-
ing the charter, that Jackson made a major issue of the matter.
He vetoed the bill, calling the Bank unconstitutional (although
the Supreme Court had recently declared the reverse), and an
economic burden upon the West. In the Presidential elections
of that year Jackson was re-elected triumphantly. Thereupon he
undertook to destroy the Bank at once. Its charter still had four
years to run, but Jackson decided to withdraw all Government
funds from it. His Secretary of the Treasury refused to do this, so
he was promoted to the State Department. The new Secretary of
the Treasury also refused, so he was dismissed, and a man was
found who was docile enough to do what the enraged General demanded.

The people of the United States were delighted with this
combat. Jackson had assured them that the 'money power' was
their enemy, and they accepted the statement as obvious truth;
Jackson was destroying the chief symbol of this power, and they
thought the act both courageous and statesmanlike. The fact that
he had no alternative plan, nothing to put in the place of the one
agency that had discouraged 'wild-cat' banking and the more
insane forms of speculation, did not impress them.[1] Neither did

[1] Jackson was not, like Calhoun, seeking to build a new kind of state on the ruins
of Hamiltonian capitalism. His opposition to the Bank was emotional; he destroyed
this essential element in the Northern business system, but he would never have
permitted the North to secede and build its own system. Calhoun would have en-

the fact that the 'War on the Bank' was immediately followed by the worst financial depression the country has ever known, that for six years business was prostrate, and that 'the people' of Jackson's cherishing were the chief sufferers from this disaster.... The politicians, observing all this, learned a useful lesson about the new forces of democracy: that if a man seemed bluff and unpretentious, and talked about protecting the people, he could deprive them of every penny they possessed and they would still support him. Jackson had done this by mistake, and had made no profit; but surely a more far-sighted man could do it by intention?

Another vital problem which was becoming sicklied o'er with cant about 'the people' was the problem of the public lands. The election of 1828, in which Jackson defeated Adams, decided for all time that these lands would not be used wisely; but a further question remained, namely, in whose interest were they to be plundered? Gullible as ever, Jackson was persuaded by his advisers that the rights of the common man demanded that these lands be thrown open unconditionally to any settlers who would take them, and in 1832 he recommended this scheme. Congress, however, was not so naïve as the Executive. If the lands were to be given away, then someone (obviously not 'the people') would make enormous profit from them. In that case the giver should clearly have a reward. Furthermore, the problem was complicated by the conflicting interests of the three sections of the country. The West wanted the lands thrown open. No matter how they were settled, or who profiteered on the transaction, the West would obviously gain by having its population increase. New England, however, feared a rise in factory wages if too much cheap and fertile land were opened up; and the South feared the creation of new free States which might vote against the planting interests in the Senate. So, for the time being, nothing decisive was done. It was a question of waiting until the economic tension between North and South grew so acute that one section or

couraged the Northerners to secede. He had no wish to dictate their financial system: but if the country had to be a unit, he wished it to be run in the interests of the South.

the other forgot its fears and offered the West this enormous bribe in return for its support. Meanwhile, in 1841, Henry Clay put through a halfway measure which temporarily placated the West — a bill allowing settlers to pre-empt the public land in small lots and at a low price — ten per cent of the proceeds of such sales to go to the State in which the land lay.[1]

Less dramatic than the Peggy O'Neil affair, or the War on the Bank, the most important issue of Jackson's Presidency was that which led up to South Carolina's stand for nullification. The tariff issue had been critical throughout the South since 1828, and when, in 1832, it became clear that the Jacksonian party, so far from diminishing, was willing to increase the burden, South Carolina prepared to act according to the plans laid by Calhoun. Arguing from the premiss that the Constitution was a compact between sovereign States (the thirteen original States having been 'sovereign' from the time of the Declaration of Independence until the organization of the new government in 1789), Calhoun declared that whenever the Federal Government usurped powers that had not been granted it, any State had the right to declare the acts of the Federal Government null and void. And the protective tariff laws, according to Calhoun, were unconstitutional; so in 1832 his State declared the recent tariff law null and void. Jackson fulminated, threatening to hang Calhoun and to treat the South Carolinians as he had treated the English and the Spanish in Florida. But Congress knew that a war in South Carolina would not, at the moment, be popular; therefore, while passing a Force Bill to give Jackson all the authority for which he asked, it simultaneously passed a compromise tariff bill, providing for a progressive diminution of the rates over a period of nine years. It was a triumph for the new leader of the South; but Calhoun was too far-sighted to feel encouraged. He knew that his section was in a minority, and would be increasingly outweighed as the

[1] When a new State was admitted to the Union, the Federal Government retained title to all the lands that had not yet been allotted, though ceding jurisdiction over them.

West developed. He knew that the Northern manufacturers would never rest content with a low tariff. The South could not permanently control the Government at Washington; therefore, in the long run, she must secede. From this moment onward, Calhoun was working to create a unified South, to cut across the artificial party division of Whig and Democrat, and to build a Southern, States'-rights, free-trade, agrarian party — a party to be led by the planting aristocracy, and ready to secede the moment the business men captured the Government.

4

John Caldwell Calhoun looked exactly what he was: the brilliant, pessimistic leader of a doomed cause. Jefferson Davis remarked on his 'glorious pair of yellow-brown shining eyes,' and these stared gloomily from sunken sockets under great heavy brows. Across his pale broad forehead was a sweep of black hair that almost hid one eye. His features were rugged, his body spare and gaunt, his bearing that of one accustomed to tormented thoughts. It was said of Daniel Webster that no man could be as great as Webster looked; if any man could be as tragic as Calhoun looked, it would be the man who foresaw the murder of everything he held good in the life of his country.

When Calhoun was born, in 1782, his family had been two generations in the South Carolina uplands, and had begun to prosper. The ambitious boy, therefore, did not push West, like Jackson, but stayed at home and married his cousin, Floride, whose mother was Floride Bouneau of the tidewater aristocracy. Calhoun had been educated at Yale University, and had then become a lawyer, and after his marriage he was wealthy enough to devote himself to public life. When he first went to Congress, he became one of the 'War-Hawks' of the lower House — he and Clay being the leading figures in creating the War of 1812. His ardent patriotism lasted until the eighteen-twenties, when he suddenly realized the permanent economic and cultural antagonism between North and South. At once he abandoned nationalism and gave allegiance to his State — which was a unit small enough to be known in the way a man should know his country, a unit small enough to be loved.

Calhoun set himself to build a political philosophy by which the new South could live. He lacked Clay's charm, and he disliked the flashy rhetoric of Webster; it was by the power of intellect and character, of plain speech and logic, that he made himself an uncrowned king in Carolina and the master of the Southern mind. His programme was audacious; he knew that no halfway measures could save the agrarian South. 'My aim is fixed,' he said in a speech in 1839. 'It is no less than to turn back the government to where it commenced its operation in 1789.' So Calhoun's first demand was that the whole Hamiltonian scheme, the basis for the strong capitalist state, for government by and for the business man, must be destroyed. This involved, among other measures, the complete separation of the Government from the banks, the reduction of all the expenses of the Federal Government, the abandonment of the policy of building roads, canals, or other internal improvements, at national expense, and the abandonment of the protective tariff. The second item in Calhoun's programme was that the tyranny of majority rule must be abolished. It was for this purpose that he elaborated his States'-rights doctrine, so that the will of a nation-wide majority might be checked by a sectional referendum. Thirdly, Calhoun met the increasing Northern criticism of slavery, not with apology, but with the statement that slavery was a positive good, that all cultures are based on some form of forced labour, and that by comparison with Northern exploitation of the factory hand the Southern treatment of the black was benign. Taking the offensive against the North, Calhoun insisted that the agrarian South, based on the slave-labour of an obviously inferior people, directed by an aristocracy of great landowners, and supported by a large group of planters with moderate holdings in land and men — that such a South offered the one promise for civilization in America and must be defended to the last against the bourgeois ideals and the tyrannous democracy of the North. He was trying to erect a barrier against the triumphant middle class, and before he died he had won the allegiance of the South. He had given his section a coherent programme; it was for the next generation to fight for the privilege of adhering to it.

5

When Jackson was re-elected to the Presidency in 1832, Van Buren took Calhoun's place as Vice-President. The Peggy O'Neil affair had begun the break between Jackson and Calhoun, and the hard feeling increased when Jackson discovered that Calhoun had wanted to have him censured, back in 1819, for his conduct in the Florida affair. But the final reason for the break was Jackson's violent opposition to South Carolina's experiment in nullification. Presumably Calhoun expected Jackson's support, for on some matters Jackson was an ardent States'-rights man. When Georgia had claimed the Cherokee Indians as her subjects and tenants-at-will — in obvious violation of the treaty between the Indians and the United States Government — Chief Justice John Marshall of the Supreme Court decided that Georgia had no right whatever to molest the Indians. Jackson's comment was, 'John Marshall has made his decision. Now let him enforce it.' So the State of Georgia proceeded to defy the National Government. That was permitted because Jackson, a frontiersman, hated Indians. He was not acting upon anything so complicated as a political theory, and therefore thought nothing of adopting the opposite attitude when South Carolina defied the Federal Government.

On withdrawing from the new Democratic Party, Calhoun took his whole State with him. He did not, however, take it into the Whig Party — for within that curious grab-bag there were strong Northern, anti-slavery, and nationalistic groups. Calhoun had himself sent to the Senate, and there waited for a chance to forward his scheme for a sectional, Southern party. The chance did not come until 1843. Meanwhile, Jackson had chosen Van Buren for his heir, and in 1836 had easily secured Van Buren's nomination and election. Jackson, as soon as his second term was out, retired to 'The Hermitage,' near Nashville, Tennessee. He had little money, having left Washington poorer than when he arrived, and he made only a meagre living from his farm. During his last years he quarrelled with many of his old friends and lost all political authority. But he remained the people's hero until his death in 1845.

An observer of Jackson's career in politics could have predicted the graceless tragedy that was to overtake American public life. There are two ways in which democracy might have been made to work in the United States. The first was by following Jefferson's ideal — suppressing capitalism, discouraging industry, forcing the country to rely upon its boundless farmlands and to become a social as well as a political democracy, a nation of small-scale, independent, landowning farmers. That was a pleasing dream; but it never reached the stature of a plan. Jefferson lacked the political and economic realism to see, in time, what must be done if Hamilton was to be countered. By the time Jefferson had grasped the implications of Hamilton's scheme, it was too late to resist. Had Calhoun lived in those days, there would have been a better fight. Even two generations later he was able to undo so much of Hamilton's work that the frightened capitalists had to bribe the West and then run to arms for protection.... But even in spite of the triumph of Hamiltonianism, democracy might have been made workable if the nation had followed J. Q. Adams's plan — had controlled the growth of the West so that the new, ungainly, backwoods States would not outnumber those with a settled civilization, had kept every dollar that could be made from the public domain in the hands of the National Government and used that endowment to promote the health and education of the citizens. A well-instructed and economically independent electorate might have made a good thing of democracy.

Neither of these plans, however, was even attempted, and the planless, haphazard government which actually developed was a travesty of the democratic principle. Manhood suffrage, rotation in office, and the doctrine that the representative should mirror the opinion of the majority that elected him — these three principles were adopted by a country which was being increasingly industrialized (so that the city mobs were more numerous every year), which had only a rudimentary public education, which was already having to meet the problem of a huge immigrant population, and which was faced with new perplexing questions of adjustment between hostile sections. Obviously the stage was prepared for a distasteful form of politician — for the man who would distract the huge, uninformed electorate with fantastic shows, meanwhile going quietly about his private plunder. Only in the South (which possessed no city mobs to be bossed and bribed) was a stand made against this form of democracy. As the South grew increasingly united, conscious of the vital struggle that faced it, all classes in the community were willing to put government into the hands of their best-educated and best-trained men. As a result, there was a group of Southern statesmen in both houses of Congress, though chiefly in the Senate, who were anxious, and able, to deal with the real issues of the day. It was not until the old South was demolished by its conquerors, in the years following the Civil War, that the world was shown the full possibilities of democracy in an enormous, industrialized, uneducated and untrained country. But all this was foreshadowed, for anyone who was willing to see, as early as the election of 1840.

6

When Van Buren was inaugurated as President, in March, 1837, he must have blessed Peggy O'Neil, whose social struggle had started him toward the White House; but before he had been in office for many months it is probable that he had come to curse her. For all the evil effects of Jackson's planless, demagogic finance fell upon the country soon after Van Buren's inauguration. In this there was poetic justice; for it was Van Buren who made the political combinations that brought in the reign of

Jackson, and it was Van Buren who, at a critical moment, when the Cabinet's opposition to his Bank policy was weakening the old man's resolve, had arrived home from England and urged Jackson to go through with his destructive plans. Whether Van Buren believed in these plans is as impossible to decide as whether he believed in anything else. His contemporaries used the word, 'vanburenish,' as a synonym for suave evasiveness. It was said that a man once asked him whether the sun rose in the east, and that Van Buren answered, 'I presume the fact is according to the common impression, but as I sleep until after sunrise, I cannot speak from my own knowledge.' At the famous Jefferson-Day banquet, during the nullification crisis (when Jackson declared his open enmity to Calhoun and the Southern doctrine by giving the toast, 'Our Federal Union — it must be preserved'), Van Buren's toast was 'Mutual forbearance and reciprocal concessions.' Shrewd, tactful, suspicious, urbane, and cynical, he was never (during his years of power) the partisan of any cause, except that of political 'regularity.' Adams, in 1829, described him as by far the ablest of the men in Jackson's camp, and then added, 'wasting most of his abilities upon mere personal intrigues, [he] retains the forms of civility, and pursues enmity as if he thought it might be one day his interest to seek friendship. His principles are all subordinate to his ambition.' And, comparing Van Buren with Madison, Adams wrote, 'These are both remarkable for their extreme caution in avoiding personal collisions. Van Buren, like the Sosie of Molière's *Amphitryon*, is *l'ami de tout le monde*.' The result of this crafty and affable policy was that Van Buren had no enemies and no friends. It was as needless to hate 'Little Van' as it was impossible to love. It was, however, equally impossible to ignore him — which may have satisfied his somewhat bloodless nature. His appearance mirrored his character. Small in stature, wary and self-contained of expression, correct in dress and bearing, there was nothing to belie his reputation as 'the careful Dutchman from New York.' His long curly yellow hair, his large blue eyes, and the perfect cupid's bow of his upper lip, might have given him a misleadingly benign expression, if it had not been for the cynicism of his smile.

Van Buren was born at Kinderhook — near Albany, New York — in 1782. His ancestors, who had settled at Kinderhook early in the seventeenth century, were Dutch on both sides of the family. His father was a tavern-keeper and farmer, without the means to provide his son with more than a limited education. But at the age of fourteen, Van Buren began to spend his spare time in the study of law. At the age of nineteen, he went to New York City, where he suffered from extreme poverty; but two years later he was admitted to the bar, and a successful practice soon gave him financial independence, enabling him to give more and more of his time to politics, which had always been his chief interest.

New York State politics, in Van Buren's youth, were sordid and complicated, making the ideal training school for the man who was to be the first master at manipulating the new democracy. The Democratic-Republican Party was divided into three factions — the followers, respectively, of the Clintons, of Livingston, and of Aaron Burr. The declining Federalist Party intrigued with each group in turn, seeking to win concessions by maintaining a precarious balance of power. The fierce personal hatreds that resulted were a warning to the dispassionate young Dutchman. Shortly after Van Buren reached New York City, Hamilton's eldest son was killed in a duel at Weehawken, and two years later, on the same duelling-ground, Aaron Burr killed Alexander Hamilton himself. It is no wonder that Van Buren, by the time he had worked his way into the centre of these struggles, evolved a subtler and more ingratiating political technique.

In 1807, Van Buren married Hannah Hoes, his childhood sweetheart. She died in 1819, after bearing four sons, and there is no record that Van Buren was ever again infected with so impractical an emotion as love.... In the year following his marriage, he had obtained his first political preferment, becoming surrogate for Columbia County. Thereafter his rise was rapid, and he became a State Senator, a member of the highest court of New York, and Attorney-General for the State. He had started as a member of the Clinton clique in the Democratic-Republican Party, but soon broke with De Witt Clinton and began to form his own group. By 1820, he was a leader of the famous 'Albany Regency,' a group of politicians who controlled New York State for a generation, and who first proved to an admiring nation the simple effectiveness of the 'spoils system.' In 1821, he went to the Senate at Washington, and by 1824 he had picked Jackson as the coming man, and was beginning to lay the foundations for what was to develop into the Democratic Party.

After Jackson's election, in 1828, Van Buren was made Secretary of State. He kept on good terms with the unofficial 'kitchen cabinet,' remained as detached as possible from the Jackson-Calhoun quarrel, and made the most of the war over Peggy O'Neil. His reward was the Vice-Presidency in 1832, and the Presidency in 1836.

As might have been expected, Van Buren's inaugural message was a hymn of praise to democracy combined with an attempt to persuade both North and South that there really was no reason why they should not live together amicably. With one exception he kept all of Jackson's Cabinet, and in so far as Jackson had a policy, Van Buren continued that as well. One of his few original contributions was the Independent Treasury Bill, providing for building a treasury at Washington, and sub-treasuries throughout the country, in which (now that the Bank was defunct) the Government could lock up its funds. This bill was soon repealed by the Whigs, then re-enacted by the Democrats, remaining in force until the Civil War.

In 1840 there occurred the most ridiculous election in American history. Van Buren was renominated by the Democrats, as a matter of course; but the Whigs had trouble in choosing their candidate. Henry Clay was the obvious man; but the party leaders suspected that since his opinions on many subjects were widely known there might be a number of potential Whigs who would vote against him merely because they disagreed with him. Clay, therefore, was rejected, and the politicians looked about for someone with no known opinions, feeling that only such a man could hope to triumph over the ambiguous Van Buren. The dubious compliment of this nomination was finally given to General William Henry Harrison who, in 1811, had defeated some Indians at the battle of Tippecanoe River, in the Indiana Territory. All that was asked of Harrison, in the campaign of 1840, was that he say nothing. Nicholas Biddle, who had been President of the Bank of the United States before it was destroyed by Jackson, and who felt sure his institution would be revived if the Whigs were victorious, advised the party managers as follows: 'Let him [i.e., Harrison] say not one single word about his principles or his creed — let him say nothing — promise nothing. Let no committee, no convention — no town meeting ever extract from him a single word about what he thinks now or will do hereafter. Let the use of pen and ink be wholly forbidden.' This plan of campaign was suited to Harrison's taste and training, and was adopted almost literally. As candidate for the Vice-Presidency, the Whigs chose John Tyler, of Virginia, a man of character and experience in public life, who had recently opposed both Jackson's Bank policy and his attitude toward nullification, and who was assumed to be a Whig.

Since neither Harrison nor any party leader was to utter 'a single word about what he thinks now or will do hereafter,' it was necessary to find some other topic to discuss. This was soon supplied by an incautious Democrat. The house at North Bend, Ohio, where Harrison had been living for the past ten years, had formerly been a log cabin, and the General was reputed to drink cider with his meals rather than wine; for these reasons a Democratic orator called him the 'log-cabin and hard-cider' candidate — and the issue for the campaign was made. Seizing on this supposedly derogatory phrase, the Whigs made a virtue of it, and began picturing their candidate as a humble man of the people, a man who could be trusted to understand them and to work in their interest, a man whose whole life proved how false and unkind was

the suggestion that the Whigs favoured the moneyed classes. Log
cabins were set up all over the country, and voters were given as
much hard cider as they could hold. Log cabins were drawn on
floats in processions; log-cabin clubs were founded, log-cabin
badges distributed, log-cabin songs recited in lieu of more definite statements of policy.

Not only was Harrison made into the frontiersman's brother
and the friend of the farmer's drink, but he became a military
hero somewhat on the scale of Hannibal. The battle of Tippecanoe, it was vaguely suggested, was the crisis of American
history. 'Tippecanoe and Tyler too,' was the chief campaign
slogan; and the campaign songs were on the order of the following:

> Let Van from his coolers of silver drink wine
>   And lounge on his cushioned settee.
> Our man on his buckeye bench can recline,
>   Content with hard cider is he,
> The iron-armed soldier, the true-hearted soldier,
> The gallant old soldier of Tippecanoe.

To make the circus complete, huge balls, symbolic of the immense
majority Harrison would win, were rolled from village to village,
to the accompaniment of ditties such as this:

> As rolls the ball,
> Van's reign doth fall,
> And he may look
> To Kinderhook.

The fact that Harrison had been born and bred in Virginia, where
his father was a man of prominence and social position (having
been Governor of the State, a member of the Continental Congress
during the War of Independence, and for a time President of the
Board of War), did not interfere with the success of the log-cabin
nonsense. Similarly, the fact that Van Buren had been born and
brought up in extreme poverty, and was in fact the self-made
'man of the people' that Harrison was falsely pictured as being,
did not prevent his being attacked as an aristocrat, with lordly
manners and a love of high living, who scented his whiskers with

cologne, ate off gold plate, and laced himself up in corsets. The result of this vulgar, lying, irrelevant, and cynical campaign was that Harrison received 234 electoral votes and Van Buren 60. J. Q. Adams's comment was as follows: 'If Harrison is not found time-serving, demagogic, unsteady, and Western-sectional, he will more than satisfy my present expectations.'

It is doubtful whether Van Buren was troubled by the result. He had watched the campaign with detachment, and probably with secret, sardonic amusement. Four years later, he expected to receive the Democratic nomination and to return to the White House. However, after it seemed that the nomination was safely his, he was so unwise as to express an opinion on the most important issue of the day — the annexation of Texas — and at once the Democrats threw him over and nominated Polk instead. Van Buren never again became a commanding figure in National politics, for he identified himself with a Northern, anti-slavery faction in the Democratic Party, apparently feeling that after a lifetime of 'regularity' he could afford at least one opinion in his old age.... Having lived to see the beginning of the Civil War, he died, at Kinderhook, in 1862.

CHAPTER V

WILLIAM HENRY HARRISON TO JEFFERSON DAVIS

I

WILLIAM HENRY HARRISON was born in Charles City County, Virginia, in 1773. His father, in addition to being annoyingly successful for the parent of a log-cabin hero, was also a violent opponent of the Constitution at the Virginia ratifying convention in 1788. He had only himself to thank, therefore, for being edited out of existence in the interest of his son's election.

Harrison was educated at Hampden-Sidney College, and then began a medical course in Philadelphia. His father died in the following year. Finding himself in financial difficulties Harrison entered the army as an ensign. He had an uninspired but blameless military career, and in 1798, having risen to the rank of captain, he resigned from the army and became secretary of the Northwest Territory. Meanwhile, he married a Miss Anne Symmes, of New Jersey.

In 1800, John Adams appointed him Governor of the Indiana Territory, an office which he held until 1812. He made a series of treaties with the Indians; and when, as always, the advancing whites began to violate these treaties, the Indians attempted to form a league to fight for their lands. Harrison met this threat by leading a combined force of militia and regulars against the Indians, defeating them at Tippecanoe River.... During this period when he was Governor of the Indiana Territory, Harrison's son was born — a boy who was to have a minor political career and to become the father of the twenty-third President of the United States.

In the course of the War of 1812, Harrison rose to the rank of major-general, and to the command of all the troops in the Northwest. He accomplished nothing, however; and when the Secretary of War, without consulting him, issued an order to one of his subordinates, Harrison resigned. Under Monroe, and again under J. Q. Adams, he served for brief periods in Congress; and in 1828 Adams appointed him as the first United States Minister to Colombia. Even in this modest post, however, he did not do very well, and in 1829 Jackson recalled him. Thereafter he lived in retirement at North Bend, Ohio, earning his living as clerk of the Court of Common Pleas. In the presidential campaign of 1836, the Whigs of three States nominated him to stand against Van Buren. He made a poor showing, and there seemed every reason to suppose that his humble and harmless career was at an end. But by 1840 the party leaders were awake to the value of inconspicuous mediocrity, and Harrison became their choice. He was asked to keep quiet during the election, and to take orders with docility after the party had triumphed. Only in one respect was he a disappointment during these months. When Webster wrote an inaugural address and told Harrison to deliver it, he balked. He had composed an inflated oration of his own, which he refused to abandon. It was with difficulty that Webster even got permission to revise it — and after a day at this task he arrived late and weary at a dinner party. When his hostess wanted to know whether anything had happened, Webster answered, 'Madam, you would think something had happened, if you knew what I have done. I have killed seventeen Roman proconsuls as dead as smelts!'

Aside from keeping still and taking orders, all that was asked of Harrison was that he remain alive. Had he been capable of this unexacting task, it is possible that the South might have seceded in 1841 — and if so the break would probably have occurred without bloodshed. The Whigs, having triumphed in their buffoon of a campaign, were ready to go the whole way in the restoration of the Hamiltonian system. A high tariff and the establishment of a third Bank of the United States were their immediate projects. They had the majority in Congress; they had an obedient President. There was nothing to stop them, and there is no reason

to suppose that South Carolina would have accepted the triumph
of Hamiltonianism in 1841 any more than in 1833 or in 1860.
But on April 4, one month after coming into office, Harrison died
of pneumonia. The Whigs were to have no such chance again
until the election of Lincoln.

John Tyler, who had been made Vice-President for the sake of
Virginian votes (and with the vague feeling that because he opposed Jackson he must be a Whig), proved the antithesis of the
pliant Harrison. He was neither obedient in temperament nor
Hamiltonian in his political philosophy. Only in a time of transition, when the party alignments were not yet in keeping with the
underlying truths of the situation, could Tyler's real affiliation
have been so misunderstood. But finding himself in a thoroughly
false position, he decided to act according to his own opinions, and
to endure the charge of being a traitor to the men who had put him
in office.

2

Tyler was born in 1790, in the same county of Virginia where
Harrison had been born seventeen years earlier. Tyler's father
was a man of position and importance who served as Governor of
Virginia and as United States District Judge. The boy was
educated at William and Mary College, whence he graduated in
1807. Two years later he was admitted to the bar, and using law
as a stepping-stone to politics he was soon a member of the Virginia
House of Delegates, and of the Council of State. In 1813, he married Miss Letitia Christian, the daughter of a Virginia planter.
He took only an insignificant part in the War of 1812; but when the
war was over, Virginia sent him to the House of Representatives in
Washington. During the first two years of John Quincy Adams's
Presidency, Tyler was Governor of Virginia; and in 1827 he was
sent to the United States Senate, to succeed Randolph of Roanoke.
Throughout his career in the legislature Tyler was a strict con-
structionist in all constitutional questions — i.e., he was opposed
to strengthening the National Government at the expense of the

States. The underlying reason for this was that he was opposed to a Hamiltonian capitalist state, and that he wished to preserve agrarianism and the existing economic institutions of the South. In 1832 he supported Jackson, as the 'least objectionable' candidate; but during the crisis of 1833 he strongly favoured tariff reduction and voted against the Force Bill which gave Jackson power to coerce South Carolina. He thought South Carolina's nullification unwise; but the use of force against any State seemed to him wrong. He opposed Jackson's removal of Government funds from the National Bank, and resigned from the Senate rather than obey the Virginia Legislature when it ordered him to support a motion in favour of Jackson. The Whigs, on this account, thought they had won a convert. They should have realized that Tyler was in reality a lesser Calhoun — a man who had been driven from the Democratic Party by the activities of Jackson, but who had no sympathy with the projects of the Northern business men. Tyler interpreted the victory over Van Buren as being simply the overthrow of the tyrannical faction of Jackson and his lieutenants. He had no feeling that he was adopting an ambiguous position in allying himself for this purpose with the Whigs. The Whigs — representing men of money and position — were still the most respectable party, both in the North and in the South;[1] and it was not until after the crisis under Tyler that the country realized how completely that party was committed to the Hamiltonian system.

Tyler's first act in the Presidency was a sign of the independent attitude he intended to adopt. According to the Constitution, the Vice-President was, in case of the President's death, to be a substitute for him, and not a successor to his office. Tyler, however, insisted on becoming President, and not merely acting-President. He had his way, and the precedent he established has been followed to the present day.... At the first Cabinet meeting,

---

[1] It was about this time that Varina Howell, meeting Jefferson Davis (whose wife she was to become), wrote in surprise to her mother that Davis, although a refined and cultivated man, was a Democrat.

he had to confront another threat to his authority. He had kept
Harrison's Cabinet, and Webster, the Secretary of State, tried to
browbeat him into acting merely as the presiding officer of a
board with a vote like everyone else, but with the obligation of
accepting the decision of the majority. Tyler rejected this suggestion with finality, and the Whig leaders began to realize that
they had a problem on their hands; but they were still confident
of victory. 'Tyler dares not resist!' exclaimed Henry Clay; 'I'll
drive him before me.' Tyler's reply to such threats was, 'I pray
you to believe that my back is to the wall, and that while I shall
deplore the assaults I shall, if practicable, beat back the assail-
ants.'

It proved to be practicable. When Congress, under Clay's
leadership, repealed Van Buren's Independent Treasury Act, and
then passed a bill creating a new Bank of the United States,
Tyler vetoed the bill on the ground that the Constitution gave
the Government no power to create such a corporation within a
State unless the consent of the State had been obtained before-
hand. Clay secured the passage of a second bill, providing for the
creation of a Bank of the United States within the District of
Columbia and permitting this bank to establish branches in the
States on conditions that were intended to satisfy Tyler's scruples.
But the conditions were too ambiguous and Tyler vetoed this bill
as well. The system of centralized finance was dead until the triumph of the Hamiltonians in the Civil War. Similarly, when
Congress passed a protective tariff, Tyler vetoed it. Congress then
passed a tariff for revenue with 'incidental protection,' and with
provision for distributing the surplus revenue among the States.
On the grounds that it was merely a scheme for bribing the States
into accepting protection, Tyler vetoed this bill also. When Congress gave in and presented him with a low tariff bill that had no
distribution clause, Tyler signed it.

The third great feature of the Hamilton-Clay policy was internal
improvements at national expense. Tyler vetoed one measure
of this sort; but consented to sign a bill which referred only to

improvements on the Mississippi River, on the ground that this was a common highway for the commerce of the whole country, and that money spent on it was not a bribe to any one section at the expense of the others.

In 1842, while Tyler was in the midst of these bitter fights, his wife died. Two years later, before he had left the White House, he married again. His second wife was Miss Julia Gardiner, of New York, a convert to Roman Catholicism and an ardent worker for the faith. She was thirty years Tyler's junior, but their married life, most of which was spent in retirement at Tyler's Virginia estate, was notably happy.

The first result of Tyler's recalcitrance was that within six months of his taking office the whole Cabinet, with the exception of one man, resigned. Webster stayed on, because he was negotiating an important treaty with England, settling the long dispute about the northeastern frontier.[1] Tyler was undismayed, and chose a Cabinet of his own, which included Upshur of Virginia, Legaré of South Carolina, and Wickliffe of Kentucky. In the Congressional elections of 1842, the Whigs lost their majority in the House, and then, after Webster had finished his treaty-making and had resigned, John C. Calhoun became Secretary of State. The revolution was complete. Tyler had gone over to the Democrats and Calhoun had returned to them. The Administration, which had begun with the utter triumph of the Hamiltonians, ended with a victory for Calhoun's long-cherished policy of reforming the Democratic Party on the basis of States' rights, thus making it into the champion of his Southern slave Republic.

The work was not yet complete; the great Southern landowners were still inclined to consider themselves Whigs — chiefly on social grounds; but when Calhoun joined Tyler's Cabinet the balance of the Democratic Party shifted to the South, and the balance of Southern strength shifted to that Party. Soon the lines

[1] According to his enemies, he had still another reason for remaining; namely, that if the attempt to break Tyler were too successful, it was Henry Clay who would chiefly triumph and who would probably be elected President in 1844.

were to be drawn clear. Before Calhoun's death in 1850, he had won over his entire section. The South was a united party with a threefold policy; the defence of the agrarian Republic; the desire to remain in the Union so long as it was not administered at the expense of that Republic and for the greater profit of the Northern business men; the intention to secede whenever the Government at Washington should be captured by the bourgeois interests.

Seen against this fundamental issue, slavery becomes a mere incident. The deep South saw it as a wise and moral institution — Calhoun asserting that 'we see [slavery] now in its true light, and regard it as the most safe and stable basis for free institutions in the world.' But many of the greatest Southerners were averse to it. 'Robert E. Lee emancipated the few slaves he inherited from his mother, and owned no others. Stonewall Jackson purchased two slaves at their own request and allowed them to earn their freedom J. E. Johnston and A. P. Hill never owned a slave, and disliked slavery. J. E. B. Stuart owned but two slaves, and disposed of them for good reasons, long before the war. M. F. Maury, who called slavery a "curse," never owned but one, a family servant.' [1] These men would not have been willing to consume themselves and the whole South for a system of which they disapproved. They fought for the civilization they believed in, to save it from being forcibly transformed into the civilization they despised. The clarification of that issue throughout the South was primarily the work of Calhoun.

As part of his system for strengthening the South, Calhoun favoured the annexation by America of Texas, which had broken away from Mexico in 1835 and had existed as an independent Republic since that date. The Texans had applied for annexation; but Congress refused to act, since the North had no desire to make a present to the South of a new agrarian province larger than the whole of France. In 1844, Calhoun negotiated a treaty of annexation, which would require the consent of two-thirds of the Senate to become valid. The Senate refused its consent. A joint

[1] S. E. Morison, *Oxford History of the United States*, II, 23, note 2.

resolution of the two Houses was then attempted, and passed; and on his last day in office — the third of March, 1845 — Tyler sent word to Texas that annexation had been accomplished.

In 1844, Tyler sought the Democratic nomination; but the party was wary of him and of his complicated record. He started to campaign as an independent Democrat, then resigned in favour of the regular candidate, James K. Polk. Tyler retired to his country place on the James River, taking no further part in public life until the crisis of secession. He was then appointed by Virginia as a commissioner to consult the Government at Washington with a view to avoiding hostilities. Tyler's attitude was exactly what it had been in 1833 — that secession was inadvisable, but coercion by the National Government intolerable. As soon as he found that coercion was the probable policy of Washington, he returned to Virginia and advocated an immediate break. He was elected to the Provisional Confederate Congress, and then to the permanent Congress under the new Constitution; but he died in January, 1862, before that Congress assembled.

3

Adams and Jackson had both tried to buy Texas from Mexico. The Mexicans refused to sell; but they very foolishly offered free land on an imperial scale to Americans who would colonize that province. In the early twenties this colonization movement began, and by 1835 there were about twenty thousand ex-Americans in Texas. It was obvious that trouble must come if Mexico ever attempted to govern these foreigners. In 1835 the attempt was threatened; Texas immediately seceded from Mexico, proclaimed herself a republic, and asked for annexation to the United States. But a large number of the Texans were planters from the South, who had crossed to the rich new lands taking their slaves and their system of cotton-culture with them. It was clear, therefore, that by climate, soil, and previous history, Texas was destined to be a slave state — or possibly, in view of her immense size, a whole group of slave States. The annexation of Texas might well upset the balance of power between North and South; hence the proposal aroused a new intensity of national feeling. The legislators of Vermont protested against the admission of States that permitted slavery; Calhoun stated that the attempt to exclude a State on account of slavery would lead to the dissolution of the Union.

The more the conflict between North and South came to be stated in terms of slavery as a moral issue (rather than in the economic terms of capitalism versus agrarianism), the more inevitable became secession. The men of the deep South felt — with undue optimism — that they had found as fair a system of labour as the world had seen. They believed the Negro belonged to an inferior race, enured by heredity to the Southern climate; they believed that he was happy in his bondage, and that his labour formed the basis for a civilization that was already superior to anything attainable in the commercial North — a civilization destined to flower into one of the fairest of human achievements. They believed that in their slave-state they were on the road to solving the problem of democracy. The attempted solutions of Jefferson and J. Q. Adams had been wrecked by capitalist greed; but they believed that on the bases of agriculture and Negro slavery they could erect a civilization of free and highly developed men. And they believed that the part played by the Negro was one which he would neither resent nor suffer under. When, therefore, these Southerners were told that they were little better than monsters for permitting this institution, they developed a hostility and contempt for the North which could scarcely have been aroused by purely economic debates. In Virginia and the border States, where the seamy side of slavery was more obvious (for it was there that slaves were bred for the market), there was less enthusiasm for the institution; and since — with the approaching exhaustion of the soil — slavery was becoming less and less successful economically, those States ought to have taken the lead in an attempt to find some more ideal status for the black man. But all such chances were impaired every time the moral issue was raised. Conscious of the irony in the fact that New England made a gold mine out of the slave trade, and then began calling slavery immoral after that trade had been forbidden; conscious that the comparison between working conditions in Northern factories and Southern cotton fields was by no means unfavourable to the South; and conscious that envy of the planter's relatively spacious and leisured life had not a little to do with Northern hostility to the South, no Southerner could submit calmly to the charge that the economic basis of his life was immoral. As this charge became more common, the unification of the South became more complete. Calhoun — who never lost sight of the real issue, of the clash between two economic systems and their civilizations — exploited these misguided Northern accusations to the full.

In the last days of Tyler's Administration, there was added to the Texan issue a new territorial squabble — only this one, instead of threatening a split between North and South, threatened a war with England. Ever since 1818 the huge Oregon Territory had been held under joint occupancy by England and the United States. J. Q. Adams had three times offered to settle the question by taking latitude 49°, which was already the boundary line east of the Rockies, as the boundary to the west of the Rockies as well. But the British had refused — hoping in the end to secure the Columbia River as the southern limit of English territory. The question did not become serious until 1842, when 'Oregon fever' set in along the American frontier and caravans of covered wagons began to be seen on the Oregon Trail. Immediately the Westerners started an agitation for the annexation of the whole of Oregon, up to latitude 54° 40′, which was the boundary of Russian Alaska. In 1844, Calhoun renewed J. Q. Adams's offer of accepting latitude 49° as the boundary; but again this was refused. Thus the matter rested when it came to nominating candidates for the Presidential election of 1844.

The Democratic Convention was expected to nominate Van Buren; but when so many delegates had been pledged to him that his nomination seemed certain, he incautiously let it be known that he was opposed to the annexation of Texas. Immediately, a number of Southern delegates decided to ignore their instructions, while in some States the Party held new meetings and ordered the delegates to vote against Van Buren. He still had a majority; but not the necessary two-thirds for a Democratic nomination. After a period of deadlock, Polk was brought forward as a dark horse. He was known as an ardent expansionist, as one who was in favour both of annexing Texas and of taking a firm stand in regard to Oregon. Chiefly because of the Southern desire for Texas, Polk was nominated.

'Who is James K. Polk?' was the campaign cry of the Whigs, and it is a question that many Americans today might echo, if they chanced to hear the name. For although some of the most important episodes in American history took place during his Administration and as a result of his policies, the man himself was so colourless that he left nothing but a few facts to remember him by. He was a man without intimate friends, and quite without magnetism. Formal and punctilious in bearing, stiff and angular in appearance, he looked as insignificant as he had always hitherto been.

'Who is James K. Polk?,' though an apt comment on his career, was a flimsy slogan when compared with the two that were evolved by the Democrats. 'The Reoccupation of Oregon and the Reannexation of Texas' was the first of these. The prefix 're-,' which must have made both proceedings seem more moral, was introduced, in the case of Texas, on the grounds that the Louisiana Purchase had included Texas and that J. Q. Adams had wrongly surrendered this territory to Spain in the treaty of 1819; [1] and in regard to Oregon, there was even less justification for the expression. American traders and explorers had been in Oregon from time to time; but the notion that any of them had 'occupied' that vast domain had never previously been put into words. But the slogan was effective and exciting — as was the second slogan of the Democratic Party, 'Fifty-four Forty, or

---

[1] The warrant for this claim was the fact that Napoleon intended to seize Texas, had he occupied Louisiana.

fight!', expressing the determination to re-occupy the *whole* of Oregon, straight to the Alaskan border. The campaign was almost as insane, though not so trivial, as that of 1840. Its chief interest is that it proved the fallacy of the theory that a democracy is likely to be pacific. A responsible government would have hesitated to push blithely toward simultaneous wars with both England and Mexico; but the anonymous and unknown 'people' had no scruples. Henry Clay, the Whig candidate, tried to avoid taking any stand on the Texas question, with the result that he lost votes both North and South. Polk was elected.[1]

Polk was born in North Carolina in 1795. His family had been in America since about 1680, and his grandfather had been an officer in the Revolutionary Army; but none of the Polks had ever acquired wealth, distinction, or high social position. When he was eleven his parents crossed the mountains into Tennessee. His adolescence was spent on the frontier; but his parents had money enough to send him back east to the University of North Carolina. After graduating, he studied law in Nashville, Tennessee, and was admitted to the bar in 1820. Three years later he began his political career by going to the State Legislature. In 1824 he married Sarah Childers, the daughter of a prosperous Tennessee farmer. She had the social charm which Polk lacked, and in after years was one of the most popular hostesses that the White House had known.

During the Presidencies of J. Q. Adams, Jackson, and Van Buren, Polk was in the House of Representatives at Washington. He was undistinguished and sometimes notably silly, but became a faithful partisan of Jackson, and the Administration's leader in the lower House during the War on the Bank. As a reward he was made Speaker of the House from 1835 to 1839, when he resigned to become Governor of Tennessee. In 1841 he went into retirement, to emerge as the successful 'dark horse' of the Convention of 1844.

The Tyler Administration cheated Polk of his chance to 're-annex' Texas; but this was only a minor item in his grandiose

[1] The fact that quantities of depreciated Texan bonds were held throughout the North influenced many people to vote for the Democrats.

schemes. Beyond Texas, Polk saw California, which he told his Cabinet he intended to annex. Since 1796, New England merchantmen had been carrying on a rich trade in California, arriving there with knives, gunpowder, rum, beads, and the like; exchanging them for furs; selling the furs in China and buying silks, tea, and luxury articles to carry home to Boston. But the Spanish, and later the Mexican, law forbade foreign trade with California; and though the law was never enforced, there was always the chance that it might be, and it seemed clear to President Polk that the most reasonable solution was for the United States to own California. Between Texas and California there lay a vast Mexican territory; and that, too, thought Polk, was 'destined' to belong to the United States. And north of California lay Oregon.... Polk's method of dealing with this threefold expansionist project was more skilful and cautious than his language would suggest. Although in his inaugural message he defied Great Britain, and a few months later asserted that the American title to the whole of Oregon was 'clear and unquestionable,' when it came to negotiation he was mild and conciliatory. By that time he already had a war with Mexico on his hands, and the irresponsibility of the campaign was a thing of the past. When the English revived the old project for extending the forty-ninth parallel to the Pacific, Polk accepted the compromise. In the Senate the treaty was handled roughly, for the Northerners felt that, Oregon and Texas having been coupled in the campaign cry, and the South having gained its Texas, it was unfair that the North should be offered only half of Oregon. 'Oh, Mountain that was delivered of a mouse!' cried Benton; 'thy name shall be fifty-four forty.' But in the end the treaty was ratified.

Meanwhile, in dealing with Mexico, Polk had forced his war with as sure a touch as was ever shown by Cavour or Bismarck. After telling the American Consul on the Pacific Coast that the United States Government would protect the people of California if they cut loose from Mexico, Polk turned his attention to winning the land between Texas and California. This could only be done by purchase or by war. Mexico refused to sell; and although she was unwilling to recognize the annexation of Texas she was also unwilling to fight because of that alone. Fortunately, there was a dispute as to the southern boundary of Texas — the Texans claiming it was the Rio Grande, the Mexicans claiming it was the Nueces, which lay considerably farther north. The facts were on the side of Mexico; for until the young Republic of Texas made her large claim, the Nueces River had been the established boundary of the province for a century past. Polk, however, ordered General Taylor to lead an American army across the Nueces and to occupy the left bank of the Rio Grande. Even then the exasperating Mexicans would not start a war. Early in May, 1846, Polk told his Cabinet that he was about to send a war message to Congress. The Cabinet agreed, but regretted that Mexico had not committed some overt act, for as things stood the American action might seem unduly barefaced. That very afternoon news came that a Mexican force had crossed the river and killed some American soldiers. Polk could now go ahead happily. 'The cup of forbearance has been exhausted,' he informed Congress. 'Mexico... has invaded our territory and shed American blood upon the American soil.' Congress promptly declared that 'by the act of the Republic of Mexico, a state of war exists between that Government and the United States.'

Abraham Lincoln, then serving as Congressman from Illinois, watched these proceedings with disgust. He demanded that the President indicate the exact spot where the war began, so that the nation could decide for itself whether the United States had been invaded. And at the close of the war, he voted for a resolution giving thanks to the American officers for their conduct 'in a war unnecessarily and unconstitutionally begun by the President of the United States.'

In the meantime the Americans in California had taken Polk's hint, and had declared themselves an independent State. The Mexican War — to which the Whig (and especially the New England) minority in Congress was violently hostile — was brief and successful, the American army proving a far more useful force than it had been during the last expansionist attempt in 1812. As a result, early in 1848 Mexico signed a peace which recognized the annexation of Texas, and ceded Upper California and New Mexico — a territory larger than France and Germany combined. At the very time that the treaty was being prepared, gold was discovered in California.

Aside from his lust for new land, Polk's policies were those of the orthodox Jacksonian. He reduced the tariff, and re-established Van Buren's Independent Treasury system. It is interesting to notice that he succeeded in everything he attempted during his Administration — not because he was strong, but because he exactly represented the will of the majority at the moment. He was so thorough a democrat that he believed this to be the whole task of a ruler. If he had ever tried to control or dominate the people, his colourlessness would have been fatal, but as a mirror he was adequate to his task.

On accepting the nomination in 1844, Polk had written that he had 'a settled purpose of not being a candidate for re-election.' Much to everyone's surprise this was still his purpose as his first term drew to an end, and on March 4, 1849, he retired to his home in Nashville. Three months later he was dead.

4

General Zachary Taylor, who succeeded Polk in the White House, has been pushed off the pages of history, not so much because of his unimportance (for he was more of a man than most of the post-Jacksonian Presidents), as because his brief term of office coincided with the last impressive struggle between the three men who dominated American public life in this period. Clay and Webster on the one side, Calhoun on the other, waged a superb fight in the Senate, which all men felt to mark a crisis in the country's life. It was the final effort for each of them, and as they struggled Taylor came to the Presidency, died, and was succeeded by a bland nonentity. And no one paid much attention to either of them.

Born in Orange County, Virginia, in 1784, Taylor was the son of an unsuccessful farmer who had been a colonel in the War of Independence. The family — from Carlisle, on the English border — had been in America since 1658, but had never prospered. The year after Taylor was born, his father moved west to Kentucky, and the boy was brought up under frontier conditions, receiving almost no formal education. When it seemed as if war with England threatened and the army was being enlarged, Zachary Taylor received a commission as first lieutenant in an infantry regiment. Shortly after this he married a Miss Margaret Smith, of Maryland, who shared his dangerous and lonely frontier life throughout his army career. Before the War of 1812 was over, he had become a major. At the end of the war, he left the service; but he returned to it in 1816, rising steadily until, at the time of the Black Hawk War, in 1832, he was in command of a regiment. About this time there was a young officer in his regiment named Jefferson Davis, who fell in love with his colonel's daughter. Taylor forbade the marriage; so the girl went to visit a friendly aunt in Kentucky; Davis resigned his commission, followed Miss Sarah Taylor to Kentucky, and there married her. They set out at once for Davis's plantation in Mississippi; but the romance had a tragic ending, for Mrs. Davis died of malarial fever three months after her marriage.

By 1845, Taylor was in New Orleans, and had become a brigadier-General and the owner of a fairly prosperous plantation. In that year he received orders from President Polk to march his troops into Texas, and in 1846 he was told to advance to the Rio Grande. War ensued; Taylor was made a major-general and conquered the northeastern states of Mexico. He was popular with his troops, who named him 'Old Rough and Ready,' and his success was making him a hero with the people. Since his political affiliations were vaguely Whiggish, this was displeasing to the Democratic Polk, who determined to create a rival general. So Winfield Scott was sent to take Mexico City from Vera Cruz, and Taylor's army was depleted to supply Scott with troops. The result was the reverse of what Polk had intended; for when Taylor's force had been reduced to five thousand men, it was attacked by Santa Anna with twenty thousand Mexicans. Taylor made a magnificent stand in the glaring heat at Buena Vista — February, 1847 — finally routing the Mexicans and adding the finishing touch to his own reputation. Within a month, a Whig Convention at Iowa had nominated him for the Presidency.

Another future American President established his national reputation at Buena Vista. Colonel Jefferson Davis, of the 'Mississippi Rifles,' had saved the day with a gallant defence against a Mexican cavalry charge, and his name was almost as widely applauded as was his General's.

Taylor had never taken any part, or any interest, in politics. At first, he was unwilling to accept the nomination, but finally gave in to the flattering popular clamour. He was emphatically the people's choice, the politicians doing all they could to sidetrack him. He had no views, and the Whigs — remembering the Harrison campaign — were careful not to handicap him by expressing any opinions or suggesting that they had any policies or plans for the future. Taylor ran as a military hero whom the people wished to reward. As a nominal Whig, he could count on strength in the North; and as a slave-owner and the father-in-law of Jefferson Davis, he won many Southerners from the Democratic Party — which unwisely nominated Lewis Cass, a Northwestern frontier Democrat who made small appeal to the planting aristocracy.

Taylor was an honest man, with a contempt for political chicanery and for the obvious forms of nonsense. Being an outsider, he was unentangled in political jobbery, saw no reason why any Whig should be preferred for a particular job to any Democrat, and fought against the spoils system.[1] But there his merits ended. He was pathetically inadequate for the crisis that followed his inauguration. In his first message to Congress, he advised that body to 'abstain from the introduction of those exciting

[1] Nevertheless, about 3400 Democratic office-holders were replaced by Whigs.

topics of sectional character which have hitherto produced painful apprehensions in the public mind.' So far from abstaining from these topics, Congress indulged in the most important debate upon them, and the most determined effort to cope with them, that was ever made. In July, 1850, in the midst of this dramatic contest, President Taylor contracted a fever. In six days he was dead, leaving the Presidency to Millard Fillmore.

5

The territory acquired by the peace treaty with Mexico was the cause of the struggle in the Senate. Congress, at the instigation of Representative Wilmot, from Pennsylvania, had tried to prohibit slavery forever from this new land. The Southern Senators blocked the attempt, and the Northern Senators blocked every effort to provide for administering the territories with this proviso omitted. Tired of the deadlock, California organized itself and asked for admission as a State, with a constitution that prohibited slavery. No action was taken.

Superficially, it seemed like a foolish quarrel, for New Mexico was a desert land where no Southern slave-owner could imagine settling, and California had already declared her intention of becoming a free State.[1] But Calhoun, who led the Southern forces in the Senate, knew what he was about. He countered the Wilmot Proviso by advancing the extreme doctrine that Congress had no power to prohibit slavery in the Territories, since slaves were common-law property. It was Congress's duty to protect the lawful property of American citizens, not to deprive them of it. If this doctrine were accepted (and in 1857 it was, in fact, endorsed by the Supreme Court), the famous Missouri Compromise of 1820, as a result of which slavery was prohibited in the Territories north of 36° 30', would become null and void.

Calhoun well knew that such a suggestion would cause a storm in the North. He wished to force the issue, hoping for one of two

---

[1] The Southerners had hoped, originally, that this State might be divided in two, and the southern half of it be given over to the plantation system.

results: either secession (before the North was strong enough to resist), or a constitutional amendment creating a dual executive, one President elected by the North and one by the South, and each with a legislative veto. In either case the Southern civilization would be protected; and Calhoun knew that this was the last chance. The North already far outnumbered the South, and with the rapid growth of industrialism it was becoming incomparably more wealthy. In a few years the railways would have created a new Northwest, tied to the Northeast by lines of commerce and by a common aversion to the 'peculiar institution' of slavery. When that happened, the North would finally get control of the Government at Washington and reinstate all the Hamiltonian policies — which meant the doom of Southern agriculture and Southern life. If they waited until then for secession, the Southerners would find themselves too weak, and would be constrained to remain in the Union under Northern domination. Now was the time to force the issue; and if it should prove that Union sentiment in the North was strong enough to secure a constitutional amendment protecting the South forever against economic exploitation, so much the better. That was the only compromise the South could afford to accept.

Unhappily for Calhoun's plans, a very different compromise was actually accepted. Henry Clay, who had patched up the quarrel in 1820, and again in 1833, produced his last and greatest effort in the way of avoiding issues. Early in 1850 he brought forward the following proposals: (a) that California be admitted as a free State; (b) that Territorial governments be organized in New Mexico and Utah, without any provision as to slavery or its absence (which meant that the inhabitants could decide the question later on); (c) that Congress pass a new and strict Fugitive Slave Law, to provide for the return of slaves who escaped into the North; (d) that the domestic slave trade be abolished in the District of Columbia. Clay defended the proposals in one of his greatest speeches, declaring that only by adopting this compromise could the Union be peacefully preserved and warning the South that secession would mean war, since the millions who lived in the upper Mississippi Valley could never permit the mouth of that river to be held by a foreign power.

When Calhoun made his reply he was a dying man, and he made a grim, savage exposition of a dying cause. The issue, he declared, was not one on which compromise was possible. Either the South must leave the Union, or it must be assured of a permanent equilibrium of power, so that the Union could not be used as a means of oppression.... The speech was read by Senator Mason of Virginia, while Calhoun, who had almost lost his voice, sat staring at the Senate with tragic eyes.

The decisive speech was made by Webster. It was well known that New England would not accept that part of the compromise referring to a new Fugitive Slave Act unless it were backed by the whole power of Webster's prestige. And if the new Fugitive Slave Act were rejected, the South would reject the rest of Clay's measures, and Calhoun would have his way. But it was obvious from Webster's first sentence that he had risen to defend the whole of Clay's proposals. 'I speak today,' he began, 'for the preservation of the Union.' This was to be his last great effort also, and it was given added dignity by the knowledge that the young men of his own section would undoubtedly turn on him and call him traitor for recommending concessions to the South.... For the last time, the Senate was under the spell of that amazing presence. Carlyle had written of Webster's 'crag-like face; the dull black eyes under the precipice of brows, like dull anthracite furnaces, needing only to be *blown;* the mastiff mouth accurately closed.' Old age had destroyed none of this impressiveness; and when, with a weakened voice but with the strength of conviction, Webster pleaded for conciliation in the name of patriotism, it was hard for Southerners to remember the reasoning of Calhoun. Within the next few months all of the compromise measures were accepted. And in the meantime, Calhoun died. He had united his section, but failed to force it into action at the decisive moment. The

South waited another ten years, then struck when it was too
late.

The only part President Fillmore played in these great events
was to sign bills when they were passed him. If he had opinions,
nobody cared. Fillmore would have been a nonentity in any company, or at any period in history; but in Washington during the
crisis of 1850 he was so overshadowed as to be indiscernible.

Fillmore was born in 1800. His parents — who came from New
England, where the Fillmore family had been settled since the
early eighteenth century — had just moved to the northwest
section of New York State. Millard Fillmore, therefore, grew up
on a frontier farm. He had little school education, and his father's
library consisted of two books — the Bible and a collection of
hymns. He never saw a Shakespeare, a history of the United
States, or even a map of the country, until he was nineteen. Nevertheless he secured a job teaching school, thus supporting himself
while he studied law. In 1823 he was admitted to the bar, and
five years later he was sent to the State Legislature as a protégé
of Thurlow Weed, one of New York's ablest political bosses. In
1834, Weed became an anti-Jackson man, and Fillmore, who
by this time was a member of Congress, followed him into the
Whig Party.

After a commonplace career at Washington, Fillmore became
the Whig nominee for Governor of New York, but was defeated
at the election. Four years later, in 1848, his party nominated
him for Vice-President — chiefly because the Clay Whigs were
angry at the nomination of Taylor and demanded the minor
office for one of their own group. Fillmore was harmless, and
since nobody had heard of him he could scarcely lose the party
any votes. In appearance he was a good type for the public platform — a large man with a big smooth face and big features.
He had an impressive presence, kindly blue eyes, and a gracious
manner. The historian Rhodes describes him as 'strictly tem-
perate, industrious, orderly.'

When Fillmore became President, in 1850, it was soon obvious that he was not going to be a second Tyler and develop ideas of his own. Because of his docility in signing the bills of Congress, Southern Whigs were in favour of renominating him in 1852; but the Party Convention passed him over in favour of General Winfield Scott. The only two Presidents the Whigs had ever elected had been generals; and, undiscouraged by the fact that both had quickly died, the Whigs thought it was worth trying a third. On this occasion it was the party, not the general, that died.

With the deaths of Webster and of Clay in 1852, and the crushing defeat at the polls in the same year, the Whig Party began to fall to pieces. It had always been an anomaly. Its economic doctrines were purely Hamiltonian, and therefore sectional in their appeal; yet it had remained a national party, partly because of the prestige and patriotism of its two great leaders, partly because it re-mained the party for gentlemen, as opposed to the Jacksonian rabble of the Democrats. But now its leaders were gone, and the men who took their place in the Senate (such as Seward of New York, Sumner of Massachusetts, Chase of Ohio) were Northern or Western, rather than Unionist, in their sentiments.

Meanwhile, as a result of Calhoun's long planning, the Democratic Party, in the South, had been taken over by the planters. In the North it was still the party of 'the people,' who supplied the necessary votes in Presidential elections. The South supplied the leaders and the policy. It was an admirable system, from the Southern point of view; but it could not last for long, in view of the great Northern superiority in numbers and in money. That superiority could not be asserted effectively, however, until two changes had occurred: first, the Whig Party had to be absorbed into a more consciously sectional, Hamiltonian, anti-Southern group; second, the West, which had long wavered in its allegiance between South and East, had to be bound finally to the latter. Both of these steps were accomplished by 1860, and then the Southerners learned the full wisdom of Calhoun, learned that they should have been watching the trade statistics in 1850, instead of listening to the rhetoric of Webster. They had refused, when their leader urged them, to break the Union; and now the Union was ready to break them. The election of Lincoln threatened no man's property in slaves; but it promised the full application of the Hamiltonian programme, which meant that the staple-producing, free-trade, plantation system of the South would be sacrificed in the interest of Northern business.

Fillmore's last important appearance was in the election of 1856, when, appropriately enough, he was the candidate of the Know-Nothing Party.[1] This was an organization directed against the immigrants — chiefly German and Irish — who were now first becoming a serious problem in politics. Although strong in certain States, the Know-Nothings had little national importance, and Fillmore, in spite of being nominated by the dissolving Whig Party as well as by the Know-Nothings, ran a bad third to the candidates of the Democratic and of the new Republican Party. Although he lived until 1874, Fillmore was never again politically prominent.

The most interesting thing Fillmore ever did was to refuse the degree of D.C.L. from Oxford University, on the ground that he had no literary or scientific attainments.

6

In 1852, when the Whigs nominated General Winfield Scott, the Democrats chose Franklin Pierce, of New Hampshire, who was also a general. Pierce carried every State but four, and won 254 electoral votes, Scott receiving 42. Southerners felt they had been wise to stay in the Union, that with their leadership and the votes of the poorer farmers and mechanics throughout the North, they could run the country forever. In their overconfidence they took a step which destroyed whatever good will had been created by the Compromise of 1850, intensified sectional feeling on the slavery issue, and played into the hands of those who were trying to create an effective Hamiltonian and anti-Southern party.

[1] Officially, the American Party; it had many of the attributes of a secret society and its members were told that if asked about its principles they should answer, 'I know nothing.'

There had long been a struggle between the two sections over the building of a Pacific Railway. The objection to the southern route had been that the railway would have to pass through some Mexican territory, but this was overcome in 1853 when Jefferson Davis, Secretary of War, induced President Pierce to buy the land from Mexico for ten million dollars. The objection to the northern route had been that it would have to pass through a large unsettled region where there was no organized government — and the Southerners had blocked various attempts to organize this district as the Territory of Nebraska. But the leading Democrat of the North, Senator Stephen A. Douglas, of Illinois, was a speculator in Western lands and naturally wished to see them opened up by a railway. So in 1854 he introduced a new bill for organizing this Territory, and tried to sweeten it for the South with the provision that the settlers in the new Territory were to be allowed to decide for themselves whether or not they would have slavery.

Southerners pointed out that since Nebraska lay wholly north of the Missouri Compromise line, the Missouri Compromise Act of 1820 should be explicitly repealed. Douglas agreed to this, and also to the division of Nebraska into two new Territories — Nebraska to the north, and Kansas to the south — so that one could be settled by Northerners and become a free State, the other by Southerners and become a slave State. Jefferson Davis, less farsighted than his teacher, Calhoun, induced President Pierce to use the full force of the Administration to secure Northern Democratic support for the Kansas-Nebraska Bill. The bill passed; the Compromise of 1850 was destroyed as effectively as the Compromise of 1820 had been; the organizers of the new Northern party were given a popular issue to add to their economic programme. The South, no longer content with Calhoun's plan for security (either through secession or through obtaining a Presidential veto), appeared to be reaching out and trying to force its 'peculiar institution' on the rest of the country. It failed to realize the genuine horror that the thought of creating new slave States aroused throughout the North, or the effect of this horror on future election returns.

The immediate result of the Kansas-Nebraska Act was the formation of the Republican Party, on the one issue of opposing slavery extension. It fought the Presidential election of 1856 on this issue, expressly disavowing any connection with the old Whig or Federalist doctrines. It won almost a million and a half votes, 600,000 more than the Whig-Know-Nothing coalition. At once the practical politicians in the dying Whig Party realized that here was an organization with which they could control the country. If they could add the votes of those who opposed the extension of slavery to the votes of those who favoured the old Hamiltonian-Whig economics, they could elect a President. The plan succeeded. By 1860, the Hamiltonians controlled the new Republican Party; in the Civil War they destroyed their chief economic rivals; with brief interludes they have run the National Government ever since.

Franklin Pierce, who was the Democratic President when his party prepared its own ruin by passing the Kansas-Nebraska Act, was almost as much of a nonentity as Millard Fillmore. Pierce — whose father was a farmer and an ex-officer in the Revolutionary Army — was born in 1804, at Hillsborough, New Hampshire. He was educated at Bowdoin College, Maine, then studied law, and was admitted to the bar in 1827. Two years later he was in the State Legislature, and in 1833 he was sent to the House of Representatives at Washington. Both there and in the Senate (which he entered in 1837), he supported the Jacksonian policies. In 1842 he resigned from the Senate and returned to the practice of law. Ten years later, his State Legislature presented him to the country as a Presidential candidate, and when the Democratic Convention of that year found itself deadlocked, it turned to Pierce as an inoffensive, malleable man. Since the Southerners intended to run the Administration, they felt it was just as well to have a Northerner in the supposedly chief position. Pierce was a fine-looking man, with a good record in the Mexican

War (having enlisted as private and ended the war as a brigadier-general of volunteers), courtly manners, and considerable personal magnetism. He also had an unusually distinguished and attractive wife, who would be an asset in the White House.[1]

In 1856, the Northern Democrats refused to nominate Pierce for a second term, because of the marked pro-slavery bias of his Administration — a bias which was entirely the result of Pierce's pliability in the hands of Jefferson Davis. Buchanan was nominated instead, and won another easy victory — though Southerners should have taken warning from the fact that if the Republican vote had been added to that of the Whigs and the Know-Nothings, Buchanan would have been defeated. After leaving Washington Pierce went abroad for three years, and then returned to Concord, New Hampshire. He discouraged the attempt to nominate him in 1860, and lived in retirement until his death in 1869. A tranquil, colourless man, he had been used (quite without knowing it) to forward one of the decisive events in his country's history.

7

James Buchanan won the election of 1856 by 171 electoral votes to 114 for the Republican candidate, and 8 for Fillmore. Buchanan said he stood for the finality of the Compromise of 1850 — a remark that showed the quality of his mind, since the Compromise of 1850 was already as dead as mutton. It had been supposed to end the controversy over slavery, and to take the question forever out of politics; yet the question had never before been so emphatically 'in' politics as during the years 1856 and 1857. The ill-fated Kansas-Nebraska Act had led to a small civil war in Kansas, between Northern and Southern settlers, each group trying to win the Territory for its own social system. Which of the two groups the new Administration would encourage was the chief question of the day; and it soon was clear that Buchanan, like his predecessor, was to be under the influence of the Southern leaders at

[1] Two months before the inauguration, the Pierces' third and only surviving son was killed before their eyes in a railway accident.

Washington. In his inaugural address, he stated that in regard to the problem of slavery in the Territories, the whole country should agree in advance to accept the decision that would soon be handed down, on this question, by the Supreme Court. A few days later, the Court announced the famous Dred Scott decision. Scott was a slave who had been taken into one of the Northern Territories in the days when the Missouri Compromise was still supposed to be in effect. After being returned to the State of Missouri, he there sued for his liberty on the grounds that he had been in a free Territory, and had therefore become a free man. In settling the case, the Supreme Court went out of its way to declare that Congress had no power to prohibit slavery in any Territory of the United States. The Missouri Compromise, in effect, had been null and void from the beginning. This was the extreme Calhoun position, and it had now been made a part of the Constitution of the country.

Angry Northerners charged that President Buchanan's pious advice — that the country should accept the coming decision, no matter what it turned out to be — was a trick, and that Buchanan had known all along what the Supreme Court was going to say. This was a shocking charge, and those who made it were properly rebuked; nevertheless, the charge has since been proved to be true. Contrary to all precedent, the Court had informed the President in advance as to what its decision would be; and Buchanan, by taking advantage of this information, sought to give an air of impartiality to his advice that the nation accept the Dred Scott decision as final. Though a Northern man, he was completely under the influence of the Southern Democrats.

So far from accepting the Dred Scott decision, a large part of Northern opinion repudiated it with violence. Lincoln pointed out that the Supreme Court had often, in the past, overruled its own decisions, and he added, 'We shall do what we can to have it overrule this.' By 'doing what we can,' he meant capturing the Federal Government for the Republican Party and then making sure that new appointees to the Supreme Court shared the Northern view on slavery in the Territories. The Republican Party profited almost as much by this decision as it had profited by the Kansas-Nebraska Act. Meanwhile, Northern numbers and Northern wealth grew astonishingly; it was folly for Southerners to believe that they could long hold their domination at Washington. Instead of spending the decade of the fifties in irritating the North, they should have spent it placating the North, winning concessions before it was too late. But now that the grim pessimistic Calhoun was gone, a mad self-confidence seemed to possess the South.

How mad this self-confidence was is suggested by the following figures: During the fifties, the output of domestic manufactures (including fisheries) increased by about ninety-five per cent, while the output of Southern crops increased a little over twenty per cent. By the end of that decade the value of those manufactures (again including fisheries) was over nine times the value of the Southern crops. Also, with the rapid extension of railways through the Middle West, manufactures began to spread into what had recently been frontier country, and Ohio and Indiana began to share the Eastern desire for a tariff. More and more were the economic requirements of the South becoming different from those of any other section of the country, just as its social system had already become a thing apart. The population of the country increased, during this decade, from twenty-three millions to thirty-one — twenty-two millions in the North, and nine millions (one third of whom were slaves) in the South. Almost sixty-six per cent of the banking capital of the country was in the Northeast, and the per capita circulation in that district was $16.50 as compared with about $6 for the rest of the country.

In the face of these figures, the Southerners had no right to believe that they could go on dictating the economic policy of the country in their own interests. They pointed out, of course, that the North did not seem to be suffering from that dictation, that the country as a whole could prosper without the thorough-going economic capitalism of Hamilton, whereas the South could not prosper with it. That was reasonable; but as statesmen they should have realized that if the section which would soon be dominant saw the hope of making still more money by destroying the South, the South would unquestionably be destroyed. And as for the attempt to maintain the balance of power by forcing the North to allow new slave States to be created, that was insanity. It merely gave the North a moral excuse for doing what it was fated to do anyway, on economic grounds. But in spite of Calhoun, in spite of men like William Lowndes Yancey of Alabama (who as early as 1846 saw that the South's only hope lay in secession, and who then withdrew from Congress and gave the rest of his life to that cause), the Southerners could not be brought to secede while they were still supreme at Washington. If the Hamiltonians ever captured the Government, then, they thought, it would be time enough to secede — their Southern arrogance convincing them that they could never be forcibly restrained.

Buchanan's Administration, therefore, was a replica of Pierce's. Again there was a Northern President under the influence of Southern advisers who were using their last few years of power in unifying Northern opinion against them, rather than in preparing realistically for what must come. The worst service that the Southern leaders of this period did for their country was to permit the argument to be shifted from its true economic basis to the false issue of slavery. Angered by exaggerated and hypocritical attacks on this institution, they allowed themselves to be goaded into defending slavery, when what they really stood for, what they believed in and ultimately died for, was an agrarian civilization.

Slavery in the fifties was a dying institution, wasteful economically and deplored by many of the finest spirits in the South; yet to judge by Southern oratory in Congress, and by the policy of the Buchanan Administration, slavery might have been the one thing dear to Southern hearts. This was the blind reaction of Southerners to being attacked on moral grounds.

In 1858, while the country was still angry and excited over the Dred Scott decision, the Administration showed its bias once again by favouring the admission of Kansas to statehood with a pro-slavery constitution. Congress blocked the attempt; but again this meant many converts to the new Republican Party, again the Northern Democrats were given a motive for breaking with their Southern fellows.

If Buchanan had possessed more force, he might have taught his Southern followers to understand the Northern temper. But Buchanan was not the man to influence, or instruct, those about him.... Born in Pennsylvania, in 1791, Buchanan came of Scotch-Irish stock. His father, a successful store-keeper, had settled in America in 1783. Buchanan went to a local school, and then to Dickinson College. He read law after his graduation and was ad-mitted to the bar in 1812. He was most successful, and soon had a moderate fortune. In 1815 he became engaged to be married. His fiancée broke the engagement, and while Buchanan was hoping soon to patch up the quarrel, the girl suddenly died. It was a terrible blow to Buchanan, and the wound stayed with him per-manently. He never married.

After six years in State politics, Buchanan, in 1820, was elected to Congress. He belonged to the Federalist Party; but when, in the next few years, that party dissolved, he did not, like most of his fellows, follow Adams and Clay into what later became the Whig Party; he joined the Jacksonian Democrats. In 1828 he took an active part in Jackson's campaign, and was rewarded with an im-portant chairmanship in the new Congress. Four years later Jackson appointed him American Minister to Russia, and on re-turning from that post he entered the United States Senate. During Van Buren's Presidency, he was offered the Attorney-Generalship, but preferred his post in the Senate. Under President Polk, he became Secretary of State, and in 1849, when the Whigs came into office, Buchanan bought a country estate in Pennsyl-vania and prepared for a life of retirement. In four years, however, his party was back in power, and President Pierce sent him as Minister to England. His most important diplomatic problem at the Court of St. James's was the question of his own wardrobe.

The American Secretary of State had just issued a circular to the effect that Ministers should appear only in 'the simple dress of an American citizen,' instead of in the uniform previously prescribed, except when such dress was found to interfere with their conduct. Buchanan, attempting to conform to these ambiguous instructions, was very nearly excluded from court functions. In the end, he interpreted 'the simple dress of an American citizen' as including a plain dress sword, with the help of which he hoped, at any rate, to be distinguishable.

The only other event of interest during Buchanan's diplomatic career was the 'Ostend Manifesto' of 1854. Buchanan and the American Ministers at Madrid and Paris issued this singular document without authority from Washington. The Manifesto suggested that the time had come for the United States to buy Cuba from Spain, adding that if Spain refused to sell, the United States would have every right to seize the island. Puerile as the performance was from the point of view of diplomacy, it had a gratifying effect on Buchanan's career. For the annexation of Cuba had long been a Southern ambition; and, although nothing came of the Ostend Manifesto (except embarrassment to Washington), Southern statesmen had their attention called to still another Northern Democrat who seemed to be amenable to their influence. This, combined with the fact that Buchanan was out of the country during the bitter quarrels over the Kansas-Nebraska Bill, secured him the Democratic nomination in 1856. His election followed as a matter of course.

Spain may have wondered about the fate of Cuba when one of the authors of the Ostend Manifesto was sent to the White House. But, although Buchanan wished to take steps toward buying the island, he could not secure the necessary money from Congress. And not even Buchanan felt that the United States had the right to seize Cuba until after Spain had refused a fair offer.

By the time of the Nominating Convention of 1860, the situation in the Democratic Party was ominous. Buchanan's thorough-going support of the Southern wing had caused a break within the party, the Northern Democrats rallying about Senator Douglas. If the party split in two, there would be an end of Southern domination at Washington, and hence, presumably, an end of the Union, for the South was obviously preparing to secede if a so-called Black Republican should be elected. Nevertheless, there seemed no candidate on whom the party could agree. Buchanan, who in any case was too weak for such an emergency, refused to stand again. He favoured Breckinridge of Kentucky, who had been Vice-President during Buchanan's term; but Breckinridge was unacceptable to the Northerners, and Douglas had lost all hold over the South. His Kansas-Nebraska Bill had given him a brief popularity in that section — a popularity which died when he took the stand that in spite of the Dred Scott decision the settlers in a Territory had it in their power to exclude slavery, if they chose.... In the end, the Democratic Party split in two, each section holding its own convention. Douglas was nominated by the Northerners, Breckinridge by the Southerners. Yancey of Alabama had his way at last, and in a great speech he explained to the South what it should have seen ten years before: that, having become a minority with a special interest to be protected, the choice was to surrender or to secede.

The Republican Convention, in 1860, marked the capture of the new Party by the Hamiltonians. The Party continued to oppose the extension of slavery into the Territories, but it combined this doctrine with the tariff and banking programme that had for so long been dear to the business interests, and with the recommendation of internal improvements in the form of Government aid for the Pacific Railway. Finally, the Republicans ensured victory by offering to the West the long-withheld bribe of free land.

In the jockeying for position that had been going on between North and South throughout the last generation, it was clearly seen that either section could buy the support of the West by the free distribution of public land. Since the time of John Q. Adams no leader had refrained from this distribution for high-minded motives. The South had refrained because it feared the growth of new free States, the North because free land would raise the cost of labour. In the fifties, however, the rapid growth of industrialism led to the first serious labour troubles the country had known. Northern manufacturers were frightened at the threat of militant trade-unionism, and distribution of the public property seemed the cheapest way out. So a free-homestead act was promised, and in the campaign of 1860 the battle-cry in the West was, 'Vote yourself a farm'; in the East it was, 'Vote yourself a tariff.' The alliance of the East with the upper Mississippi Valley was now complete. The railways had begun it, binding these two sections together, and weakening the natural alliance of agrarian West and South which had been the foundation of Jacksonian Democracy and which had held even after leadership in the Democratic Party passed to the Southern plantation-owners. Opposition to the spread of slavery helped unite the Northeast and Northwest, and the promise of the Homestead Act completed the process. The South was isolated and in a minority.

In choosing its candidate for the Presidency, the Republican Party passed over Senator Seward, its most prominent leader, because he was too much identified with the anti-slavery agitation. It was important to keep the party from being tainted with abolitionist doctrines, for not even the bait of Hamiltonianism would win Northern business men to a party that proposed such wholesale confiscation of property. Lincoln's record on the slave question was clear and satisfactory. He would tolerate no extension of the system, but he stated that 'we must not interfere with the institution of slavery in the States where it exists, because the Constitution forbids it and the general welfare does not require us to do so.' Also, Lincoln came from the new West; he was a man of the people, who could win votes from among the old Jacksonian Democrats. He had no national reputation and therefore no powerful enemies, and he had proved himself an adroit, amusing, and popular stump speaker. These assets, helped out by some rather unclean bartering on the part of his friends, secured him the nomination on the second ballot. The split in the Democratic

Party secured him the election by 180 electoral votes to 12 for Douglas and 72 for Breckinridge.[1]

A little over a month after the election, South Carolina seceded. By the first of February she had been joined by all the other States of the deep South, and on February 8 they banded together to form the Confederate States of America, with Jefferson Davis as provisional President and A. H. Stephens as Vice-President. The Northern tier of slaveholding States was still wavering, and in this extraordinary state of indecision the Buchanan Administration dragged on its discredited life. The Secretary of the Treasury was a Georgian, the Secretary of War a Virginian; the President denied the South's right to secede, but confessed that he had no power to prevent secession. While waiting in misery for the fourth of March and the end of his responsibility, Buchanan pleased neither the North nor the South, and accomplished nothing at all. General Scott advised him to reinforce the garrisons in the South; but Buchanan refused, whereupon his Northern Secretary of State resigned in disgust.[2] When Buchanan reiterated that the South had no right to secede, his Secretary of the Treasury also resigned. The Administration was falling to pieces, and the South began to say that there would soon be nothing left to secede from.... But at last Buchanan's ordeal was over. He attended Lincoln's inauguration, then retired to his country place in Pennsylvania where he lived quietly until his death in 1868. His last years were mainly given to the composition of a book explaining why he had done nothing at the crisis of his career.

8

During the last month of Buchanan's Administration, there were two Presidents in the once United States. Jefferson Davis, Sen-

[1] The vote in the Electoral College, which is determined by States, gives a false picture of the popular vote at this election. Lincoln received 1,866,452 votes, Douglas 1,376,957, and Breckinridge 849,781. In spite of Douglas's large vote the only State in which he received a plurality was Missouri.

[2] Buchanan finally sent the *Star of the West*, an unarmed steamer, to reinforce Fort Sumter. She was fired on by a battery in Charleston Harbour and forced to return North.

ator from Mississippi, had announced his State's secession on January 21 and then withdrawn from the Washington Government. A little over a fortnight later, the Confederacy chose him as its chief.

Davis was born in Kentucky, in 1808. He was the grandson of a Welsh immigrant, and although his father had been an officer in the Revolutionary Army, the family was very poor, and Jefferson Davis, being the tenth child, had small prospects. Before long, the family moved to Mississippi, where the eldest son began to prosper. He acquired an education, made himself an important position, and in the end became one of the wealthiest men in the South. As a result, young Jefferson Davis had a good education, going first to Transylvania University and then to the Military Academy at West Point, where he was a contemporary of the two Johnstons and of Robert E. Lee. Graduating as a second lieutenant, he spent years of service at little Western posts, taking part in the Black Hawk War of 1832. The following year he met Colonel Zachary Taylor's daughter, and the tragic romance which resulted led to his resigning from the army and returning to Mississippi.

Between 1835, when his first wife died, and 1845, when he married Varina Howell — a spirited, accomplished woman of the highest social rank, who was one of the famous beauties of the South — Davis lived the life of a Mississippi planter. These years formed him and determined his future. He acquired a sense of the soil, a love and respect for the social system of the deep South, and above all a local patriotism. The fascination of the Gulf States closed upon him, and he could never again feel that his first loyalty was to the nation. Here was his home, in a world that had nothing in common with the North. The prodigal soil, the misty languid air, the heat, the lazy voices — what had these to do with that brisk bourgeois paradise beyond the Potomac?

> The white wolf-winter, hungry and frore,
> Can prowl the North by a frozen door;
> But here we have fed him on bacon fat,
> And he sleeps by the stove like a lazy cat.

This contrast between the harsh Northern winter and the year-long friendliness of the Gulf climate, where spring was in the air by January and autumn lingered on till Christmas — this contrast must have seemed typical of the two worlds, to the man who had fallen in love with Mississippi. The slaves were content and well-cared-for on the Davis plantation. They were lazy and inefficient — there was a saying in the South that it took two slaves to help one to do nothing; but they were cheerful, and they were numerous, and with that bountiful soil their slow work sufficed to provide plenty. Davis himself worked harder than any of his slaves, and yet the background to his life was a spacious, leisured, orderly society such as was disappearing from the Western world. He studied hard during these ten years, reading widely in history and politics, and he learned nothing to make him belittle his world as compared with the North. In fact, for any man bred in that turmoil, that formless unbeautiful world of buyers and sellers, to pretend that the South was immoral and unwholesome, must have seemed to Jefferson Davis pathetic as well as impudent.

On his marriage with Varina Howell, Davis took up politics, and was elected to the House of Representatives at Washington. Almost immediately, however, the Mexican War broke out, and Davis resigned from Congress in order to command a volunteer regiment from his own State. After he had made a national reputation for himself, at the battle of Buena Vista, he was sent back to Washington as a Senator. In 1851 he resigned from the Senate in order to stand for Governor of Mississippi. This was the time when the South was still undecided as to whether to follow Calhoun's advice, and secede rather than accept the Compromise of 1850, or whether to swallow that Compromise for the sake of the Union. Davis's opponent in the campaign for the governorship was a Compromise man; Davis himself wished to make sure of the support of other Southern States, and then secede. He lost the election by less than one thousand votes; and instead of continuing to work for secession, he tried during the next few years to make the South a nation within the Union, by extending it territorially

and developing it economically so that it could be politically equal
to the North. This is the explanation of his policy while in President Pierce's Cabinet — a policy that was bound to fail, for in the
race for wealth and numbers the North had every natural advantage. On returning to the Senate after the inauguration of
Buchanan, Davis began to work for a form of duality within the
Union, which would give the South something resembling a Dominion status, which would save the Union and still safeguard the
economic interests of that minority section. Davis bears a heavy
responsibility for the final destruction of the South, for he helped
to waste this precious decade, helped to postpone secession until
there was a new strong Northern party to deal with it, and until
the railways, the cheap immigrant labour, and the expanding factory system had given that party the power to do so.

During their twelve years at Washington the Davises' house was
a centre for social life. They were a handsome and gracious couple,
each with rare social and intellectual gifts; and even his political
enemies were grieved when, in January, 1861, Davis announced
his State's secession and withdrew from the Senate.

9

During the first few weeks of Lincoln's Presidency it looked as if
the new Administration would be as undecided as the old. All but
two of the forts and navy yards in the South had fallen into Confederate hands before Lincoln's inauguration; if he let either of the
remaining two go without a struggle, it would be a tacit admission
of Northern impotence to prevent secession. Major Anderson,
commanding at Fort Sumter, sent word that his supplies were
running short; but Lincoln delayed action, for he was watching the
border States, debating whether, if he let Fort Sumter go, they
could be saved from joining the South. Virginia was the prize for
which both sides were angling; and toward the end of March, Lincoln rightly decided that in case of war Virginia would join the
South no matter what he did about Sumter, so he ordered the relief of that fort. General Beauregard was in command at Charles-

ton, and on April 13 — Major Anderson having refused to surrender — he opened fire on the fort. The Civil War had begun.

Senator Mason of Virginia described this conflict as 'a war of sentiment and opinion by one form of society against another form of society.' This is the essential truth, underlying all the talk about slavery and States' rights and constitutional interpretation. One way of life had come into conflict with another way; their economic needs clashed; the weaker side was presented with the old alternative: to die immediately, or to fight first and die later.

CHAPTER VI

LINCOLN

I

LINCOLN was born in Kentucky in 1809, close to where Jefferson Davis had been born the previous year. When Lincoln was seven, his family, like Davis's, moved on under economic pressure. But the Lincolns, who were destitute, moved north across the Ohio River into Indiana, whereas the Davises, who had a little money, went south to the Gulf. By the time the two boys were adult, they represented worlds so far apart that there was no common ground. Davis looked an aristocrat. Clear-cut, beautiful features; a scholar's brow; wide, fearless eyes; he seemed the product of generations of fostering — yet his grandfather had been a Welsh immigrant. Accustomed to command men, with a strong sense of *noblesse oblige* and a contempt for the opinions of the multitude, Davis recognized only three careers for a man of his class — the land, politics, and the army. Before middle age he had excelled in all three. Lincoln, by contrast, was a gnarled, unkempt man — ugly, common, prematurely lined, but with a baffling look of wisdom and sympathy in his eyes. He was accustomed to any sort of odd job, by way of keeping himself clothed and fed; and by middle-age he was a failure, in the strictly worldly sense, at everything he had tried.... No one looking at the two men, in 1850, could have imagined that there was ever a period when their lives had a point in common.

Lincoln's first American ancestor landed in Massachusetts, in 1637, from Norfolk. The family stayed in Massachusetts for three generations, then moved to Virginia, and then (in the time of Lincoln's grandfather) to Kentucky. The next move was to Indiana, and finally, in the year Lincoln came of age, his father pushed west to Illinois. This constant wandering from one frontier settlement to another was characteristic of the shiftless and un-successful — the class to which Lincoln's father belonged. His mother, Nancy Hanks (the illegitimate daughter of a Virginia girl who had moved West soon after her child was born), was far superior to his father both in mind and character. From her, presumably, the boy inherited some of the traits which distinguished him from his Lincoln ancestors.

Two years after the move to Indiana, Nancy Hanks died; and a year later, when Lincoln was ten, his father married a Mrs. Sarah (Bush) Johnston. Again the feckless and poverty-stricken frontiers-man had married a woman who was in every way his better. And again the boy profited. Lincoln was devoted to his stepmother, who had a deep and happy influence on him, encouraging his astonishing thirst for knowledge — a thirst which his father viewed as a discreditable malady. Years later, when Lincoln had left home, his father still harped uneasily on the subject. 'I suppose Abe is still fooling hisself with eddication,' he said one day to a visitor. 'I tried to stop it, but he has got that fool idea in his head, and it can't be got out.'

It is hard to imagine the efforts Abe had to make in order to go on 'fooling hisself with eddication.' In his whole life he had less than twelve months of formal schooling; and the only books he could lay his hands on, during his childhood, were the Bible, Æsop, *Robinson Crusoe*, *Pilgrim's Progress*, and Parson Weems's *Life of Washington*. His days were spent in exhausting work. In addition to the usual labour of frontier farming, each of the family moves meant clearing fresh land, fencing it, building a new cabin. Lincoln grew into a physical giant — six feet four inches in height, and with a strength that became famous even in that world where physical vigour could be assumed of anyone who managed to survive. But in spite of the energy that went into such growth, and the wear of his daily work, Lincoln never faltered in his desire to learn. At night he would read by firelight; and he was always willing to walk miles to borrow a book. His difficulty was in finding anyone who had a book to lend. 'The things I want to know are in books,' he said. 'My best friend is the man who'll get me a book I ain't read.'

Combined with Lincoln's passion for reading books was the far more unusual passion for thinking about them. Lincoln belonged to the small minority of people who actually think, even when they are neither reading nor writing nor talking. Books were for him not mere information, nor mere diversion; they were the means of deepening experience, of intensifying life by giving his imagination more material with which to work. Lincoln brooded over Man, and God, and the meaning of his country's history. Like Carlyle's heroes, he lived with the Great Fact of Existence staring him in the face. He did not chatter about these things; he thought about them with reverence and humility — as a boy, while working alone with his axe in a frontier clearing; as a man, while driving alone over the prairie between the far-scattered court-houses where he practised law.

When Shakespeare and Burns came into his possession, the richness and mystery of life grew still more painfully obsessing. But he was born to face the eternal questioning, to try and understand, never to take refuge in any of the time-honoured protections: work, love, drink, sport, cynicism. The boy who was never too tired, after a day with plough or axe, to lie by the fire and study, grew into the man who could never take law or politics or money-making quite seriously enough to absolve him from the burden of thought. A fellow-lawyer noticed him once in court, 'sitting alone in a corner of the bar, remote from anyone, wrapped in abstraction and gloom. He seemed to be pursuing in his mind some specific painful subject, regularly and systematically through various sinuosities, and his sad face would assume, at times, deeper phases of grief. No relief came till he was roused by the adjournment of court, when he emerged from his cage of gloom, like one awakened from sleep.' These fits of abstraction were characteristic of Lincoln from his twelfth year onward. There was no state of trance connected with them, no mystic detachment; he was merely, like Socrates on similar occasions, trying to think. The two men, indeed, had much in common. If Lincoln had been born into a society that provided his mind and spirit with rich fare, and gave him time for thought, he might have found more peace as a Socratic philosopher, a gadfly to the world's conscience, than he ever found as a disillusioned leader of men.

In regard to religion, Lincoln's position is hard to define. He was not a Christian in the accurate sense of the word. He was a theist — but also a fatalist. Once, on being asked point-blank what his religion was, he said that it seemed to be his fate to go on as in a twilight, feeling and reasoning his way through life. Then he compared himself to the man in Saint Mark who spoke that most human and despairing sentence: 'Lord, I believe; help Thou mine unbelief.' Lincoln's religion, however vague the formulation he could reach, included reverence and the tragic sense of life.

Lincoln never stopped growing. There were no years of education to his life, to be followed by years of experience. The two went side by side. He was always learning, always increasing in wisdom. At forty the change that had come over him astonished an Eastern lawyer who had not seen him for ten years; at fifty he was twice the man he had seemed a decade earlier. His greatest speeches were made in the last two years of his life; and had he lived to old age and retirement, he might have had time to explain what he had learned. He was the most sincerely thoughtful man America has produced — probably the wisest in sympathy and understanding — and he died before he had expressed his wisdom. All he accomplished was to save the American Union; he never explained why he thought it worth saving. Lincoln would not have fought the Civil War for the sordid end that resulted. But for what end did he fight it? What was this Union of his dreams? He must have defined it in his own mind, for he was not a man of empty words. The few things he believed in, he could state. Behind the Gettysburg Address, and the Second Inaugural Speech, the reader feels some formed and definite picture of a future America. But it was never made clear. The one great democrat of the modern world died without telling us his vision of democracy. Unable, therefore, to know what Lincoln wanted his country to become, we can only lament the beauty that he killed to give this vision birth, and the ugliness that was the end of all his effort.

2

At the age of nineteen, Lincoln went on a flatboat to New Orleans, via the Ohio and Mississippi. The journey gave him a new picture of his country, and started his imagination working, on the subject of slavery, along disturbing lines. Shortly after this, his father moved to Illinois, and again Lincoln helped in the weary work of starting a new farm. He served as clerk in a store, then went again to New Orleans. The store in which he worked was about to close, leaving him without a job, when the Black Hawk Indian War began. Lincoln volunteered, and was chosen as captain by the local company; but he saw no fighting. The same year, 1832, he stood as Whig candidate for the State Legislature, and was defeated, though his showing in the district proved his popularity among those who knew him.

Lincoln, who had lived his life in backwoods districts where Jacksonian Democracy was strongest, was a Whig for two main reasons: first, he had, while a young man, a deep admiration for Clay, whose patriotism and feeling for the Union roused in him an eager response; and second, Lincoln had a strong feeling for property, and the Hamiltonian banking programme of the Whigs made for a security of property values that was threatened by the financial demagogy of Jackson. For a man who was too much interested in trying to understand life to pay much attention to acquiring property for himself, it is astonishing how uncritically Lincoln accepted the developments of the institution of private property that were taking place in America during his lifetime. When the business interests which had annexed the Republican Party between 1856 and 1860 investigated Lincoln's record as a lawyer, they found it sound, from their point of view, on every point. A frontiersman would be expected to feel strongly about the sanctity of the more immediate forms of private property;

but Lincoln carried this feeling over, unchanged, to such corporate property as railways, banks, and public utilities. He never
saw that the democracy which was his deepest faith, the America for which he was willing to give half a million lives, was to be
killed in the interests of this new form of property, and that by wag-
ing and winning the Civil War for his business masters he was to be
a chief agent in the murder.

After an unsuccessful venture at joint-ownership of a store
(which left him with debts that it took fifteen years to clear),
Lincoln, in 1834, was elected to the State Legislature, where he
served for the next eight years. During these years he was admitted
to the bar, and moved from the village of New Salem to Springfield, a town which was soon to become the capital of the State.

In the spring of 1835, Lincoln became engaged to Ann Rutledge, daughter of a local tavern-keeper and farmer. Lincoln was
in love, with all his intense passionate being. His melancholy was
in abeyance; hope and ambition were freed. He would get clear
of his debts; he would go to Illinois College between sessions of
the Legislature, while Ann, who was twenty-two, would go to a
young ladies' academy in the same town. Then they would be
married. But in August, Ann Rutledge died of malaria, and for
weeks Lincoln's sanity was in danger. He would sit for hours, unaware when he was spoken to; he was found wandering about the
woods, talking incoherently to himself; he was found lying in the
graveyard, with an arm across Ann Rutledge's grave. Friends
took him to their house and tried to care for him. One wild night
of storm he stood in their doorway, watching the tempest. 'I can't
bear to think of her out there alone.... The rain and the storm
shan't beat on her grave.' It is the theme of one of Baudelaire's
greatest poems, and through this summer and autumn Lincoln was
living in that shadow-land of guilt and defeated memory where
nothing flourishes but the *fleurs du mal*. He returned slowly to his
normal state; but the streak of morbidity in his nature was more
apparent than ever, the contrast more striking between his moods
of sorrowful brooding and of vulgar, bawdy laughter.

Lincoln's personal appearance reflected his enigmatic nature. His long awkward body and dangling arms expressed physical strength and lack of even rudimentary social training. His father said that his body 'looked like he needed a carpenter's plane put to him,' and his mind and spirit might have profited by a similar finish. Lincoln made no virtue of his roughness; he would have been glad to conform to the conventions of the world in which he wished to succeed; but there was something angular and unkempt in his soul, and it was fitting (and seemingly inevitable) that his clothes should always look like sacking, and his coarse black hair always be rumpled. But it was Lincoln's face that was most disturbingly expressive. His big, deep-set eyes, under bushy black eyebrows, revealed a probing, insatiable mind. No such mind could have peace on earth, and there was no peace in Lincoln's eyes — laughter, or quizzical friendliness, or baffled pain; but never peace. And Lincoln's mouth showed the other side of him — the impudent, broad-humoured, bawdy defence against the sorrowful vision of his eyes; a large, flexible mouth that could twist itself into endless caricatures of emotion. Lincoln was the most famous story-teller in the West, and the cruellest mimic. He could collect a crowd at a crossroads store and keep them in ribald laughter for as long as he chose. He could break up a serious talk with a moment's mimicry. He could make a witness look and sound so absurd that the jury would be ashamed to pay attention to him.[1] But every so often, Lincoln's mouth would droop, sharing the nameless melancholy of his eyes; it was a sign that his one protection was gone and that he was given over entirely to depression.

It was the combination of racy, horse-sense humour and true thoughtfulness that made the success of Lincoln's speeches, and hence of his whole political career. He could not use the cheap, easy phrase or the rhetorical abstraction. He had thought too long about his subject-matter not to know when he was saying nothing. He had worked and suffered for what little understanding,

---

[1] He did this very seldom. He was famous for the consideration with which he usually handled witnesses.

what few fixed ideas, he possessed, and when he spoke he was trying to help others reach the same end with less pain. Therefore, as Mr. Sandburg said, Lincoln talked·'to thousands of people as if he and another man were driving in a buggy across the prairie, exchanging their thoughts.' This was flattering, and exciting; but it might get monotonous, and it was there that Lincoln's crazy humour saved his speech. To illustrate a point, to make fun of an opponent, to satirize an idea, he had a store of homely ridiculous anecdotes that in themselves were worth half a dozen ordinary political orations.

After the death of Ann Rutledge, Lincoln gave himself to politics and law for five years. Then he became engaged to Miss Mary Todd, who had come to Springfield from Lexington, Kentucky, and whose social background was far superior to Lincoln's. The wedding was set for January 1, 1841 — but, when the time came, Lincoln did not appear. Once before he had tried to break the engagement; but at the sight of Mary's tears he had immediately capitulated. Now he sought to solve the problem by staying away from the wedding. For a time this was effective in separating him from Mary Todd; but in less than two years they were engaged again, and in November, 1842, Lincoln went through with the marriage. A friend who was with him that day said he 'looked as if he were going to the slaughter.' While Lincoln was dressing for the wedding, at a friend's house, a son of the house asked him where he was going. 'To Hell, I suppose,' was the answer, and it was not given facetiously.

Whatever tangle of motives and memories explained this wedding, it was an inauspicious union from the beginning. Mrs. Lincoln became something of a shrew — trying to Lincoln, and so trying to outsiders that Lincoln had sometimes to make friendly appeals and apologies to the local tradesmen to induce them to go near the house for orders or deliveries. In the White House, matters grew worse; and in the last years of Lincoln's life there were scenes that are embarrassing to recall. Only one of the four children of the marriage lived to maturity.

In 1846, Lincoln was elected to the House of Representatives at Washington — the only Whig from Illinois who was elected that year. His opposition to the Mexican War, however, was not popular with his constituents, and two years later, when the Whigs elected Zachary Taylor to the Presidency, Lincoln failed to retain his seat. During the Taylor campaign he made a trip East, delivering a number of speeches in Massachusetts, and thus for the first time winning attention outside his own State. He then returned to his law practice at Springfield, and for the next eight years had little direct connection with politics.

These were important years in Lincoln's life. He was forty-seven years old at the end of this period, and had at last developed to something like his full stature. He had a long way to travel yet before he could be capable of his last great speeches, or of the self-confident yet humble forbearance with which he handled men and events during the Civil War; nevertheless, by the end of these eight years of retirement from politics there was a recognizable similarity between the man he was and the man he would become. The buffoon in Lincoln became less and less obvious, though his sense of the ridiculous remained keen as ever, showing in the quick detection of pose and artificiality which made him a deadly debater. His uncouthness and lack of manner began to be submerged during these years, under the dignity of a great personality. Gradually he became a leader of the Illinois bar and began to receive important corporation cases, winning a reputation among the new lords of capitalism for economic and social 'soundness.' But the most important aspect of his life during these years was his growing absorption in the problems of slavery and the preservation of the Union.

In spite of his instinctive abhorrence of slavery, Lincoln could never bring himself to be an Abolitionist, for two main reasons: first, his regard for the property rights of the Southerners; second, and more important, his realization of the evil chaos that would result from immediate emancipation. In spite of all the furore and humanitarian oratory in the North, Lincoln seems to have been one of the few people who really thought about the plight of the Negro. Charles Francis Adams, Jr., the grandson of John Quincy Adams, stated the problem which the self-styled 'friends of the Negro' chose, disastrously, to ignore. 'My impression, from what I see,' wrote Adams, when he was serving as an officer in the Union army 'is that emancipation as a Government measure would be a terrible calamity to the blacks as a race; that rapid emancipation as the result of an economic revolution destroying their value as agricultural machines would be a calamity, though less severe; and finally, that the only transition to freedom absolutely beneficial to them as a race would be one proportioned in length to the length of their captivity, such a one in fact as destroyed villeinage in the wreck of the feudal system.... The blacks must be cared for or they will perish, and who is to care for them when they cease to be of value?' Lincoln grasped this problem, and taught himself that there was no easy answer. The blacks had been sacrificed once to the white man's greed; were they now to be sacrificed to his sentimentality? A field-hand cost over a thousand dollars — which was a good reason why the least kindly Southern master did not abuse him physically, or overwork him, or underfeed him. It was customary to import day labourers from the North to drain swamps on the plantations or to dig ditches in malarial regions. Negroes were too valuable for such work. But what value would they have, once they were free? Untrained, illiterate, shiftless, inefficient — who would protect them when their well-being was to nobody's interest? They could not clothe themselves in citizenship or eat the Declaration of Independence.

It was knowledge of all this that led Lincoln to say in a speech, in 1854, 'When Southern people tell us they are no more responsible for the origin of slavery than we are, I acknowledge the fact. When it is said that the institution exists, and that it is very difficult to get rid of it in any satisfactory way, I can understand and appreciate the saying. I surely will not blame them for not doing what I should not know how to do myself.'

Lincoln, therefore, was never an Abolitionist. Yet his deepest faith in life was outraged by the existence of slavery. He had to teach himself that there was no quick way out, and to hope that in time the institution would die and that during the transition period the Negro would be prepared for citizenship. But all this led him to one further conclusion — that slavery must never be allowed to spread. The more he realized how hard it was to get rid of slavery in the South, the more he knew that this problem must not be foisted on the new Territories. 'We must give them a clean bed,' he said, 'with no snakes in it.' Having come to these two conclusions, having learned them painfully and made them a part of him, Lincoln was ready to become a leader in the new Republican Party, which was formed to forward exactly those ideas.

Still another conviction had been growing in Lincoln's mind during these years. As the Southern threats of secession grew more frequent, and as many Northerners contended that the South should be allowed to go whenever it chose, Lincoln's feeling for the Union crystallized, becoming one of his dominant emotions. In this he was a true representative of his section, for the Middle-Western States felt they could not afford to lose the lower Mississippi Valley. Vinton of Ohio stated the feelings of these States. 'Disunion,' he said, 'is ruin to them. They have no alternative but to resist it whenever or wherever attempted.... Massachusetts and South Carolina might, for all I know, find a dividing line that would be mutually satisfactory to them, but, sir, they can find no such line to which the Western country can assent.' But there was more to Lincoln's feeling for the Union than this economic motive. There was his patriotism, and, dominating all, his belief in democracy. That the great experiment should fail was to Lincoln an intolerable idea. That it was actually failing under his eyes was a fact he did not perceive — probably because he lived his life in the Middle West, in the Valley of Democracy, and had no knowledge of the economic revolution that was taking place, no prevision of its effects on politics. It is this ignorance that accounts for Lincoln's belief that the Southerners were seceding because of what they thought was a threat to slavery. When they disregarded his honest and explicit promises that their slave property would not be touched, Lincoln thought they were bemused by disloyal leaders. The issue, in his mind, became the simple one of preserving the Union. And on that issue he made war. There is no telling whether he would have made it if he had realized that the South was fighting for an agrarian society against the threat of a business man's oligarchy. Lincoln would have hated that oligarchy almost as much as did Jefferson Davis. and if he had grasped the main issue, Lincoln might have felt that his real fight lay elsewhere.

By the time of the campaign of 1856, Lincoln was prominent in the Republican Party in Illinois, and two years later the Republican State Convention made him the party choice for the United States Senate. His opponent in the campaign was Senator Douglas, the leader of the Democratic Party in the North.[1] In accepting the nomination, Lincoln made a speech that gained him a national hearing. He pointed out that agitation in the slavery question had been increasing ever since the passage of the Kansas-Nebraska Act, adding that the agitation would not cease 'until a crisis should have been reached and passed. "A house divided against itself cannot stand." I believe this government cannot endure permanently half slave and half free.... Either the opponents of slavery will arrest the further spread of it, and place it where the public mind shall rest in the belief that it is in the course of ultimate extinction; or its advocates will push it forward till it shall become alike lawful in all the States, old as well as new, North as well as South.'

Lincoln believed that if the Democratic Party, with its Southern leaders, was to remain in power, either disunion or the spread of slavery must result. Therefore, 'To meet and overthrow the power

[1] Senators were chosen by the State Legislatures, so the real question in the election was which party would control the legislature. The Republicans declared in advance that they would choose Lincoln if they controlled the legislature, and the Democrats would, of course, appoint Douglas to succeed himself.

of that dynasty is the work now before all those who would prevent that consummation.' That was in 1858. The mission of the Republican Party was, in Lincoln's mind, clear — to save the Union and to arrest the spread of slavery. Two years later the issue, for Lincoln, had not changed; but his party had changed. It had been taken over by the enthusiasts for a high tariff and a National Bank, and was buying (with the promise of free land) the votes of thousands who had never given thought to Lincoln's issues. The implications of this change seemed lost on Lincoln.

Although he failed of election in 1858, Lincoln added to his reputation by the campaign. He showed, in a series of debates with Senator Douglas, that not only could he hold his own with the leading orator of the Senate, but that his thoughtful, conversational speeches had more appeal, as well as more sense, than the flowery efforts of his opponent. There was something ingratiating about Lincoln's way of explaining his ideas, even to people who disagreed with them. In 1860, therefore, when the party sought to ingratiate itself with as many different groups as possible, men like Seward and Chase, who had expressed bitter anti-Southern opinions, were passed over, and Lincoln became the logical candidate for the Presidency. He did not win the nomination, however, without the help of chicanery on the part of his managers. The vote of the Indiana delegation was secured by promising that Caleb Smith would be made Secretary of the Interior and William Dole Commissioner of Indian Affairs. The managers then telegraphed Lincoln, who had stayed in Springfield, that the Pennsylvania vote could be had if he would promise the Treasury Department to Simon Cameron. Lincoln replied, 'I authorize no bargains and will be bound by none.' His managers were discouraged; but they soon recovered. 'Lincoln ain't here,' said one of them, 'and don't know what we have to meet, so we'll go ahead as if we hadn't heard from him, and he must ratify it.' They made the promise, and secured the Pennsylvania vote at the critical moment. During the third and decisive ballot, a Lincoln manager approached an

Ohio leader. 'If you can throw the Ohio delegation for Lincoln, Chase can have anything he wants.' 'How d'ye know?' 'I know, and you know I couldn't promise if I didn't know.'

Lincoln subsequently told Thurlow Weed, 'I have not promised an office to any man.' Nevertheless, his Cabinet included Cameron of Pennsylvania, Salmon P. Chase of Ohio, and Caleb Smith of Indiana. Seward became Secretary of State, and Lincoln had the awkward task of handling a Cabinet which contained two of his defeated rivals for the Presidency.

In his dealings with this Cabinet — the members of which had been chosen, not because Lincoln thought he could work with them, or because he had a high opinion of their abilities, but purely for political reasons — Lincoln showed his acumen, his tact, and his moral superiority. Seward expected to run the Administration, and set to work, from the beginning, to dominate the Western clodhopper. The whole Cabinet thought Lincoln something of a joke, and there is no question that they had superficial cause for thinking so. The account given by Charles Francis Adams of his call at the White House shows the worst of Lincoln. Adams had been appointed Minister to Great Britain, and called to receive any communications the President might want to make. Seward introduced him to Lincoln, who was shabbily dressed, even for him, and had on a pair of worn-out slippers. Adams expressed his gratitude for the confidence that had been shown in him, and Lincoln replied, ungraciously, that 'Governor Seward' was the man Adams ought to thank. He then stretched his long legs out comfortably in front of him, turned to Seward, and remarked, 'Well, Governor, I've decided that Chicago Post-Office appointment.' The interview was at an end.

No wonder Adams went to London with the impression that his President was a charlatan as well as a buffoon. So far, since the election, his conduct seemed to portend the worst. During the critical months while the country was falling to pieces under Buchanan's nerveless rule, Lincoln had ignored the leaders of his party, and had spent his time, in Adams' words, 'perambulating the country, kissing little girls, and growing whiskers.'[1] And then, instead of showing interest in his country's relations with England (relations which were soon to determine the fate of the Civil War and hence the future of America), Lincoln made a parade of the cheap-politician side of his nature. Yet Adams, before long, came to realize that there was genuine greatness in his chief, and so did the disgruntled and discordant Cabinet. Lincoln got the best possible service out of that jealous, ill-assorted group. He appeared humble before their arrogant self-confidence, diffident before their cock-sureness; but he never gave an inch on any essential matter, and he somehow evoked co-operation and a kind of rough loyalty from men who had never previously shown signs of such virtue.

The impressive thing about Lincoln's dealings with his associates, while he was President, is that he never took the chance to assert himself and never missed the chance of asserting his cause. Always he was trying to show those about him, and the nation at large, that more than the Union was at stake; that democracy, the entire American experiment, would stand or fall depending on which side won the war. With this conviction at heart, it became increasingly difficult for Lincoln to bother about whether or not some member of his Cabinet patronized him or some newspaper editor insulted him. His dedication gave him an impressive detachment and moral strength; it added little to his stature as a statesman, however, since it was based on a misapprehension of the facts. Did he come to suspect this, before the end? About a year before he died, in the spring of 1864, he wrote: 'I claim not to have controlled events, but confess plainly that events have controlled me. Now at the end of three years' struggle, the nation's condition is not what either party or any man devised or expected. God alone can claim it. Whither it is tending seems plain.' Did he have a vision of what the future really held? If so, it would explain his increasing melancholy.

[1] Lincoln had always been clean-shaven; but as soon as he was elected President he provided himself with a beard. Perhaps this was a symbolic recognition of his new need for dignity.

3

The clearest illustration of the way in which events controlled Lincoln is the story of emancipation. When Fort Sumter was attacked, Lincoln decided on war in order to save the Union. He had no desire to force quick emancipation on the South; but the Northern Abolitionists hailed the struggle as a war for freedom, and there were numerous politicians and business men who saw that the easiest way of avoiding a revival of Southern leadership in Congress, after the war had been won, was to confiscate the Southern slave property, thus pauperizing the upper class in that section. So there was steady pressure on Lincoln, from the very beginning, to emancipate the slaves. Had he done so at the opening of the war, the slave-owning border States would have joined the South; Washington (which was surrounded by slave territory) would have fallen into Southern hands, and the strategical problem of the war would have been made so much more difficult that there is little doubt that the large Northern minority which opposed the war would have had its way, and the South would have gone unmolested. But Lincoln refused to emancipate the slaves, and he revoked the orders of two of his military governors who had freed the slaves in the territories under their control. In 1862, Lincoln had Congress pass a bill offering financial assistance to any State that wished to provide for gradual abolition.[1] The border States that had sided with the Union should have seized this chance to get compensation. But they made no move — showing clearly that in their eyes at least it was a war to preserve the Union and not a war against slavery.

As the Abolitionist pressure on Lincoln became more insistent, he wrote, 'My paramount object is to save the Union, and not either to save or to destroy slavery.' And again, 'I view this matter as a practical war measure, to be decided in accord to the advantages or disadvantages it may offer to the suppression of the rebellion.' Finally, however, after a slight turn of the tide in the

[1] In the same year, slaves in the District of Columbia were set free — and there was no compensation to their masters.

Union favour during the summer of 1862, Lincoln decided that the border States would now put up with emancipation so long as it did not affect them, and that Northern enthusiasm for the war would be stimulated by such a step. So in September he announced that on the first of the following January he would declare free all the slaves in any State, or any part of any State, which was still in rebellion against the Federal Government. When the time came, he made his proclamation. It did not affect the border States, for they were not in rebellion. And it did not affect the unconquered Confederate States, for Lincoln had no power over them. Actually, therefore, Lincoln's reluctant and long-delayed proclamation freed very few slaves; it is somewhat ironical that he should be known to history as the Great Emancipator.[1]

The political effect of the Emancipation Proclamation throughout the North was all that could have been desired. It is probable that without it the Republicans would have lost the election of 1864. For the old Democratic Party in the North was by no means dead, and though there were many War Democrats, there were even more who had disapproved of the war from the beginning, and whose disapproval grew more and more intense as the carnage dragged on vainly through the years. In 1864, they nominated McClellan, a deposed and dissatisfied general, declaring that the war had been a failure and demanding an end of hostilities on whatever terms could be obtained. The Republicans renominated Lincoln, and, in order to attract the War Democrats, Andrew Johnson of Tennessee (a Democrat who had split with his State on the question of preserving the Union) was put forward for the Vice-Presidency. McClellan received 1,808,727 votes, Lincoln 2,216,076.[2]

When the news of this election reached the South, it is probable that all the leaders except Davis knew that the game was up.

---

[1] In 1865, after Lincoln's death, the Thirteenth Amendment to the Constitution was adopted. This amendment, proclaimed by President Johnson, abolished slavery throughout the country, without compensation.

[2] In the Electoral College McClellan received 21 votes, Lincoln 212!

Davis was incapable of facing that idea. Until the last mournful week he was assuring his people that confidence and moral superiority would still bring them out on top. At the Hampton Roads Conference, in February, 1865, two months before the end, Lincoln offered the South practically any terms it chose in return for accepting the Union and Emancipation. Davis would accept nothing short of independence. Such an attitude, at that date, was blindness; for the three factors on which the Southern leaders had counted for victory had by then all been proved to be delusive. These factors were: first, that the Southerners, man for man, would be better soldiers than the Northerners.[1] Second, that the anti-war minority in the North would grow stronger as time passed, and finally force a negotiated peace.[2] Third, that Cotton was King, and that a Northern blockade of the South would cause England to enter the war, or at least to recognize the Confederate States and to break the blockade.

This last was the most sensible hope of all; for the Civil War presented England with a unique opportunity. Here was a raw-material-producing section of the world which was not only willing but anxious to remain non-industrialized, and therefore to maintain free trade. Southern statesmen regarded England as the natural complement to their own country. England was the only industrial nation strong enough to dispense with tariffs, and the Southerners wished to make a permanent trade alliance, shipping to England their raw materials and buying her manufactured goods. It had not seemed to them that any nation could be so obtuse as to refuse this opportunity. But the economic causes of the war, so clear to the Southerners, were for the most part unknown in England. English liberals quickly persuaded themselves that this was a war for human freedom; John Bright toured the country and convinced the workingman that democracy, as well as liberty,

[1] This was quite true, but the difference had not been enough to compensate for the fact that there were nine million Southerners — including slaves — against twenty-two million Northerners.

[2] This was no longer a reasonable hope after November, 1864.

was at stake — with the startling result that the very operatives who were thrown out of work by the cotton shortage petitioned the Government not to help the South by breaking the blockade. The English ruling class had every interest, financial and sentimental, in siding with the South. Parts of the English working-class were in danger of starvation if England did not side with the South. And yet she held aloof. Largely this was the work of John Bright and his followers; partly it was the result of the excellent diplomacy of Charles Francis Adams; and partly it followed from the accident that there was a failure of food crops in England in 1861 and 1862, so that immense quantities of wheat were being imported from the Northern States. By chance Northern wheat had for the time being become as important to England as Southern cotton. By 1863, when this unnatural state of affairs was ended, the Southern cause was no longer a good bet.

Toward the end of the war, Davis made a last bid for English intervention by promising to emancipate the slaves, in return for England's support. He was told that the offer had been made too late.

In April, 1865, Davis and the Confederate Government had to flee from Richmond. Throughout the war, Davis had insisted on the protection of that city, thus hampering Lee's movements and committing the best Southern army to the defence of a useless capital. Within a week of the fall of Richmond, Lee had surrendered, and three days later Johnston surrendered the last Southern army to Sherman. But still Davis was opposed to yielding, and it was not until the very end of the month that he could be prevailed on to admit that the Confederacy was dead. On the tenth of May he was captured in Georgia, and sent to prison at Fortress Monroe. Two years later he was released — for the interesting reason that the Government lawyers had failed to find any charge on which they thought it safe to try him. The legal arguments in favour of the constitutionality of secession were dangerously strong.

With his fortune gone, his home destroyed, and his health apparently wrecked, Davis had a chance to show that, in his own life at least, the unbreakable will with which he had tried to animate the South was capable of miracles. He lived for twenty-two years after leaving prison. He tried to recoup his fortunes by business ventures; but he was not made for that world, and the ventures all failed. He rebuilt his health by sheer force of character, and was stronger at the age of seventy than he had ever seemed before in his life. Returning with his wife to a farm, on the Gulf of Mexico, he managed to keep going, financially, and to write *The Rise and Fall of the Confederate Government*. The State of Mississippi wanted to send him back to Washington as Senator; but he refused to ask for the necessary Federal pardon.... In December, 1889, he died in New Orleans.

On the evening of April 14, 1865, while Jefferson Davis was wandering about the South trying to pretend that the Confederacy still existed, and to avoid capture by the Union soldiers, Lincoln went to Ford's Theatre, in Washington. There he was shot, and killed, by John Wilkes Booth, a member of a band who had plotted to kill several leaders of the Government. Lincoln's death was the last fatal blow to the old South. There had been, until then, a little chance of preserving some continuity of leadership, and hence some of the values of that pre-war world — but now there was no chance at all. At his last Cabinet meeting, a few hours before he was murdered, Lincoln had said: 'I think it providential that this great rebellion is crushed just as Congress has adjourned and there are none of the disturbing elements of that body to hinder and embarrass us. If we are wise and discreet, we shall reanimate the States and get their governments in successful operation, with order prevailing and the Union re-established before Congress comes together in December.... I hope there will be no persecution, no bloody work after the war is over.'

It is clear that Lincoln realized the task he would be faced with in trying to secure civilized treatment for the South. With his politician's sharpness, and the prestige he had slowly won, he might have succeeded. But more probably he would have been broken as Andrew Johnson was broken.

For the forces of vindictiveness and greed were about to be un-chained throughout the North, and they are more terrible than the dogs of war. The darkest days for the South were still to come — and the darkest days, too, for the things Lincoln believed in: democracy, equality, a certain compassion in public life, the in-dividualism of a farming or a backwoods community. The Union was saved; but everything the Union symbolized for Lincoln was gone. Professor Morison, after quoting Lowell's jubilant ode to freedom and peace, comments: 'Lowell was, in fact, delivering the swan-song of the New England intellectuals and reformers. In the generation to come, that region would no longer furnish the nation with teachers and men of letters, but with a mongrel breed of politicians, sired by abolition out of pro-fiteering. Industrialism and commercialism had the Middle States firmly in their grasp, and were extending tentacles through-out the Middle West. The old simplicity and idealism retreated beyond the Mississippi, and materialism soon overtook them there.' [1] And along with all these losses, there was gone out of American life the stability, the self-confidence, which characterized the old South. Henry Adams, making friendly fun of the Southern statesmen, wrote: 'All were supported, lifted, inspired by the moral certainty of rightness. To them the universe was serious, even solemn, but it was their universe, a Southern conception of right.... Slavery was only a part of the Southern system, and the life of it all — the vigor — the poetry — was its moral certainty of self.' With this certainty there died the ideal for which three generations of Southerners had worked:

> ... Bury the purple dream
> Of the America we have not been.
> The tropic empire, seeking the warm sea,
> The last foray of aristocracy
> Based... on a certain code, a manner of birth,
> A certain manner of knowing how to live,
> The pastoral rebellion of the earth
> Against machines, against the Age of Steam.

[1] *Oxford History of the United States*, II, 325.

PART THREE
PLUTOCRACY

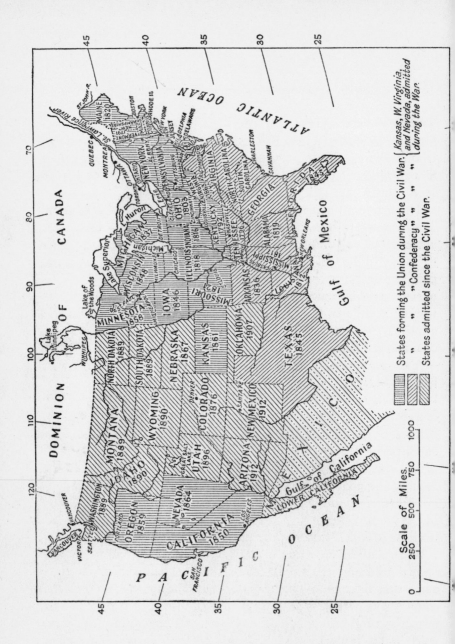

Scale of Miles.

States forming the Union during the Civil War. Kansas, W. Virginia, and Nevada, admitted during the War.
"   "   "   "   Confederacy   "   "   "   "
"   "   States admitted since the Civil War.

INTRODUCTION TO PART THREE

THE second attempt at a planned society had failed. Of the three forms of democracy that had existed in America, the worst had triumphed: the democracy of massed city populations, ignorant foreign labour, graft, and 'machine politics' — the democracy, in other words, that was really plutocracy.

The new masters of America had no vision of an ordered state. They wanted to be let alone, so that they could make a great deal of money. To gain this freedom, they were willing to do what was necessary in the way of corrupting the Government. Beyond that, they had no interest in politics. This third period, therefore, was one of growing anarchy. The only reason the Government worked at all was that the country had such huge riches it could afford to waste most of them and still be better off than many countries. But the system was hard on posterity.

A keen observer, as early as Grant's Presidency, could see what had happened. 'The system of 1789,' wrote Henry Adams, 'had broken down, and with it the eighteenth-century fabric of *a priori*, or moral, principles. Politicians had tacitly given it up, and Grant's Administration marked the avowal. Nine-tenths of men's political energies must henceforth be wasted on expedients to piece out — to patch — or, in vulgar language, to tinker — the political machine as often as it broke down. Such a system, or want of system, might last centuries, if tempered by an occasional revolution or civil war; but as a machine, it was, or soon would be, the poorest in the world — the clumsiest — the most inefficient.'

When the country began to fill up, when, in 1890, the old frontier disappeared and there was little more free land, when the time came that intelligent planning was needed in order to keep the country prosperous, trouble began. By the end of the century, a farmer's revolt and a labourer's revolt had appeared. These revolts found political expression in the Progressive Movement, which, for a few years, improved the moral tone of politics, but which came to nothing because it, too, was without a plan. It was too late to revive the America of Adams, or of Calhoun, or of Lincoln; and the formless plutocracy could not be made a good thing merely by honest administration. Yet the Progressives had no new, thought-out vision of an organized State. So their movement died, and Harding became President.

At the beginning of this third period, there were about thirty-four million people in the United States; when Harding died, in 1923, there were a hundred and twenty-four million. In the decade between 1870 and 1880, there were almost three million immigrants to the United States; in the next decade there were over five million. Then immigration dropped to below four million; but it rose to seven and three-quarters million between 1900 and 1910. The World War then intervened; and after the War the United States turned to a policy of immigration restriction, and soon to what was virtually a policy of exclusion. It was high time, for large sections of the country were polyglot and without the semblance of social or cultural unity.

CHAPTER VII

JOHNSON AND GRANT

I

As THE election of 1864 approached, Lincoln felt it was more than likely that he would be defeated, and the South be allowed to go free. In August of that summer he wrote, and signed, the following private memorandum: 'This morning, as for some days past, it seems exceedingly probable that this Administration will not be re-elected, then it will be my duty to co-operate with the President-elect so as to save the Union between the election and the inauguration, as he will have secured his election on such grounds that he cannot possibly save it afterwards.' Lincoln's pessimism was shared by most of the Republican leaders, which explains their willingness to let him have his way at the Convention and to dictate a mild and conciliatory policy, calculated to keep the border States on the side of the Union and to win the votes of the War Democrats. The temporary chairman at the Convention was the Reverend Doctor Breckinridge, a War Democrat from a border State, and he made it plain that this was not to be a Republican, but a pro-Union, Convention. And a delegate from New York said: 'We meet here not as Republicans.... If we meet as Republicans I have no place in this Convention. I have been a lifelong Democrat.' The party name, for this campaign, was changed from Republican to National Union, and Andrew Johnson, a Democrat from a seceding State, was nominated for Vice-President. Johnson had been Senator from Tennessee when the war broke out, and had won nation-wide praise and obloquy by being the only Southern member of Congress who repudiated the secession of his State.

Born in North Carolina, in 1808, Andrew Johnson knew extreme poverty during his childhood. His father died in 1812, and when Johnson was ten years old he was apprenticed to a tailor. He learned how to read simple words — which is all the education he

acquired as a child. At the age of eighteen, he moved to Greenville in Eastern Tennessee, where he set up a shop of his own. The
following year he fell in love with, and married, Eliza McCardle.
She was eighteen, and Johnson nineteen, and they had not a penny
between them. The girl, however, had a fair education, and she
set to work at once teaching her husband to write, and to read
words of some complication. It was a number of years, however,
before Johnson had time to acquire the ordinary school learning.
He had none of Lincoln's deep need of food for the imagination —
only the ordinary ambitious man's desire for training.

While building up his tailor's business — with the profits of
which he acquired a hundred-acre farm and a number of slaves —
Johnson took part in local politics. East Tennessee was a region of
poor farmers, in contrast to the western end of the State where the
well-to-do planters lived. Johnson became a Jacksonian Democrat, a champion of the common man. There was a large element
of class-consciousness, of hatred of the rich planters, in Johnson's
democracy, and this was accentuated by his position as a poor
farmer in a slave State, where the division between rich and poor
was more striking than in much of rural America.

In the early thirties Johnson was Mayor of Greenville; then, for
eight years, he was in the State Legislature; and in 1843 he went to
the House of Representatives at Washington. After ten years in
Congress, he failed of re-election, but became Governor of Tennessee; and in 1857 he was sent to the United States Senate. All these
political triumphs he won entirely on his popularity, without the
aid of a political machine. In fact, by the fifties, when the planting
aristocracy had joined (and for the most part taken over) the
Democratic Party, Johnson found himself in the awkward position
of having as alleged allies the men whose privileges he had been
fighting all his life. But he kept his hold on the people in his own
end of the State, though the other Slave-State Senators at Washington were cold to him because of his plebeian manners. Johnson,
however, was no mere demagogue; he had complete sincerity, with
a deep love for democracy and for the country that he regarded

(reasonably enough, in view of his own experience) as the home of freedom and opportunity. In Washington, he was an Administration Democrat, except that in season and out he persisted in advocating a Homestead Act for the free distribution of land. He had much to do with keeping this subject a live political issue, and therefore with its final adoption by the Republican Party during the war.

In the campaign of 1860, Johnson was a good Southern Democrat, supporting Breckinridge and attacking both Lincoln and Douglas. After the election came the critical decision of his career. He was a slave-owner and a low-tariff man, who believed that the South would be grievously wronged by Lincoln's Administration. On the other hand, he was, above everything else, a democrat, a believer in the common people. Like Lincoln, he felt that the Union was the safeguard of democracy, that if secession succeeded the democratic experiment in government would have failed. And like Lincoln, he was unaware of the menace to democracy from triumphant Northern business. He was presented, therefore, with a conflict in loyalties — and he chose to stand by democracy and desert the South. During the last dismal months of the Buchanan Administration, he made two patriotic speeches, denouncing secession, that made him a figure of national importance. It gave heart to the Unionists in the North, that a Southern Senator should take this stand. And politicians told one another that if weather-wise Andrew Johnson was opposing the Southern cause, there must be more hope of holding the Union together than there seemed. But Johnson was not playing politics when he sided against his own State; he was following his deepest conviction.

Lincoln's views on the Union, and on the meaning of the war, were the same as Johnson's; so it was natural that the new President often consulted Johnson on the problem of handling the border States that had not seceded. And when, in March, 1862, the North had conquered a large section of Tennessee, Lincoln appointed Johnson military governor of that district. The post, especially for a Tennessee man, was one of extreme danger. Johnson acquitted himself well, governed firmly but not tyrannically, and prepared his section of the State for emancipation and amicable reunion with the North.

In March, 1864, when he was inaugurated Vice-President, there came the first serious set-back of Johnson's career. He had been unwell, and had wished to postpone his inauguration. But Lincoln urged him not to do this, so he made the trip to Washington. On a doctor's advice, to fortify himself against the ordeal, he took some whiskey. He was not an habitual drinker, and on this occasion he took a great deal too much, with the result that his inaugural remarks were a cheap stump speech in which he prided himself on his humble origin and embarrassed his audience most painfully. The Senate was shocked, and talked of demanding his resignation; but when the incident was reported to Lincoln, his response was characteristic: 'Oh, well, don't you bother about Andy Johnson's drinking. He made a bad slip the other day, but I have known Andy a great many years, and he ain't no drunkard.'

2

When Lincoln was assassinated, there were many important people in the North who felt that this was, perhaps, a blessing. The dominant Republicans in Congress — known as 'Radicals' because they wished to take drastic punitive measures against the South — scarcely attempted to conceal their pleasure that the soft-hearted President was out of the way; and in the many eulogies delivered on Lincoln, there were a surprising number of references to the theory that it might have been God's will to call Lincoln, now that the war was over, and to leave the problem of dealing with the conquered South to a sterner man. God, in other words, was assumed to have used Lincoln to trick the border States — and many Democrats — into helping win the war, and then to have put Lincoln out of the way to make room for a more whole-souled 'Radical.' The foresight of the Deity must have begun to seem questionable, to these people, when they discovered that Andrew Johnson intended to be as conciliatory as Lincoln.

At first the Radicals were confident that they would now have everything their own way, for Johnson had been making fiery threats of what he would like to do to the South. He wished to hang Davis, and if possible Lee, and to treat the whole district with Roman severity. But suddenly, within a few months of becoming President, his tone changed. He had been picturing the South in terms of the proud and haughty plantation-owners who had snubbed him all his life, and he had felt that for such people no humiliation was too extreme; but as he learned the facts, he came to realize that the South was a ruined land, where there was nothing to eat and nothing to wear, no money, no credit, and (since the Negroes had taken to lounging about and playing banjos while waiting for the Federal Government to provide them each with forty acres and a mule) very few able-bodied labourers to plough the deserted fields.

As soon as Johnson grasped this picture of the South, his lifelong sympathy for the under dog asserted itself and he became as humane as Lincoln, whose reconstruction policy he proceeded to carry out. He appointed provisional civil governors in the Confederate States, who then summoned constitutional conventions. The conventions were elected by those former rebels who were willing to take an oath of allegiance to the Union — with the exception of certain classes who were considered the ringleaders of the rebellion, and who were not allowed to vote.[1] These conventions were to amend the former State constitutions, declaring slavery abolished, to repudiate the Confederate debt, and to declare the secession ordinances invalid. Having done all that, they could hold elections and proceed to re-create their ordinary civil governments, subject to the necessity of adopting the Thirteenth Amendment. By the summer of 1866, all the ex-Confederate States except Texas had

[1] These included officers of the Confederate and State Governments, general officers of the Southern army, former United States Congressmen or United States Army officers who had resigned their positions to join with the South, and most of the wealthy ex-Confederates.

gone through the necessary forms, and the President declared that the insurrection was at an end. But Congress was still to be heard from, and within a few months this peaceful and wise work had been undone.

The Congress that had been elected in November, 1864, met for the first time in December, 1865 — both Lincoln and Johnson having refrained from summoning it in special session. By that time most of the Southern States had been 'reconstructed' according to the President's plan, and had sent members to sit in the new Congress. They were not received. Instead, a joint committee of both Houses was appointed to investigate the title of the Southern candidates. From the beginning, the committee took the attitude that the Southern Governments were still disloyal and were seeking to find a new way of enslaving the blacks. They pointed with indignation to the 'black codes' which contained provisions such as that any Negro over eighteen, who was without employment, could be fined or imprisoned or hired out at the discretion of the court. Many of these codes were repressive, and they made no pretence that the Negroes were to be given political equality with the whites. To Northern theorists and ex-Abolitionists, this was intolerable; and the Radicals in Congress (who wished to keep the South prostrate for political purposes of their own) made skilful use of the indignation.

The leader of the Congressional Radicals was Thaddeus Stevens of Pennsylvania, of whom a leading American historian has written that he is 'perhaps the most despicable, malevolent, and morally deformed character who has ever risen to high power in America.'[1] He was a bitter, friendless, uneducated old man, whose hatred of the South was intensified when his iron-works were destroyed during Lee's raid into Pennsylvania. But for all his malignancy, Stevens was an able parliamentarian, a vitriolic orator, and a man who knew exactly what he wanted. For two years he became the real ruler at Washington, and if he had not died at the end of that time he might have provoked a second civil war.

[1] J. T. Adams, *The Epic of America*, 275.

Under Stevens's leadership, Congress refused to accept Johnson's work of reconstruction; and in March, 1867, it passed, over the President's veto, a reconstruction measure of its own. This bill abolished Johnson's State Governments; it divided the South into five military departments, each to be administered by a Northern general, with the support of troops; it authorized the military governors to call new State Conventions, for which all adult males (black and white, except for the disfranchised whites) were to be allowed to vote; and it provided that the Governments created by these new conventions could then enter the Union, if they first ratified a Fourteenth Amendment to the Federal Constitution. This amendment had been submitted to the States the previous summer, and had been rejected by the governments of Johnson's reconstructed States. It provided: first, that all people born or naturalized in the United States are citizens of the United States and of the States in which they reside; second, that if any State does not enfranchise all its adult males, its representation in Congress is to be reduced in proportion to the number of adult males who are disfranchised; third, that ex-Confederates should suffer certain political disabilities unless these were removed by special act of Congress.[1]

The excuse for this rigorous policy was humanitarian: it was all done to protect the Negro. The real reason was less pretty. In the first place, if the Southern States were allowed to return to the fold without having Negro suffrage thrust upon them, they would (in spite of the disfranchisement of their old leaders) send a solid block of Democratic Representatives and Senators to Congress. This Democratic block would be even larger than before the war, since, in apportioning representation, five slaves counted only as three people, whereas five ex-slaves would count as five people. There was danger, therefore, that the control of Congress might be taken away from the Republicans and all their hard-won economic

---

[1] One purpose of the amendment was to compel Southern States to enfranchise the Negro by the threat of having their representation in Congress reduced, on the average, by thirty-three per cent.

measures undone. But if many Southern whites were disfranchised and all Southern Negroes given the vote, the reconstructed States could be counted on to send Republican members to Congress and the fruits of the Civil War would be safe.... And in the second place, the Radicals in Congress planned to break Johnson's power and prestige and to create a centralized government at Washington, in which the Legislature was to be paramount over the President and the Supreme Court.

In 1866, the Supreme Court had held that the military tribunals were illegal and could not function in time of peace. In the following year, it was considering the case of a Mississippi editor who, on being arrested by military order, sued out a writ of *habeas corpus*, charging that military reconstruction was unconstitutional. The military governor refused to obey the writ of the United States Circuit Court, and appeal was taken to the Supreme Court. In view of its previous decision, it seemed certain what action the Court would take, and if that were permitted, the whole scheme of Congressional reconstruction would be killed. Before the day of the hearing, therefore, Congress repealed the law allowing appeals in such cases. The Supreme Court made no protest. Meanwhile, Congress had been taking an equally high hand with the executive.

On the same day on which it passed its reconstruction act, Congress passed the Tenure-of-Office Bill, depriving the President of the power to dismiss his more important appointees (such as members of the Cabinet) without the advice and consent of the Senate. Johnson declared the law unconstitutional and removed his Secretary of War without the consent of the Senate, whereupon the House of Representatives impeached him.

Johnson, by this time, had lost his popularity with the public. Infuriated by the attitude of Congress, he had behaved in a grossly undignified way. Making a tour of the country in order to arouse public opinion in his support, he allowed himself to be goaded by hecklers into silly threats and helpless displays of anger. His enemies recalled the unhappy lapse at the time of his inauguration, and spread the story that he was drunk every time he appeared on the platform. His reasonable treatment of the South was said to be a betrayal of the Union by a man who had clearly always been a secessionist at heart, and his fight for the constitutional powers of the Executive was carried on with such ill grace that few people realized how completely he was in the right.

The impeachment trial before the Senate, with Chief Justice Chase presiding, was a disgraceful scene. Even if the Tenure-of-Office act were constitutional,[1] Johnson had the legal right to remove his Secretary of War, Stanton, who had been appointed by Lincoln and whose appointment did not come under the terms of the act. And even if the removal had been an infringement of the act, it was ludicrous to call it a 'high crime and misdemeanour.' Nevertheless, the Radicals came within one vote of impeaching Johnson. Thirty-five Senators voted for conviction, and nineteen for acquittal. Thirty-six votes would have made the necessary two-thirds for conviction; and it was the Radicals' plan to impeach the Chief Justice next, which would have left Congress in possession of all power in the Government.

Although he survived the impeachment, Johnson's authority as President was gone. Congress was supreme. Johnson continued to veto all reconstruction measures, but they were easily passed over his veto.

Johnson's last hours as President were further embittered by the behaviour of Grant, the President-elect. Grant had played a part in the struggle over the removal of Stanton which led Johnson to accuse him of bad faith. Grant, in return, refused to ride in the same carriage with the outgoing President in the inaugural procession.... Johnson, on retiring to Tennessee, was apparently more discredited than any President had ever been at the end of his term. Six years later, however, the State of Tennessee returned him to the United States Senate. It was an interesting scene when Johnson re-entered the chamber where he had last appeared to meet the charges of impeachment. The temper of the country had now changed; the tragedy of Congressional reconstruction had been

[1] Many years later, the Supreme Court declared that it was not.

played to its ugly end, and it seemed as if Johnson might regain his lost prestige at the expense of the Republican Administration. But in the summer of that same year he died of a stroke.

In the course of the years, the Supreme Court has held that Johnson was within his rights in all his important vetoes, and that the Tenure-of-Office Act was invalid from the beginning. 'In short,' writes a recent biographer of Johnson, 'it is held today by the courts, and generally agreed by historians, that nearly every particle of reconstruction legislation after peace was restored was null and void and that Andrew Johnson was correct in his veto messages. It follows that the Fourteenth and Fifteenth Amendments, so far as the Southern States are concerned, were adopted under compulsion and by means of illegal statutes disfranchising whites and enfranchising blacks.' Johnson was broken for trying to win fair treatment for the South and to maintain the power of the Executive. He helped defeat himself by his rashness and ill-temper; but public opinion in the North was against the conciliatory policy, and it is not unlikely that Lincoln, had he lived, would have been broken in the same cause. It is easier for a Thaddeus Stevens to sink the public into bitterness than for any man to lift it into reason.

3

It would have been small consolation for the ruined South to know that the Supreme Court, in the course of years, would find the reconstruction acts unconstitutional. Meanwhile, they were bitter realities, and they produced a state of affairs such as no other civilized nation in Christendom has forced upon a conquered enemy. The constitutional conventions elected under the Congressional reconstruction laws were made up largely of Negroes and poor whites; they adopted constitutions that gave the votes to all blacks and disfranchised all ex-Confederates. The Governments that were finally created under these new constitutions were, of course, Republican, consisting of black men and their degraded white leaders. These whites belonged to two groups. First came the 'carpet-baggers' from the North, drawn South by the high odour of corruption. They had come to gobble up the Federal offices, which could not be given to ex-rebels. By manipulating the Negro vote, they also wormed their way into the new State Governments, where they made quick fortunes out of the public funds.[1] The second group were the 'scalawags,' Southern whites who were willing to play the same malign game, fattening on the last resources of their country. Southern property-owners had suffered the confiscation of about $4,000,000,000 worth of slave property. In addition to that, all of their loans to the Confederate Government and to the States in the Confederacy (which consisted in most cases of everything they could raise by mortgages or by liquidation of investments) had been wiped off. Meanwhile, their land had gone out of cultivation, and most of the cotton they had stored away was confiscated by the Federal Government on the ground that it had been sold to the Confederacy. And now they were forced to submit to such conditions as the following: 'Here' (in the South Carolina House of Representatives), wrote an observer from the North, 'sit 124 members. Of these, 23 are white men, representing the remains of the old civilization.... Deducting the 23 members referred to, who compromise the entire strength of the opposition, we find 101 remaining. Of this 101, 94 are coloured and 7 are their white allies.... The Speaker is black, the clerk is black, the doorkeeper is black, the little pages are black, the chairman of the Ways and Means is black, and the chaplain is coal black. At some of the desks sit coloured men whose types it would be hard to find outside the Congo.... It must be remembered, also, that these men, with not more than half a dozen exceptions, had themselves been slaves.'[2]

Professor Morison describes the activities of this same Legislature as follows: 'The Radical majority, whose members paid an

---

[1] A few carpet-baggers went South with honest intentions, hoping to help the freedmen. They were revolted by what they found, and either returned home or made common cause with the Southern whites.

[2] James S. Pike, *The Prostrate State*.

aggregate annual tax of $340, increased the property tax until it amounted to confiscation, stripped the State Treasury, issued bonds until they could float no more, and sold charters to corporations. Under the head of legislative supplies members were furnished at the public expense with such articles as champagne, Westphalia hams, oval library tables with carved legs, Brussels carpets, gold watches, carriages, and ornamental cuspidors.' [1] It was 'government' such as this that raised the State debt of Louisiana, in four years, from seven to fifty million dollars.

One result of this sad farce was that the Negro was being more pitilessly exploited than he had ever been in the days of slavery. Knowing that such a feast of corruption would not last, his new political masters were making use of him to line their own pockets before the reaction set in. Nothing was done to improve his economic status, and the money voted for his education was for the most part stolen. An illustration of the way his new Northern friends treated the Negro is the South Carolina land-swindle. The white leaders in the Legislature, after buying up most of the swamps and worthless sand-stretches in the State for twenty-five or fifty cents an acre, introduced a bill for establishing the Negroes on the land. The grateful Negro Legislature appropriated over $800,000. The land Commission then bought back the swamps and the sand for more than five dollars an acre, and solemnly put the Negroes on it.

While the blacks were being made fools of in this fashion, they were also being led to behave in a way that would embitter their relations with the white man who must soon return to leadership in the South. In the meantime, Northern Republicans, who might have been expected to show some concern over the Negro's plight, contented themselves with two measures. One was the Fifteenth Amendment, forced through in 1870, declaring that no State may deny the vote to any of its citizens 'on account of race, colour, or previous condition of servitude.' As soon as the whites returned to power in the South, this amendment was evaded, and neither it,

[1] *Op. cit.*, II, 341.

nor that part of the Fourteenth Amendment which should result in a reduction of Southern representation, has ever accomplished anything except to increase American disrespect for law. The other measure in favour of the Southern Negro was the creation of the Freedman's Bureau. This was set up by the Legislature as a welfare league for the black man and an agency to supervise contracts between Negroes and former masters. It opened a few schools for Negroes, and began doing good work. Then it, too, got into the hands of politicians and thieves. It organized a Freedman's Savings Bank, with headquarters in Washington, to teach the ex-slaves the advantages of thrift. After collecting millions of small savings, the bank failed. In the course of the next thirty years, the black depositors were paid back a few cents on the dollar.

After a few years of shocked hopelessness, the white man's answer to the Carpet-Bag Governments was the Ku-Klux Klan. This had started in Tennessee in 1865, as a secret society for amusement, but it was soon turned into a terrorist organization, to enable Southerners to run their country according to their own ideas. Its victims were first given ghostly warnings; if they disregarded these, they were beaten; if they still disobeyed, they were murdered. By this means the blacks were coerced into going back to work and into remaining away from the polls. Carpet-baggers and scalawags were driven out of the South, and the attempts of the Federal Courts to bring members of the Invisible Empire to justice were met by refusals on the part of whole communities to give evidence. By 1877, the Carpet-Bag Governments were overthrown in all the Confederate States except Louisiana and South Carolina, and in the latter State two governments existed side by side: a black government, supported by troops, and a white government whose orders were obeyed by the people. In April of that year, the President withdrew the troops from both those States, and the whites and the Democrats controlled the entire South once again. Meanwhile, affairs in the North, though more prosperous, were almost as disgraceful.

4

The war had been bad for the soul of the Northern people. Like most modern wars, it had been waged in the name of the most difficult virtues, the noblest ideals. The rise to power of the middle-class capitalist, which was both the cause and the chief result of the Civil War, did not of itself seem to justify the casualties. Self-respect led the North to believe that it was fighting for freedom, patriotism, brotherly love; and the suppression of thought, the half-conscious hypocrisy, required for the protection of this pretence had a corroding effect on character. The final result was not to elevate the war, but to debase the virtues which had been named in vain. Meanwhile, quite apart from the war, the character and ability of men in public life had been steadily declining, as a result of political democracy in a huge, uneducated country with a proletarian class made up largely of recent immigrants. In the decade following the war, therefore, there appeared for the first time two of the more sinister aspects of modern American life: a Congress which taken as a whole was beneath contempt, and a public which was well aware of the fact and which found cynical, disinterested pleasure in calling attention to it.

Henry Adams went to Washington during this period, fresh from seven years in England, and full of hopes for a political reformation under President Grant. He found that 'newspapermen as a rule had no great respect for the lower House; Senators had less; and Cabinet officers had none at all. Indeed, one day when Adams was pleading with a Cabinet officer for patience and tact in dealing with Representatives, the Secretary impatiently broke out: "You can't use tact with a Congressman! A Congressman is a hog! You must take a stick and hit him on the snout!"' As for Senators, Adams found that 'the comic side of their egotism partly disguised its extravagance, but faction had gone so far under Andrew Johnson that at times the whole Senate seemed to catch hysterics of nervous bucking without apparent reason. Great leaders, like Sumner and Conkling, could not be burlesqued; they were more grotesque than ridicule could make them; even

Grant, who rarely sparkled in epigram, became witty on their account; but their egotism and factiousness were no laughing matter. They did permanent and terrible mischief.'

That these descriptions of Congress are, on the whole, flattering, will be recognized by anyone who reads the debates of the period or the newspapers and magazines in which the doings of these politicians are chronicled. For there was no pretence on the part of the general public that Congress was worthy of respect. To quote Adams again: 'A young man fresh from the rustic simplicity of London noticed with horror that the grossest satires on the American Senators and politicians never failed to excite the laughter and applause of any audience. Rich and poor joined in throwing contempt on their own representatives. Society laughed a vacant and meaningless derision over its own failures... The people... stood helpless before the chaos; some laughed and some raved; all were disgusted; but they had to content themselves by turning their backs and going to work harder than ever on their railroads and foundries.'

In the last sentence Adams is inclined to flatter 'the people' — an unusual mistake for a member of his family. The people did not have to turn their backs and leave Washington to the hands of wild Congressmen; they chose to do so, having something more interesting than Government to think about, i.e., the exploitation of a continent, the making of money in hitherto undreamed quantities. With the Southerners (and their irritating agrarian economics) disposed of, with a high tariff at last, with gold on the Pacific Coast, silver in the western mountains, iron in Pennsylvania, endless timber everywhere, with cheap workmen arriving by the millions from Europe, with industries freed from foreign competition and thousands of miles of railroads to finance and build — with all these blessings to choose from, the new rulers of America asked nothing of Congress except a few colossal land grants and the favour of being let alone. They knew that the country would not object so long as business boomed, and they saw no reason why it should not boom forever — or at least until they had all grown rich.

There was only one possible danger to this system: Grant was to be inaugurated as President in 1869, and nobody could predict what he would turn out to be. In view of his Civil War record, there was no keeping him from the Presidency if he wanted it. After some hesitation he decided that he did want it; so the Republican Party annexed him, and elected him. Grant's only previous contact with National politics had been in 1856 when he voted for Buchanan, a Democrat. On being asked why he had done this, he gave the wholly satisfying answer, 'I knew Frémont.'[1]

From this one episode, however, little could be deduced as to the General's politics. He entered office with prestige such as no President had possessed since Washington; he had no party commitments; he was under no pledges; he was a man of proved force, decision, and authority. If, therefore, Grant had an ideal in mind for what America might be; if, as seemed possible, he had a soldier's distaste for seeing his country become a promoter's paradise, he had only to give leadership and the country would follow him. His inauguration was awaited with anxiety by the politicians and by the men behind them, but by the time he had been in office a week, their fears were allayed. It was clear that they had only to keep him from making too great a fool of himself, to re-elect him indefinitely and the spoils were theirs. Grant was the politicians' ideal of a President — a protective reputation, an obvious but unalert integrity, an inability to believe evil of any man he liked, a complete absence of plan, of thought, even of cunning.... They had to wait until the end of the World War for another President who approached Grant in perfection.

The failure of the President to provide leadership in 1869 helped produce a surreptitious and largely unrecognized change in the working of the American Constitution. The distinguishing feature of that document is its attempt to avoid giving full authority to any man or group. In all other governments, supreme authority, and hence responsibility, is centred somewhere — be it king, committee, parliament, or dictator. But the framers of the

[1] The Republican candidate.

American Constitution were afraid of unlimited power. They reserved many of the important prerogatives of government for the States; and in the circumscribed central government they tried to divide authority between the Courts, the President, and the Congress. The Civil War showed that ultimately the States had only such power as the National Government allowed them. The whole Congressional reconstruction programme was based on the assumption that the authority of the States was exercised by them only on good behaviour and by the permission of Washington.

Not only was the power of the National Government increased, but there was a strong tendency toward centralization of power within that Government. The Supreme Court was supposedly independent, but it could be, and had often been, packed by the party in power; its Dred Scott decision had been overruled by Congress; its attempt to interfere with Congressional reconstruction had been ignored; and a few years later it was packed again, in order that it might reverse its own decision on the constitutionality of a Legal Tender Act. The Court was a check; it had something like a delaying veto over the acts of Congress; but it was not an independent source of authority. Clearly, then, the real division of power was between President and Congress. In the early days of strong Presidents, the balance had been all on the side of the Executive. After the coming of democracy, when Presidents became figureheads, the old forms were observed. The Southern oligarchy chose Presidents whom it could control, but it allowed the President to exercise his authority, at least in appearance. At the end of the Civil War, however, Congress set to work to change all that. While taking to itself the powers originally reserved by the Constitution to the States, it strove to subordinate the Federal Executive at the same time. Under Johnson the struggle had been furious; and though Congress failed to impeach the President, it triumphed in all important matters of policy. If Grant had made a fight, he might have re-established the President's power; but he made no fight, because he had no plans; there was nothing for which he wished to use his power. Congress had its own way for another eight years, and from that time on it has only been the rare strong President who has been able to control the Legislature, and then only for a time, and only for causes that have wide popular appeal.

The vicious part of the system that grew up under Grant was not that authority tended to centre in Congress (if that had happened openly, as the result of a Constitutional Revolution, it might have been a blessing), but that this centralization took place unofficially, almost unnoticed, so that it involved no concentration of responsibility. Legally, Congress was still only one element in a complicated balance of powers; practically, it had destroyed the reserved powers of the States and was exercising many of the President's prerogatives. With greatly increased power and no added responsibility, and with a *personnel* which was steadily declining both in brains and character, Congress became the tool of the people who could afford to buy it. The triumph of the business man was complete, and the results of that triumph were swift and scandalous.

The first bad scandal to become known was the attempt of Jay Gould and James Fisk, Jr., to corner the gold market. Gold, at the time, had almost been driven out of circulation by the depreciated paper money issued during the war, but there was a trade in gold, on the Stock Exchange, since it was needed by business men for their dealings in foreign countries. The Treasury sold about two million dollars' worth of gold each month, in order to keep it in circulation. Gould and Fisk (two of the nastiest of the money pirates) saw they could make a fortune by buying more contracts for the delivery of gold than there was gold to be had outside the National Treasury. First of all, however, they needed an assurance that the Treasury would not break their monopoly. They thought that such an assurance should be easy enough to get from a dull President who was surrounded by knaves. With the help of Grant's brother-in-law, whom they bought, they became friends of the President, entertaining him in New York, and undertaking to persuade him that the Treasury's sales of gold were bad for business, and especially for the farmers. The plan very nearly succeeded,

Grant's personal honesty being offset by his ignorance, and by a reverence for wealth which made him not only willing, but pleased, to be seen in public as the guest of a person like Jim Fisk. The scheme went forward and the price of gold rose to 162. At last Grant suspected that something was wrong, and gave orders to the Treasury to sell. Meanwhile, Gould had made millions; but Fisk held on too long and lost heavily. The public knew that the Government had been used by a pair of thieving financiers, and that Grant had some backstairs connection with the affair. 'The worst scandals of the eighteenth century,' wrote Henry Adams, 'were relatively harmless by the side of this, which smirched executive, judiciary, banks, corporate systems, professions, and people, all the great active forces of society, in one dirty cesspool of vulgar corruption.'

In 1872 came the Crédit Mobilier scandal. The National Government had given the first transcontinental railway company, the Union Pacific, twelve million acres of land along its right of way, and had also lent the Company twenty-seven million dollars. The promoters of the company then bought up a Pennsylvania corporation called the Crédit Mobilier, which had a liberal charter permitting it to engage in almost any form of activity, and proceeded to make a contract with themselves for the building of the railway, at a price per mile that allowed them a two hundred per cent profit. Meanwhile, the non-existent railway, with its land grant, was mortgaged for thirty-seven millions, which meant that the Government had a poor chance of ever recovering its twenty-seven million dollar loan. A member of the House of Representatives was a director of the company, and in order to avoid unpleasant inquiries he sold Crédit Mobilier stock to a selected list of his fellow-Congressmen. When a Congressman said he was too poor to buy, he was told that he need not bother putting up any money; he could hold the stock and pay for it out of dividends. This proved unexpectedly easy to do, for in the year 1868, Crédit Mobilier paid dividends to the value of 805 per cent.[1] By the time

[1] Only sixty per cent of this was in cash — 745 per cent was in Union Pacific stock and first mortgage bonds.

all this leaked out the railway was built and the Crédit Mobilier had ceased to exist, having wound up its affairs after making a profit of twenty-three million dollars on an investment of less than a million.   The only effect of the revelations was the destruction of several reputations, including that of the Vice-President of the United States.

In 1874 it was discovered that the Treasury Department was conniving at a fraud in tax-collection. Grant, with his customary misplaced good-nature, protected the Secretary of the Treasury by permitting him to resign.

In 1875, the new Secretary of the Treasury discovered that the whiskey distillers of St. Louis were, with the help of Treasury clerks and officials, evading about two-thirds of the excise tax. One of the men most deeply involved in this swindle was General Babcock, Grant's secretary. When Babcock was on trial, Grant testified in his favour, declaring that he thought Babcock guiltless in thought and deed. Babcock was acquitted; and the new Secretary of the Treasury, who had unearthed these disturbing facts, was so coldly treated by Grant that he resigned. Honesty in Washington had to learn to be its own reward.

In 1876, a member of the House of Representatives demanded that Belknap, the Secretary of War, be impeached, on the ground that he had been receiving a bribe of six thousand dollars a year in connection with an appointment to a post-tradership in the Indian Territory. The Secretary of War, hearing what was on foot, dashed to the White House to hand in his resignation. Grant, as usual, accepted it, and declared he did not believe Belknap to be guilty. And the strange thing is that Grant probably meant what he said. He appeared to believe that rogues must all be some special colour or shape, and that no ordinary man, whom he knew and liked, could be dishonest. To retain such innocence in the Washington of Grant's days was an almost pathological eccentricity. Senator Hoar of Massachusetts, speaking on the proposed impeachment of Belknap, showed how inescapable, to normal minds, was the knowledge of governmental corruption. After stating that he had been in public life for only a few years, he added: 'In this brief period, I have seen five judges of a high court of the United States driven from office by threats of impeachment for corruption or maladministration. I have seen the Chairman of the Committee on Military Affairs in the House rise in his place and demand the expulsion of four of his associates for making sale of their official privilege of selecting the youths to be educated at our great military school. When the greatest railroad of the world, binding together the continent and uniting the two great seas which wash our shores, was finished, I have seen our national triumph and exaltation turned to bitterness and shame by the unanimous reports of three Committees of Congress — two of the House and one here — that every step of that mighty enterprise had been taken in fraud.... I have heard that suspicion haunts the footsteps of the trusted companions of the President.'

5

When Henry Adams met President Grant, his impressions were as follows: 'First and last, he [i.e., Adams] saw a dozen Presidents in the White House,... but he found Grant the most curious object of study among them all.... A single word with Grant satisfied him that, for his own good, the fewer words he risked the better. Thus far in life he had met with but one man of the same intellectual type — Garibaldi. Of the two, Garibaldi seemed to him a trifle the more intellectual, but, in both, the intellect counted for nothing; only the energy counted. The type was pre-intellectual, archaic, and would have seemed so even to the cave-dwellers. Adam, according to legend, was such a man.' But Grant was an even more 'curious object of study' than Adams pictures. Grant was more complicated and perplexing than the ordinary man of action of the Garibaldi type. During most of his life, Grant was not a man of action at all; he was a passive, feckless failure, incompetent at his various jobs and quite without interest either in the external world or in his own inner life. At the age of thirty-nine he seemed a total loss. He had been forced out of the army for drunkenness, and had proved a failure as farmer, as real estate agent, and as clerk in a country store. Morose and alcoholic, and with a wife and children to support, he was living at the expense of his grudging family. Then came the war and four years of astounding success — to be followed by twenty years of failure that were almost equally spectacular. No honest man could have been a worse President than Grant; and when, after serving two terms, he went into business, the result was the loss of over sixteen and a half million dollars of other people's money. It seems as if there had been a lifelong curse on Grant, which was mysteriously lifted for those four years of war.

Grant was born in Ohio in 1822. His first American ancestor had landed in Massachusetts in 1630, and the family had remained in New England until after the Revolution, when a Captain Noah Grant moved to Pennsylvania, and later to Ohio. His son became a tanner at Point Pleasant, Ohio, and the tanner's eldest child was the future General Grant, who was christened Hiram Ulysses. The subsequent history of this quaint name is amusing. When he was appointed to the Military Academy, Grant foresaw the torment awaiting any boy whose initials spelled the word 'Hug.' Wisely, therefore, he reversed his names and became Ulysses Hiram Grant. But when he registered under that name at the Academy, the Adjutant told him that his papers had all been made out in the name of Ulysses Simpson Grant.[1] The Adjutant was worried, complaining that he had no authority to accept a Ulysses Hiram: the whole affair would have to be referred back to Washington. Grant was in danger of being lost forever among his three names, and of wandering like a Pirandello hero through the intense inane. He evaded this fate with characteristic matter-of-factness, by assuming the name Ulysses Simpson on the spot. His initials, however, had now become U. S., or Uncle Sam. This was not as funny as 'Hug,' but it was funny enough, and his classmates promptly rechristened him, so that in the memoirs of the officers

---

[1] Simpson was the name of Grant's mother, and the Congressman who had secured Grant's appointment assumed it was the boy's middle name.

who had known him in West Point days, he is usually referred to
as 'Sam' Grant.

Grant's mother, the cause of all this trouble, was a silent, un-
demonstrative, hard-headed woman, who appears never to have
shown the least interest either in Grant's failure or in his world-
fame. His father was shrewd, aggressive, and unliked; but he was
moderately successful in business and was able to send his son to
school from the time he was six until he was seventeen, and then
to secure him an appointment to the Military Academy. During
his school days Grant worked on the family farm in all his spare
time. He grew into a shy youth, devoid of small-talk or *camaraderie*,
and with a fondness for horses. In appearance he was short and
sturdy, but with something delicate, something almost feminine,
about his face and hands, a fact which was concealed in later life
by his marked sloppiness of dress, his beard, and his endless cigars.
In his early days in the army he was known as 'Little Beauty,' and
in an amateur dramatic show, one winter when his regiment was
camped in Texas, he played the part of Desdemona. This feminin-
ity appeared in his character as well, in the guise of an exaggerated
physical modesty [1] and an almost morbid distaste for the killing of
animals, an unexpected trait in the General who became famous
for his indifference, when it served an important purpose, to the
most terrifying casualties.

At West Point, Grant made a commonplace record, ranking
below the middle of his class. On graduating, he was appointed to
the Fourth Infantry, in spite of being a brilliant horseman. Two
years later, the Mexican War gave him the chance for active
service. Grant hated the war, being convinced of its immorality.
'I have never altogether forgiven myself for going into that,' he
wrote years later. 'I do not think there was ever a more wicked
war than that waged by the United States against Mexico. I
thought so at the time, when I was a youngster, only I had not
moral courage enough to resign.' Grant did not even have the

---

[1] In late middle age, Grant stated that since his early childhood no one had seen
him naked.

compensation of enjoying the war from the professional point of view, for the strangest thing about this enigmatic man is that he was bored by the military profession. On a visit to Germany at the height of his world-fame, he was invited to a military review. He attended with reluctance, confessing to Bismarck: 'The truth is, I am more of a farmer than a soldier. I take little or no interest in military affairs.... I never went into the army without regret and never retired without pleasure.'

It was during the Mexican War that Grant first took to serious drinking. He was a lonely, uncompanionable man, who was bored with his work. Alcohol was the obvious refuge; but during the war Grant never drank enough to interfere with his usefulness. He first saw active service under General Taylor, whose rough, unkempt ways combined with hard sense and efficiency became a model for Grant himself in later years. He was transferred to General Scott's army before the battle of Buena Vista, and served well, but inconspicuously, in the campaign against Mexico City.

When the war was ended, Grant married Miss Julia Dent of St. Louis, to whom he had been engaged for four years. The lack of enthusiasm which characterizes most of Grant's life does not seem to have been broken by his courtship or marriage. Grant, throughout this period of his life, was only half alive; neither imagination nor animal vitality was ever thoroughly awakened. After four years of dreary barracks service, he was transferred to the Pacific Coast. Mrs. Grant remained in St. Louis, not feeling well enough to face the trip. Again Grant was alone and bored, and this time there was not even a war to distract him. So his drinking increased, and was soon attracting the unfavourable attention of his colonel. It was an age of heavy drinking, but there was also a wave of prohibition sentiment, which by 1855 had led thirteen States to go 'dry.' The divided temper of the public mind is shown by the Baptist church in Illinois, whose trustees suspended the local schoolmaster for joining the temperance reform movement. Shortly afterward, they suspended another church member for getting dead drunk, whereupon a puzzled member of the congregation stood up in church and took a half-full whiskey bottle from his pocket, shaking it up and down as he drawled, 'Brethering, you have turned one member out because he would not drink, and another because he got drunk, and now I want to ask a question. How much of this 'ere critter does a man have to drink to remain in full fellership in this church?' [1]

Grant might, in such a world, have found a colonel who paid no attention to his drinking; but in fact he found one who disapproved. After a talk on the subject, Grant wrote out his resignation and gave it to the colonel with the understanding that it was not to be sent to Washington unless his drinking was again excessive. Not long afterward, Grant was noticeably drunk while paying off his men, and the colonel sent the resignation to the War Department. Grant had to borrow money for his passage East. The next seven years were a time of complete failure — in farming, in real estate, and as an unwanted clerk in his brother's store. Grant even tried to turn a penny by selling, or hiring out, his wife's two slaves.

In April, 1861, when the Civil War began, Grant took the Union side with enthusiasm. It was a matter of instinctive patriotism. Grant had no feeling on the question of slavery. His wife owned slaves, and kept them during the Civil War, and in 1862 Grant wrote to his father, 'I have no hobby of my own in regard to the Negro, either to effect his freedom or to continue his bondage.' And Grant had no political opinions — not even on the tariff, or on the constitutional question of secession and States' rights. But he had a deep feeling for the Union, and the attack on it liberated his powers from their long sleep. The result was the application to the military problem of a clear and honest mind that had confidence in its own judgment and a rare capacity to trust subordinates. In peace-time this capacity was tne ruin of Grant's reputation, but in war it served him well.

In June, 1861, Grant was still a discredited failure, whose application for a commission in the new army had not even been

[1] Carl Sandburg, *The Prairie Years*, I, 166.

answered by the War Department. Eight months later, he was a major-general with the most brilliant victory to his credit that had yet been won in the war — the capture of Forts Henry and Donelson and of half a Confederate army. These two forts guarded the Tennessee and Cumberland Rivers, and guarded the Confederate West. The Union had found a general who saw the two essential points of the war: first, that so long as the Confederacy remained a unit it would be unbreakable, but that it could be cut into parts by an attack from the West; and second, that the capture of localities would not end the war — only the destruction of the Southern armies would do that. When he gained command in the West, Grant effected the first of these ends, in a campaign culminating in the capture of Vicksburg, on the Mississippi, in the summer of 1863. And when he became Commander-in-Chief, in the spring of 1864, he advanced toward the second end of his policy, by engaging all the Southern armies at once so that they could not reinforce one another, and by accepting the most ruinous-sounding casualties in his campaign against Lee, since Northern reinforcements were plentiful and Southern reinforcements, by that time, were almost non-existent. In a little over a month Grant had 54,926 casualties in an army of 118,000. But in the end he beat Lee, which his five predecessors in Virginia had failed to do.

Even during the days of his great success, Grant's drinking remained a problem. There was an occasion during the siege of Vicksburg when he was dead drunk. This naturally led to gossip and to suggestions that he be removed. But Lincoln knew he had found somebody real. 'I don't know what to make of Grant,' he said, 'he's such a quiet little fellow.' But he noticed that Grant produced results — whereas the noisy generals who abounded in Washington did not. Perhaps Lincoln's chief direct contribution to victory was in standing by Grant.

When the war was over, Grant's new strength stayed with him for a few months. During the first anti-Southern frenzy, when there was a plan to try Lee for treason, Grant protested to President Johnson, saying that so long as Lee and the other officers and men who had surrendered to Grant at Appomattox kept their paroles they could not be touched. He said he would resign from the army if they were.... It was not long, however, before the flame began to burn low again within Grant. He got into the hands of the radicals in Congress and began opposing Johnson for his liberality to the South. Probably this was because he had no political knowledge or capacity and was therefore easily managed by those about him. But a more discreditable explanation is possible, and would be probable in the case of anyone less naïve than Grant. For in 1868, when he was elected President on the Republican ticket, Grant would have been defeated except for the Negro vote in the South, which had not yet been suppressed. In other words, if President Johnson's reconstruction programme had not been destroyed by the savage Radicals in Congress, Grant would not have become President.[1] Possibly he foresaw this, and hence altered his first magnanimous attitude toward his late foes. But as Grant never seems to have foreseen anything else to his own advantage, or to have grasped a political manœuvre even after it had all become history, it seems only fair to ascribe his change of heart in regard to the South to the influence of his new associates and to the flickering out of his own authentic greatness.

Grant's first term as President was so disastrous to the country that in 1872 his party split in two, the 'regular' politicians gratefully renominating Grant, and a group of 'Liberal Republicans' (including such men as Carl Schurz and C. F. Adams) leading a revolt against the corruption. The Democrats, instead of taking advantage of the split, joined with the Liberal Republicans and endorsed their nomination of the feeble Horace Greeley. The result was an easy victory for Grant. His second term was as unseemly as his first, so far as scandal among his associates went; and it was also marred by the financial panic of 1873. One of the few times that Grant, as President, showed independent courage was in vetoing a popular inflation bill, which would have added to the unbacked paper currency that had been issued during the war,

[1] The vote was: Grant 3,015,071; Seymour, the Democratic candidate, 2,709,613.

creating a dangerous peace-time precedent for permitting Congress to dally with paper-money cures. But the crisis, which Grant faced with some intelligence, did more harm to his reputation than all his previous incompetence. In 1876, the New York *Nation* described the hero of Vicksburg as 'an ignorant soldier, coarse in his taste and blunt in his perceptions, fond of money and material enjoyment and of low company.'

After serving his second term, Grant went abroad, returning in time to spoil the plans of the Republican machine to nominate him for a third term. Grant wanted this nomination, and if he had stayed out of the country the 'regular' politicians would probably have got it for him. But he returned in time to attract attention to what was on foot, giving the opposition a chance to organize and to remind the public that Grant had been an atrocious President and that the tradition against a third term should not be broken in his favour.

It might have been cheaper, in the end, for the country to have had him again as President, rather than let him go into business, which was his next venture. For Grant fell into the hands of one of the most thoroughly dishonest men in the history of modern finance — young Ferdinand Ward. Grant's son, Ulysses, Jr., appears to have been a chip off the old block, for it was he who first found Ward and trustfully started the banking and brokerage firm of Grant and Ward. General Grant joined the firm, giving it national prestige and providing (in all innocence) a respectable false front behind which Ward could go about his stealing. Grant's innocence was shocking. When Ward asked him to use his influence to get Government contracts, Grant very properly refused. But when Ward went about among the bankers and whispered that the General was bringing large Government contracts to the firm, Grant never suspected what was happening. Ward would borrow money, ostensibly to help the firm finance the great contracts Grant was getting from the Government. Ward's excuse for never showing the contracts was that Grant's position was such a difficult one, in view of his nice sense of honour; but Ward was always happy to produce forged telegrams from Washington, giving large orders at high prices. On receiving the loans, Ward would gamble with them on the Stock Exchange. What Grant did, all day long at the office, is a mystery. Ward seems to have provided him with twenty-five good cigars every morning, and perhaps smoking these and giving them away to callers was all Grant had time for. It came out at the trial that he had signed, without reading it, a letter in which the full power of his name and influence was used to cover up Ward's tricks.[1]

At the end of three years Grant and Ward failed. The firm had liabilities amounting to $16,792,640, and its assets came to $67,174. On the official balance sheets, the firm's assets had been shown as $27,000,000. Ward was sent to prison for ten years.

Grant's career ended as it began, in total failure. He lost everything he owned in the crash of Grant and Ward, and everything of his family's, and the savings of thousands of old soldiers and of simple people throughout the country who thought that anything with the great General's name attached to it must be safe. 'I have made it the rule of my life,' he said, 'to trust a man long after other people gave him up; but I don't see how I can trust any human being again.' Remorseful and bewildered, Grant had come to the end of his days. A little over a year after the crash, he died of cancer of the throat. But during the pain and depression of that last year, he wrote his *Memoirs*, having been assured by Mark Twain that the book would make money for his family. Grant worked almost to the end, producing a dry and colourless book. Fortunately, however, almost five-sixths of it is devoted to the Civil War, and nothing that Grant wrote on that subject could be really dull or unimportant. The *Memoirs* earned almost half a million dollars. The preface is dated July 1, 1885. On July 23, Grant died.

Had Grant been in Washington on the night of Lincoln's murder, he too was to have been killed. Perhaps if that had happened, his reputation today would be almost as high as Lincoln's. The early failures would have been no more than an artistic prelude to

[1] W. E. Woodward, *Meet General Grant*, 484 ff.

the later glory; and the heart-lifting generosity of Grant's behaviour at Appomattox would have been a noble end to the tale. But with Appomattox the brave days were done, not only for Grant but for his generation. The fog of corruption, the dull respect for wealth, the descent into Wall Street, the crash, the remorse — in all these Grant was a symbol of his country's malady. Was it for this that the old South was destroyed?

CHAPTER VIII

HAYES TO McKINLEY

I

'WITH capital at hand, with natural resources to be had for the asking or the taking, with stalwart labour ready for the fray, with a domestic market assured, with politicians impatient to co-operate and share the fruits, and unhampered by a powerful aristocracy, lay or clerical, attached to other manners and other ideals, American business men leaped forward as strong runners to the race when the news of Lee's surrender boomed throughout the land.' With this sentence Professor Beard prefaces a passage on American business expansion — a passage in which even that sardonic historian appears unduly impressed by the size and glitter of the spectacle. It is customary to write of the rise of Big Business as if it were one of mankind's major accomplishments, and Professor Beard's description of the business men leaping forward as strong runners to the race suggests that he shares this view. An apter metaphor, however, would be 'strong pirates to the boarding-party,' for it was the plunder of a continent to which these men leaped. They were offered a unique, gaudy chance to sack their country, and those of them who prospered most in the ensuing mêlée must have had rare gifts of greed and ferocity, and a talent for organization. Little else was required of them; the conditions were too easy to breed great men, or even great burglars.

The building of the Union Pacific Railroad is typical of their inglorious triumphs. On the one hand, the railway was built with reasonable speed, and it worked with reasonable efficiency; on the other hand, the enterprise was carried forward with a wasteful corruption that made quick wealth attainable by the most commonplace knaves. Charles Francis Adams commented at the time, that 'every expedient which the mind of man can devise has been brought into play to secure to the capitalist the largest possible

profit with the least possible risk.' Since the phrase, 'every expedient,' was the literal truth, since no expedients were ruled out
for moral, religious, or humanitarian reasons, it is not surprising
that some of the capitalists actually succeeded in making large
profits. And the fact that they left behind them some constructive
achievements, such as a completed railway or an efficient oil
trust is less impressive than the fact that they destroyed the pros
perity of American agriculture and treated their own wage-earner
so evilly that there resulted a series of strikes and private wars which
exceeded Calhoun's bitterest prophecies as to what would happen
if the Northern business men were given their way.

It was during this period that there was played out the last act
in the drama of the Western lands — those lands in which J. Q.
Adams foresaw ages upon ages of material and cultural welfare for
the American people. The railway companies, the mine-owners,
and the lumbermen now descended on these lands — buying them
for a pittance, receiving them as a gift, or stealing them in full certainty that the Government would acquiesce. The railways alone
received over one hundred and fifty million acres — a territory the
size of the whole of New England with a large part of New York
State added. When it was all over, a commission was appointed to
report on what had been done, and its conclusion was that scarcely
a single great Western holding had a title that was not tainted by
fraud. And as for the homesteads, which had actually been given
for nothing to the poor (in order to win their votes for the youthful Republican Party) — many of them did not linger for long in
the possessions of their new owners. For as a result of the financial
policy of the new régime, the farms of the nation tended to fall into
the hands of mortgage-holders.

At about the time of the Civil War, the Industrial Revolution
began to exercise its full influence on American farming. Progress
came to the countryside in the form of new farm machinery: the
reaper, the automatic self-binder, the corn-planter, the tractor,
etc. Year by year the machinery became more elaborate, more
ingenious, and more expensive. It saved the farmer much time and

trouble; and in many cases it lost him his farm. For he had no choice but to buy the new machinery. Once it was forced on the market, the price of grain was determined by the production costs of mechanized farms. Investing in the latest machinery called for capital, which meant mortgages, which meant that the farmer sank steadily into debt, becoming more and more dependent on the banker. But while the farmer was thus drawn into the capitalist system, he did not enter it on terms of equality. He no longer controlled the Government, whose promises were sometimes made for his benefit, but whose performance was all for the business man. And the farmer was at a cruel disadvantage as compared with the business man, when it came to bankruptcy. Like Antæus, after contact with Mother Earth, the man of money seemed to emerge from bankruptcy fresher and stronger than before; but the man of land, if he went bankrupt, came out as naked as Adam.

Another result of the Industrial Revolution in agriculture was specialization of crops. The full benefit of mechanized farming could only be had on a fairly large unit of land, so the diversified farming of the old days had to go. This meant that the farmer became no more self-sufficient than a clerk in a grocer's shop. To the world-old hazard of crop failure, there was added a new hazard, namely, that a fall in prices (resulting from the opening-up of new land, or a bumper crop on the other side of the world, or some fresh triumph of human inventiveness) might leave him with no spare cash, after he had paid his mortgages, and with nothing to eat except a few hundred acres of barley or of cotton. During the seventies and eighties, just such a state of affairs was produced, on a large scale, by the monetary policy of the business men whose orders were carried out at Washington. This led to an agrarian revolt, a belated stand for the old Jeffersonian dream of a nation sustained by independent, home-owning farmers. It was too late. The issue had been settled by the Civil War. Nevertheless, the attempt of desperate farmers to reverse that decision, to force a fiscal policy that would cheat the capitalists of half their victory, is the key to American politics during these decades. The labour dis-

putes, and the first stirrings of political reform, were premonitions
of the twentieth century. But the nineteenth century was to end as
it began, with an unsuccessful stand of the countryman against
the lords of business. In 1800, Jefferson tried to break the Hamiltonian system; but though he was elected President, he was not
strong enough to alter the economic drift. In 1896, Bryan tried
to break the Hamiltonian system, and though he failed of election,
he aroused such passions of assent and hatred that the money-men
were frightened for the first time since the Civil War, and there
was talk on Wall Street of an Eastern secession if the Democrats
should win.

The currency problem has always been a critical one in American politics. In the first years after the War of Independence, in the
days of the Articles of Confederation, it was chiefly the inflationist
tendencies of the State Governments that led men of property to
overcome their separatist tradition and to create the Federal
Constitution. It was Hamilton's bill for creating a National Bank
to control the currency in the interest of sound business principles,
i.e., of capitalism, which led to the formation of parties during
Washington's first Administration. The Jeffersonians, in 1811,
allowed the charter to lapse; but the Bank was revived in 1816, as
a result of the wave of nationalism that followed the War of 1812.
The most popular of Jackson's acts was his 'War on the Bank,'
which destroyed this second national institution in 1836, leaving the
creation of currency in the hands of the State banks. From then
until the Civil War the State banks were supreme, with the result
that money was issued generously (wildly, from the point of view
of business) and there was a steady tendency toward inflation.
Cheap money meant rising prices; and the farmer (unless he was
caught by one of the periodic deflations) could generally pay back
his borrowings, or pay off his mortgages, in dollars that were
worth a little less than the dollars he had received. To the money-
lender this seemed a highly immoral process, and the financial
interests could be counted on to reverse the process if ever they
came into power.

The Civil War, therefore, brought about a revolution in American public finance. The State banks of issue were suppressed and a National banking system created. At first there was no protest from the agrarians, for one of the ways in which the Union financed the war was by issuing a large quantity of paper money, not founded on gold. These greenbacks, as the legal-tender notes were called, were no sounder than the old State notes; so the era of inflation continued, much to the gratification of the farmers who had joined the new party. But once the war was over, there came from the business centres a steady demand for deflation. The greenbacks must either be withdrawn or put on a metallic basis. The Western farmers opposed this demand, asking that the greenbacks be kept in circulation, or even increased. But the Republican Party belonged to the business men, and in 1875 a bill was passed providing for the redemption in specie of the greenbacks when presented at the Treasury in sums of not less than fifty dollars. This bill was passed just at the time when the farmers were sinking most heavily into debt, for the reasons given above. And the bitterness aroused by the bill of 1875 was increased when the farmer came to realize that two years earlier, in 1873, an even more drastic deflationary measure had been put through inconspicuously, without anyone realizing the issues involved.

The United States had long had a bimetallic currency; but Congress had never found a satisfactory way of adjusting the proportionate value of gold and silver. If silver were undervalued in terms of gold, if a silver dollar were really worth more than its face value, then the silver coins would be hoarded and would go out of circulation. And if silver were overvalued, the reverse would happen and gold would be driven out of circulation. Ostensibly in order to avoid this nuisance, Congress, in 1873, stopped the coinage of silver dollars. The bill was passed in all innocence on the part of most of the Representatives who voted for it; but it is hard to believe that the orders to demonetize silver had not been issued by men who knew what they were doing. For 'The

Crime of '73,' as this bill was later described by its victims, was committed just in time to prevent the new silver mines, which were being opened up throughout the West, from making a large addition to the American currency and thus starting a new era of rising prices. The opportune withdrawal of silver led, instead, to a startling fall in prices — or at any rate, it was accompanied by such a fall, and the American farmers were convinced that there was a relation of cause and effect. By 1890, wheat was selling at half the price which obtained in 1865; and silver, too, had fallen to half its earlier value, now that it was no longer used for coins. There arose, therefore, a desperate demand for the free and unlimited coinage of silver at the old ratio of sixteen to one, i.e., sixteen ounces of silver being declared equal in value to one ounce of gold. The friends of silver contended that it would soon return to this old value if it were restored to its place in the American currency system. And even if it didn't, the overvaluation of silver would merely result in extra inflation, which the farmer could face with tranquillity.

In 1878, an attempt was made to quiet the silver advocates by a bill providing for a monthly coinage of two to four million silver dollars. This had no effect on the situation, and the farmers continued to demand the unlimited coinage of silver. In 1890, a further concession was made in the form of a Silver Purchase Act, repealing the Act of 1878, and requiring the Treasury to buy four and one-half million ounces of silver each month, and to issue against this bullion, up to its full value, legal-tender notes redeemable on demand in coin — either gold or silver, at the discretion of the Secretary of the Treasury. But this act, too, failed to stop the fall in prices, and the demand for the free coinage of silver grew more and more impassioned.

It was not until the last years of the century that the currency question became an issue between the two major parties. Throughout the seventies and eighties there were no real issues. Since the withdrawal of Southern leadership, the Democratic Party in the North had for the most part fallen into the hands of the political 'machines' in the big Eastern cities. The urban politician, with his well-drilled immigrant voters, had no positive interests, no programme, in common with the rural Southerner. Both groups wanted to get the Republicans out of office — that was their only basis for co-operation. In policy, therefore, the Democrats became almost indistinguishable from the Republicans. Both parties began to agitate for civil service reform; both became frightened at the increasing labour troubles. The Democrats cried out against Republican corruption, but so did many Republicans. The Democrats pretended that they wished to lower the tariff, but failed to do so when they were given the chance. There was no issue, except the personal one of who should wield the power and the patronage. Both parties were ignoring the fate of the farmers, and public life grew increasingly dreary and trivial — qualities which are reflected in the Presidents chosen during this period.

2

In 1876, toward the close of Grant's second term, the Democrats nominated Samuel J. Tilden for the Presidency — a rich New York lawyer, who had been Governor of that State and who had a reputation for honesty and courage. In view of Grant's disgraceful record, it was thought that the Democrats would elect Tilden, and after the election it appeared that they had done so. The Republicans, however, contested the returns in three Southern States and also in the State of Oregon. If Tilden had received a single one of the contested electoral votes, he would have become President.[1] The matter was settled by a commission which had a majority of Republicans on it; so every decision was given in avour of that party, and Tilden's opponent, Rutherford B. Hayes, was declared to have been elected by 185 to 184 electoral votes.

There was bitter feeling during the period of uncertainty, and

[1] He would, of course, have received all the electoral votes of the three Southern States if 'reconstruction' had not still been in progress, i.e., if the Negro vote had not been upheld by Northern troops.

the Southerners would not have accepted the verdict had not their leaders made a good bargain with the Republicans, whereby the withdrawal of the last Northern troops was promised in return for the election of Hayes. The restoration of white rule meant more to the Southerners than the Presidency.

Hayes was the son of an Ohio farmer, and the descendant of a family that had emigrated from Scotland to New England in the middle of the seventeenth century. He was born in 1822, and received a good schooling, first in Ohio and later in the East. After graduating from an Ohio college, he went East again to the Harvard Law School. In 1850, he opened a law office in Cincinnati. Two years later he married, and about the same time he entered politics as a Whig. The war gave him his first chance to distinguish himself, and within three years he had risen to the rank of brigadier-general. Meanwhile he was elected to the House of Representatives, but did not take his seat until after the war.

In Congress he was a regular and inconspicuous party-man, resigning in 1867 to become Governor of Ohio, in which office he served for two consecutive terms. In 1875, when the Republicans had been doing badly in Ohio, he was elected Governor for a third term, being the first man in the State to attain this honour, and thereby becoming a national figure. In spite of being an honest man, Hayes had not broken with the 'regular' Republicans in 1872, when the party had split over the re-election of Grant. He was therefore an 'available' candidate in 1876, being tolerated alike by the reform group and by the machine.

On becoming President, Hayes adhered to the bargain that had been made with the South. He recalled all the Union troops and put an ex-Confederate in his Cabinet.[1] For the rest, his Administration was placid and harmless. Henry Ward Beecher referred to it as 'a bread poultice' for the country. The one measure on which Hayes had set his heart was a thorough-going reform of the Civil Service, including appointment for ability only, security

[1] He had wished to appoint General Joseph E. Johnston as Secretary of War, but was advised that this would be too unpopular in the North.

of tenure, and exemption from demands of partisan service. The spoils system had finally been developed to such perfection that it applied even to the charwomen in Government offices. There were almost 120,000 executive appointments, and in addition to all the other evils of the system, the demands on the President's time and energy were killing. All that Hayes could accomplish, however, was to instruct the heads of departments to make appointments on merit. This would, of course, have no effect on subsequent Administrations, and Congress refused to pass a law for civil service reform. When Hayes tried to clean out the New York Custom House, which had long been one of the prizes of the spoils system, he had difficulty in getting the Senate to confirm his appointments.

On the currency question, Hayes was even more conservative than his party. He vetoed the Act of 1878, providing for the monthly purchase of two to four million ounces of silver; but the act was passed over his veto.

Hayes had stated, on accepting the nomination, that he would not serve a second term. Since he proved to be a stubborn and ungraciously honest President, the party leaders were glad to take him at his word, and in 1881 he retired to his Ohio home, where he lived until his death in 1889. The politicians had named him 'Granny' Hayes, and thought him something of a joke; but both in pacifying the South and in focusing public attention on the need for civil service reform, Hayes had done useful work.

James A. Garfield, who succeeded Hayes in the Presidency, called attention to the need for civil service reform in a still more startling fashion. Four months after his inauguration, he was shot by a disappointed office-seeker, and died after eleven weeks of pain.

Garfield, like Hayes, was the son of an Ohio farmer, and like Hayes he was descended from one of the early settlers of New England. Garfield's father, however, was very poor, and he died in 1832 when the boy was two years old; so throughout his childhood Garfield knew real frontier hardship. He had to struggle to find time for education, but was finally able to work his way through Williams College. Two years later he married. Like his father before him, he was a member of the Disciples of Christ, and as a lay preacher in the organization he developed notable powers of oratory.

During the war Garfield rose rapidly to prominence; for unlike many of the volunteer officers, he took soldiering seriously, studying hard at his new job, and quickly rising to the rank of brigadier-general and chief of staff in Rosecrans's army. After the battle of Chickamauga, he was made major-general; but at the end of 1863 he went to the House of Representatives at Washington, where he served for nine terms. He became a finished parliamentarian, and the leader of his party in the lower House. Although a cultivated and well-read man, he contributed no original, or even interesting, thoughts to the dreary waste of politics in the seventies. He appears to have been involved in the Crédit Mobilier scandal, though there is no final proof; and he certainly accepted a retaining fee from a company that was angling for a Government contract during his term of office. This did him no harm, however; in fact the moderation of his alleged corruption appears to have been what chiefly impressed his contemporaries — the *Milwaukee Sentinel* remarking that his name 'is exceptionally clean for a man who has been engaged for twenty years in active politics.'

In 1880 he was elected to the Senate, but he never took his seat, for he became President instead. He attended the Republican Convention of that year as manager of the campaign to nominate Senator Sherman. Grant and Blaine were the leading aspirants, but Garfield and the Sherman forces succeeded in blocking them both. They could make no headway for their own candidate, however; and when finally the State of Wisconsin voted for Garfield himself, this seemed to Garfield a reasonable compromise. He was nominated on the next ballot. Although he defeated the obscure General whom the Democrats nominated (presumably as a sign of their patriotism), Garfield's chances for a successful Administration were slight; for the 'stalwarts,' i.e., the 'Old Guard' of the party, who had favoured Grant, never forgave him for the part he played in the Convention. The Vice-Presidential nomination had been given to Chester A. Arthur of New York — a leading 'stalwart,' and the man whom Hayes (as part of his civil service reform) had ousted from the job of Collector of the Port of New York; but even this did not placate the party machine. Senator Conkling, the leader of the New York Republicans, tried to block the confirmation of several of Garfield's appointments, but in the end the President had his way.

During Garfield's brief time in office, one of the most far-reaching of the political scandals came to light, causing the dismissal of the Assistant Postmaster-General. This was known as the 'Star Route' scandal, and Garfield pressed for a thorough investigation. Before anything had been accomplished, Garfield was dead.

Chester A. Arthur became President under embarrassing circumstances. The disappointed office-seeker who had murdered Garfield was, according to his own account, a 'stalwart,' and he gave as his motive the desire to have a member of that branch of the party as President. The man was half-demented, and there was no question of his having the slightest official connection with the party. Nevertheless, there was ugly, vague suspicion in the air, and the country was disinclined to be generous to Arthur. Actually, he turned out to be a far better President than many of the men who have been elected to that office; but at the time that fact was little noticed.

Arthur, who was born in Vermont in 1830,[1] was the son of a Scotch-Irish Baptist clergyman. He was educated in Union College, New York, taught school for a time, and then began the practice of law in New York City. He had become a man of taste and cultivation, and in 1859 he married a charming woman of the world, Miss Ellen Lewis Herndon, daughter of a naval officer.

[1] It was charged that he had really been born a few years earlier, in Canada, where his father was then living, and that he was not an American citizen. On being nominated for the Vice-Presidency, it was stated, he had appropriated the birthday and the birthplace of his younger brother, who had died in infancy. This charge was probably false.

Arthur confined his fastidiousness to his private life, for in politics he soon became identified with the so-called 'Custom House Gang,' which fattened on Federal appointments and the minor spoils of office. Before long he was the friend and lieutenant of Conkling, the powerful, bullying leader of the group which had found Grant so much to their liking.

During the war Arthur held several administrative offices, serving as Engineer-in-Chief, Inspector-General, and Quartermaster-General of New York. In these positions he quickly learned more than is good for a man to know about New York State politics. Having been hardened by this experience, he was able to hold office under the 'Tweed Ring' in New York City — the most flamboyantly corrupt of all the groups which have plundered American municipal governments. Finally, in 1871, Grant appointed Arthur Collector of the Port of New York. Here, as elsewhere in his career, Arthur was honest in the handling of revenue. What endeared him to his superiors, in spite of this eccentricity, was his gift for exacting full political service from all his appointees. There were one thousand employees in the New York Custom House, which was grossly overstaffed, and Arthur saw to it that they all had a chance to show their gratitude to the party that put them there.

When Hayes became President, he issued orders that civil servants should refrain from taking part in party and campaign affairs. The order was not taken very seriously in New York, and Hayes, after a struggle with the Senate, replaced both Arthur and the Naval Officer of the Port.

In September, 1881, therefore, when Arthur became President, there was nothing about his record to inspire confidence, although on the personal side his life suggested that he might have qualities which had not yet been displayed in public. Arthur was a tall, well-built man, with a shaven chin and side whiskers. His courtesy and dignity, and his air of breeding and intelligence, made it seem unlikely that he could be the mere 'pot-house politician' that the papers called him. Socially, the new Administration was an immediate success. It was the first time since the days of Buchanan that the President had possessed social gifts, or even normally attractive manners, and the change was welcome. Arthur's wife had died about a year before his inauguration, but his sister presided at White House functions, proving an accomplished and graceful hostess.

Presumably Arthur had played politics in New York as a kind of game, a complicated and dangerous gamble which he could enjoy without the introduction of any moral issues, except that of financial honesty. On being elevated to the Presidency, his entire attitude toward politics appeared to change, and he acquired, for the first time, a sense of responsibility. To the dismay of his 'stalwart' friends, he retained Garfield's appointees, ignoring even Grant's request that he dismiss the Secretary of the Navy in order to make way for one of the Old Guard. He vetoed an extravagant appropriation bill which was popular with the politicians, and a Chinese Exclusion Bill which was popular with the people, but which happened to violate a United States treaty with China. And he did his best to secure prosecution of the men involved in the 'Star Route Frauds.' This latest scandal concerned the juggling of postal contracts on the horse-drawn mail routes (known as 'Star Routes') in such a way that big profits accrued to a ring of contractors. Ex-Senator Dorsey, the Secretary of the Republican National Committee and one of the men chiefly responsible for the election of Garfield and Arthur, was involved in this scandal. He belonged to that sinister group: the men of whom Grant thought highly.

The most surprising of Arthur's acts as President was his energetic backing of the movement for civil service reform. As a result, in 1883, Congress passed an act providing for the appointments of about twelve per cent of the civil service positions on the basis of competitive examinations, and permitting the President to enlarge this list by executive decree. Little by little, as a result of such executive action, the civil service has been rescued from the spoils system.

Arthur hoped for the Presidential nomination in 1884, but he found himself unexpectedly friendless at the Convention. The 'stalwarts' felt, quite rightly, that he had gone back on them; the reform element had never conquered its old distrust of him; and the Garfield men had never forgiven him for being the beneficiary of their leader's murder. He was, therefore, passed over, and the nomination was given to James G. Blaine, of Maine. In March, 1885, Arthur retired, and eighteen months later he was dead.

3

Blaine was the only man ever nominated to the Presidency in spite of the fact that the public knew perfectly well he was dishonest. Garfield was thought to have been dishonest, but only in the mildest sort of way; Blaine was known to have been dishonest, and on a good scale.[1] Nevertheless, he had been a brilliant party leader in both House and Senate, and he had a personal following such as no other politician had possessed since Henry Clay. He had a fascinating personality, and a gay impudence that was endearing. The leaders of the party decided that a public which had re-elected Grant, and which had made a martyred hero of Garfield, would certainly not boggle over Blaine. In this they were wrong; the tide was beginning to turn, and a considerable group of Republicans — derisively nicknamed 'Mugwumps' — openly disassociated themselves from the party, declaring themselves ready to support any honest and capable Democrat. This put the Democrats in an awkward position. They clearly had a good chance to win, but they wondered just how honest their candidate had to be. If he were too honest, it might turn out to have been hardly worth their while electing him. They decided, however, to

---

[1] In the course of a congressional investigation of his activities, Blaine had stolen a package of his own letters from a man who was about to produce them as evidence. He had asked to see the letters, promising, on his word of honour, to return them after reading them. He then put them in his pocket and walked off with them. Although he subsequently made the letters public, his explanations of the incriminating passages in them convinced few people at the time, and historians have since concluded that he was guilty of dishonesty.

take no chances, and they nominated a man of complete and obvious integrity, Stephen Grover Cleveland, of New York.

The ensuing campaign was unusually horrid. The Democrats attacked Blaine's morals with such hypocritical violence that the Republicans searched angrily for material with which to retaliate. They discovered that Cleveland was the father of an illegitimate child. They immediately published the fact, accusing Cleveland of continual and alarming immorality. Cleveland himself behaved with dignity; but the songs, cartoons, and speeches of the campaign, on both sides, were irrelevant and unworthy to an extent which marked a new low level for American politics.

The nation's agriculture was being ruined; the nation's natural resources were being stolen; the nation's working-class was being goaded to violent discontent. But the nation's political parties had no cures for any of these evils, and no real issues to discuss; so they worked the country into a cheap and superficial frenzy over the question of whether Mr. Cleveland really did have a great many illegitimate children, and if so, of what colour, and whether Mr. Blaine had married his wife only three months before their first child was born, or whether there had been a secret marriage a full year before that interesting event.

In the end Cleveland was elected — chiefly because a foolish Republican parson, speaking in New York, had referred to the Democrats as 'the party of Rum, Romanism, and Rebellion.' New York was the crucial State, whose vote would determine the election; and there were many Roman Catholics in New York, who resented this apt alliteration. As a result, Cleveland was elected. If this is what is meant by 'the voice of the people,' it is blasphemous even to remember the rest of the tag.

Grover Cleveland was born in New Jersey in 1837. He was the son of a Presbyterian clergyman, a man of good education who was descended from a Moses Cleveland who settled in Massachusetts in 1635. When Cleveland was sixteen, his father died, and from that time the boy was chiefly dependent on his own work for a livelihood, though for a while he was given a home by his mother'?

uncle, near Buffalo, New York. By 1859 he had prepared himself for admission to the bar, and four years later he became District Attorney of Erie County, New York. He took no part in the Civil War, perhaps because he was giving financial aid to his mother and could not afford to leave his work, or perhaps (since he was already identified with local Democratic politics) he felt only moderate enthusiasm for the Republican war.

After a period as District Attorney, he became Sheriff of Erie County, and in 1881 was elected Mayor of Buffalo. There was the usual corrupt city government in Buffalo, and Cleveland was elected on the promise of reform — a promise which he fulfilled. In 1882, the Democrats had a good chance to elect a Governor of the State, for the Star Route frauds were before the public; and although these frauds had nothing to do with State politics, the monotonous corruption of the Republican Party at Washington was becoming a bore and had begun to affect its popularity throughout the country. So the Democrats nominated Cleveland for the governorship of New York, hoping that his reputation for having done what he promised in Buffalo might attract some dissatisfied Republican voters. Cleveland was elected; and as Governor of New York he refused to play the political game of spoils, patronage, and party regularity. Ordinarily this would have meant his ruin; but the country was sickening for an honest man, and the fact that New York State had a Governor who meant what he said attracted as much attention as if it had a Governor with feathers. When he was disowned by John Kelly, the leader of Tammany Hall, his popularity increased markedly. Blaine's nomination made him an obvious choice for the Democrats, and much as they would have preferred a man of greater pliability, they nominated Cleveland on the second ballot.

Cleveland was forty-eight years old, and a bachelor, when he went to the White House. He was short, stolid, and fat — in character unbending and ungenial. Industrious, conscientious, ungracious, and without charm, Cleveland was an anomaly in the White House. Ordinarily, such a man would only have been elected if he had represented a cause which made popular appeal, or if the politicians had forced him on the country for dark reasons of their own. But neither of these things was true. The country had forced him on the politicians, not because it shared his ideas or his prejudices, but simply because it felt he was an honest man. ... Cleveland's enemies predicted that he would prove weak, and that he would be run by the party bosses. In fact, he was unnecessarily independent, refusing even to take advice from the regular politicians, and trying to oversee every detail of administration. He was too distrustful of subordinates to make a good executive. He never learned to use other men efficiently; during his first term, he would even answer the White House telephone himself.

In policy, Cleveland had nothing to contribute toward a solution of the real problems before the country, but was determined to force honesty and economy on the National Government and to carry out his promise for 'practical reform in the civil service.' With the latter promise in mind, Cleveland went as slowly as he could in the matter of replacing Republicans by Democratic spoilsmen. This was not very slow (within a year, for instance, eight thousand fourth-class postmasterships had been handed over to Democrats), but it was slow enough to earn him the hatred of the 'regular' party workers, who complained that they might almost as well not have elected him, for all the good they got out of it.

Early in 1886, Cleveland married Frances Folsom. Immediately his enemies, within and without the party (who had long insisted, untruthfully, that he was an habitual drunkard), began to declare that Cleveland beat his wife with fair frequency. This was false, but nevertheless hard to disprove, and for some years the story had wide circulation.

It is an interesting fact that Cleveland should have aroused such ferocious hatred merely by his stubborn efforts to impose honesty on the National Government. An example of the sort of thing that made him hated is the following: In 1886, he began, with his customary diligence, to read some of the pension bills, for Civil War veterans, that were sent him by Congress. It was customary to pass these bills (each referring to special cases) by the dozen, and no President had previously been so indiscreet as to look at them before signing. Cleveland found that pensions were being awarded to certain men who had never been in the army at all, to other men who had deserted from the army, and to still others who had been injured many years after the end of the war. Naturally, he vetoed the bills, an act which caused bitterness in Congress, where the feeling appeared to be that if a man couldn't award Civil War pensions to his more exigent constituents it was hardly worth being a politician.

There had been a rumour in the land that the Democratic Party believed in lowering the tariff, and although Cleveland was by no means a free-trader he did feel that something might be done in this direction, especially since the present tariff was bringing in a large surplus revenue, which had much the same effect on Congress that the high odour of a carcass has upon birds of prey. The attempt to lower the tariff failed; but it created an issue for the campaign of 1888. It was not much of an issue, since all it amounted to was that some of the Democrats wanted to lower the tariff a little bit. Still, it was an improvement on the problem of Mr. Cleveland's babies.

The Republicans nominated Benjamin Harrison, the grandson of the famous hero of Tippecanoe, and, with the help of Sir Lionel Sackville-West, the British Minister, Harrison was elected. Toward the close of the campaign, Sir Lionel had received a letter from a man called Murchison, who said he was an ex-Britisher and who craved Sir Lionel's advice as to how to vote in the best interests of the mother country. With a pretty trust in human nature, Sir Lionel answered that a vote for Cleveland would be useful to England. At the critical moment in the campaign, the Republicans published this letter, reminding the people that they had said all along that the low-tariff policy was adopted in the interests of England, and that Her Majesty's Government had clearly suborned Mr. Cleveland. As a result, Cleveland dismissed Sir Lionel, and the American people dismissed Cleveland.

Benjamin Harrison was born in Ohio in 1833. His childhood was spent on a farm, and he had little schooling. His family, however, were able to provide him with a tutor and to send him to Miami University, in Ohio. He then studied law, and on being admitted to the bar he settled in the town of Indianapolis. In the same year he married Miss Caroline Scott. In the second year of the war, he was commissioned as second lieutenant, and had risen to the rank of colonel by 1865, having fought in Kentucky and Tennessee, and taken part in Sherman's march on Atlanta. At the end of the war he returned to the practice of law. In 1876, he stood for the governorship of Indiana on the Republican ticket, but was defeated. His opponent was a simple homely farmer, known as 'Blue Jeans' Williams; and the Democrats, wishing to emphasize the fact that their candidate was a man of the people, called Harrison 'Kid Glove' Harrison, asserting that he was aristocratic and cold. His grandfather, born into the privileged planter class of Virginia, had been transformed, for campaign purposes, into a backwoods hero; and the grandson, born at a time when the family had declined to the status of rather seedy Western farmers, was accused of all the distinction that had been denied his grandfather.

In 1881, Harrison refused a position in Garfield's Cabinet, for the Legislature had just appointed him to the United States Senate. There he served inconspicuously for six years, favouring civil service reform and opposing the pension vetoes of Cleveland. At the end of that time he failed of re-election, and it seemed as if his meaningless political career must be at an end. He had no marked talents, no ideas, no record, no reputation. He had also, however, no enemies, no bad habits, and no taint of corruption. In 1888, the Republicans were looking for just such a man. And in addition to all his gratifying negative qualities, Harrison was descended from a vaguely remembered martyr of the Whig cause, and he came from the pivotal State of Indiana.[1] So Harrison was

---

[1] Harrison is thus far the only President to be chosen from Indiana, but that 'doubtful' State has furnished four successful candidates for the Vice-Presidency.

nominated, affording one of the best examples in American history
of the bland nonentity who is the politician's ideal for President —
both because he is easiest to elect and because he makes least
trouble after elected. Harrison made no trouble at all after he was
elected. The control of the party was in the hands of a hard
tyrannous group (men like Quay, Platt, and 'Czar' Reed), who
had no time to waste on a meek lawyer from Indiana. They went
their way, and Harrison went their way also, abandoning his ambition for serious civil service reform, and signing a pension act
that increased the annual expenditure from 98 to 157 millions.
Congressional encroachment on the presidential power appeared
to have reduced the Chief Executive to a position analogous to
that of the President of the French Republic. Congress felt supreme and irresponsible, its one vital problem being the question
as to which of the two parties should dispense the booty. It was
at about this time that Mr. Frederick Townsend Martin gave an
imprudently frank account of the point of view of the real rulers
of America — a class to which he himself belonged. 'It matters
not one iota,' he said, 'what political party is in power or what
President holds the reins of office. We are not politicians or public thinkers; we are the rich; we own America; we got it, God knows
how, but we intend to keep it if we can by throwing all the tremendous weight of our support, our influence, our money, our
political connections, our purchased Senators, our hungry Congressmen, our public-speaking demagogues into the scale against
any legislature, any political platform, any presidential campaign
that threatens the integrity of our estate.'

Harrison's Administration was committed to raising the tariff,
so in 1890 the McKinley Act was passed. In many cases the new
duties were prohibitive, and the revenue declined sharply, while
prices of protected articles went higher. The manufacturers had
overreached themselves, and an anti-tariff reaction began, a reaction which brought Cleveland again to the White House in 1892.
Both parties were still trying to evade the currency issue, and during Harrison's Presidency Congress passed the Sherman Silver

Purchase Act, which, it was well known, would have little effect, but which, it was hoped, might quiet the agrarians temporarily.

After his defeat in 1892, Harrison retired to law practice in Indiana. His wife had died during the last campaign, and in 1896 Harrison married her niece. Aside from this mild eccentricity his last years were as uneventful as the rest of his life, with one exception. In 1898, the Government of Venezuela retained him as leading counsel in the arbitration of a boundary dispute with Great Britain. He argued the case in Paris, in 1899. It was a shaky case, which Harrison could not strengthen, though he delivered a twenty-five-hour closing argument that was described as 'thorough.' Subsequently Harrison returned to Indianapolis, where two years later he died.

4

Since Cleveland, during his first term, had stood openly for tariff revision, the nation-wide discontent with the McKinley tariff found expression in a pro-Cleveland movement. Again the Democrats were faced with the knowledge that if they nominated Cleveland they would get many Republican votes. This time, however, they knew by experience that Cleveland was a sorry disappointment when it came to distributing the spoils, and a serious effort was made (especially by the New York Democrats) to head off the popular demand and find a more ingratiating candidate. The attempt failed, and Cleveland was nominated on the first ballot.

In March, 1893, when Cleveland was inaugurated, the country was on the verge of a financial panic which was at last to break down the issue-dodging of both parties. Cleveland's second term was a period of realignment, and it ended in an election campaign which for the first time in thirty-two years forced an open discussion of a problem of major importance.

Cleveland was an arch-conservative in financial policy, a convinced sound-money man who distrusted any form of inflation. When the panic struck the country, he blamed it in part on the

Silver Purchase Act of 1890, and instructed the Secretary of the Treasury to redeem in gold all the notes which were issued against the monthly purchases of silver. This neutralized the inflationary tendencies of the Silver Purchase Act, but it also created a drain on the gold reserve in the Treasury. The Government issued bonds in order to bring gold to the reserve, but it was drained out again as fast as it came in, until finally Cleveland forced the issue by calling a special session of Congress and forcing through a repeal of the Silver Purchase Act. This was in 1893, and it represented the completeness of the victory of the business man over his old rival, the farmer.

A Democratic President, the last hope of the agrarian interests, was convinced that the country's salvation lay in complete acceptance of capitalist fiscal policy, and used his full prestige and the full power of his patronage to force the repeal of the one concession made to the prostrate farmer since the Civil War. 'For a hundred years,' wrote Henry Adams in his autobiography, 'between 1793 and 1893 the American people had hesitated, vacillated, swayed forward and back, between two forces, one simply industrial, the other capitalistic, centralizing, and mechanical. In 1893, the issue came on the single gold standard, and the majority at last declared itself, once and for all, in favour of the capitalistic system with all its necessary machinery. All one's friends, all one's best citizens, reformers, churches, colleges, educated classes, had joined the banks to force submission to capitalism.'

Adams was right, in retrospect, to choose 1893 as the decisive date, for the fact that Cleveland could force the repeal of the Sherman Act showed where the real strength lay; but to contemporaries it seemed as if Cleveland's action had merely defined the issue which must be decided at the next presidential election. At once the agrarians in Congress deserted Cleveland, called him a traitor to the Democracy, and set to work to capture the Democratic Convention of 1896.

Before the end of his term, however, Cleveland enjoyed a few days of unexpected popularity. In 1895, he interfered in a long-standing boundary dispute between British Guiana and Venezuela. Lord Salisbury had refused to submit this question to international arbitration, on the ground that Venezuela's claim to more than half the British Colony was plainly ridiculous. Suddenly, in 1895, Cleveland éntered the dispute, and after sending some very high-handed notes to England, he informed Congress that he intended to determine the disputed boundary himself, and to invoke the Monroe Doctrine against any attempt by Great Britain to exercise jurisdiction beyond the boundary that he should determine. Both in his notes to England and in his message to Congress, Cleveland's language was provocative beyond excuse; presumably he was afraid that Venezuela would drift into war and that the United States would then be involved. Seeking to avoid this, he took so firm a tone that he almost precipitated the war himself. His behaviour — which was dangerously popular with the jingoistic element in America — was out of character, and may have been caused by his anger at being branded, seven years before, as the tool of England. Fortunately, the British Government agreed to arbitrate; and in 1899 the tribunal gave a unanimous decision along the line of the British claim.

Interpreting his re-election as a mandate to lower the tariff, Cleveland was outraged when his party passed a bill that was almost as protectionist as the previous Republican tariff. He described the bill as 'party perfidy and party dishonour,' and refused to sign it. This, and his actions in interfering in a railway strike, by getting the Federal Government to issue an injunction to restrain the strikers and by sending troops to maintain order, completed his break with his own party. Meanwhile, his refusal to recognize the American-made Revolution in Hawaii, and to annex the islands in accordance with the plan of the Harrison Administration, and his refusal to be drawn into hostilities with Spain over an insurrection in Cuba, made him hated by the Republicans, who were beginning to feel the sinister stirrings of Manifest Destiny and to drift toward the most disgraceful of America's wars. Cleveland ended his second term a lonely figure. He rightly opposed most of what his country was doing, but he had nothing helpful to offer instead, and could scarcely expect to have a following.

As the election of 1896 approached, the Republicans saw their opportunity, and, although they nominated for the Presidency a man who was a nonentity even among the Presidents of that period, they declared unequivocally for sound money and against bimetallism.[1]

When the Democrats met in Chicago, it was clear at once that the agrarians felt a holy passion for their cause, that they had identified free silver not only with their prosperity, but with truth and goodness and decency.   And their opponents, the more conservative Democrats from the Eastern industrial States, had made the same identification with the gold standard. The bitterness of the coming campaign was foreshadowed on the floor of the Convention; neither group would listen to the opposing spokesmen, and the transaction of business was almost impossible. But finally the tension was broken, and the immediate future of the party determined, by a speech from William Jennings Bryan. A young man from Nebraska with no national reputation, zealous, ignorant, and charming, with a beautiful voice and an evangelical fervour for what he regarded as the cause of humanity, Bryan was the perfect spokesman for this last phase of American agrarianism. Aristocratic agrarianism, the civilization of the landowner, had been killed in the Civil War; and now the poor farmer who had helped the capitalist win that war awoke to the knowledge that he had sold himself to a relentless master. It was a peasant uprising for which Bryan spoke, and his impassioned Biblical phrases sound strange and appealing, and pathetically out of date, in the America of the Standard Oil Company and the arrogant Mr. Townsend Martin. 'When you come before us,' he said to the gold delegates, 'and tell us that we are about to disturb your business interests, we reply that you have disturbed our business interests by your course.

[1] They were willing to adopt the latter if it were agreed upon by the leading European nations.

We say to you that you have made the definition of a business man too limited in its application. The man who is employed for wages is as much a business man as the employer.... The merchant at the crossroads store is as much a business man as the merchant of New York. The farmer who goes forth in the morning and toils all day — who begins in the spring and toils all summer — and who, by the application of brain and muscle to the natural resources of the country, creates wealth, is as much a business man as the man who goes upon the board of trade and bets upon the price of grain.... We come to speak for this broader class of business men. We do not come as aggressors.... We are fighting in the defence of our homes, our families, and posterity. We have petitioned, and our petitions have been scorned. We have entreated, and our entreaties have been disregarded. We have begged, and they have mocked when our calamity came.... You come to us and tell us that the great cities are in favour of the gold standard. We reply that the great cities rest upon our broad and fertile prairies. Burn down your cities and leave our farms and your cities will spring up again as if by magic, but destroy our farms, and the grass will grow in the streets of every city in the country.... If they dare to come out into the open field and defend the gold standard as a good thing, we will fight them to the uttermost. Having behind us the producing masses of this nation and the world, the labouring interests, and the toilers everywhere, we will answer their demand for a gold standard by saying to them: You shall not press down upon the brow of labour this crown of thorns. You shall not crucify mankind upon a cross of gold!'

Long before Bryan reached the end of this speech, he had to pause after each sentence for a wild howl of applause. An inhuman excitement had seized the Convention. Men believed that they were listening to the greatest of all pleas for right; men felt that years of poverty, of bitterness, of oppression, were being avenged by this golden voice. Including spectators, there were fifteen thousand people in the Convention Hall, and as Bryan ended they gave way to delight. When order returned, the free silver platform was adopted, and on the following day Bryan was nominated for the Presidency, and the Eastern 'Gold Democrats' seceded from the party.

The fallacy of the Bryan speech was the assumption that it was any longer necessary to preserve a free and moderately contented farmer class in order that capitalist America should, for a short time, prosper. There were many ways of solving that problem — all preferable, in the eyes of the owners of America, to a policy that might reduce the profits of business. Food could be brought half across the world from Russia or the Argentine; food could be raised by tenants or semi-slaves on mechanized *latifundia*. But Bryan's business men at the crossroads store, and Bryan's free farmers on whose broad and fertile prairies the great cities were alleged to rest, were as outmoded as the economics of John Taylor of Caroline County, who had once expressed Jefferson's vision of an America that was not to be.

Everything that Cleveland had stood for was repudiated by his party's Convention and his party's nominee. But his reputation for honesty and safety was high throughout the East, and when he retired from the Presidency and went to live in Princeton, New Jersey, he remained a national figure in a way which had become unusual for American ex-Presidents. As a respected 'elder statesman' he was in demand as speaker and author of articles, and a large public gave attention to his comments. Though never a popular man, because of a reserve that amounted almost to dourness, Cleveland was so obviously superior, in mind and character and earnestness, to any other President since Lincoln, that when the passions of the gold campaign were allayed, and when his stubborn integrity was no longer a danger to the politicians, he was praised and honoured by men of every opinion and party. The news of his death, in 1908, was received with sorrow.

During the campaign, the insane pro-silver ardour of the Convention crowd was matched by an equal insanity on the part of the defenders of gold. The whole machinery of finance, all the influences so cynically listed by Mr. Townsend Martin, were set in motion to convince the people that the election of Bryan would mean the end, not only of wealth, but of honour, and, quaintly enough, of Christianity. Everything was done to create a feeling of panic. Capitalists gave orders to factories on the understanding that they were not to be executed if Bryan were elected. Insurance companies holding Western mortgages let it be known that, if McKinley won, the mortgages would be extended for five years at a low rate of interest. Employers, paying off their workmen at the end of the week before the election, told them not to come back to work if Bryan were elected. The big banks brought all possible pressure on the little country banks, to convince them that the immediate future would be black unless the Republican Party came to power. In the end, Bryan met his inevitable defeat — but only by 6,502,925 votes to 7,106,779 for his opponent.[1]

The quality of the passions aroused in this contest are shown by the following comments on Bryan and his policy in the New York *Tribune*: 'The thing was conceived in iniquity and was brought forth in sin. It had its origin in a malicious conspiracy against the honour and integrity of the nation.... It has been defeated and destroyed because right is right and God is God. Its nominal head was worthy of the cause. Nominal, because the wretched, rattle-pated boy, posing in vapid vanity and mouthing resounding rottenness, was but the vocal leader of that league of hell.' The paper then goes on to speak of the 'lies and forgeries and blasphemies and all the nameless iniquities of that campaign against the Ten Commandments.'

Although the one campaign issue was free silver, the Democratic platform had also contained a declaration against the use of injunctions in restraint of strikes in labour disputes, and a demand for such 'control of railroads as will protect the people from robbery and oppression,' and for an enlargement of the powers of the Interstate Commerce Commission — a body which had been created to

[1] The Spanish War and the ameliorating effects of new supplies of gold from South Africa soon brought a decline in public interest in the silver question. In 1900 a Gold Standard Act was passed.

control, in the interests of the community, some of the activities of Big Business. This platform, in other words, while reaching back in support of a vanishing agrarianism, was also reaching forward and foreshadowing the new issues that were to face twentieth-century America. The century-long fight between landowner and business man was over. Two new fights had already begun — that between capitalist and proletarian, and that between Big Business and what was left of the American Constitution. Could the democracy control the monstrous financial organizations that it had fostered, or was it to go on being owned by them? Clearly, if a stand were to be made, it could not begin in Congress, among 'our purchased Senators, our hungry Congressmen.' Only under a President capable of leadership would such a contest be possible. And the politicians would do their best to prevent the appearance of such a President. In view of their success in electing the spineless, featureless McKinley, it seemed likely that their best would always prove sufficient.

5

In March, 1897, the owners of the Republican Party must have surveyed the past and the future with shocking complacence. They had overcome the one threat to their power that had arisen in thirty years. Their old enemy was obviously beaten once and for all, and unless they were gifted with rare foresight they would not yet be worried by their new enemies: labour and the reform movement. A few seeming concessions, which meant nothing and which had been cancelled by one golden legal victory, were all that the new enemies had extorted, or seemed likely to extort. The Civil Service Act of 1883 had been an annoying concession to the reformers — but not a dangerous concession, since the rapid centralization of Government had created so many new Federal jobs for distribution among the faithful that the loss of a few thousand of the old jobs hardly mattered. The Interstate Commerce Act of 1887 was another sop to the malcontents who resented the rapacity of Big Business; but the act had been so gently administered, and so kindly interpreted by the Supreme Court, that it proved to mean nothing at all. And the ominously named Sherman Anti-Trust Act of 1890 had been intentionally worded with such vagueness that its one result was to raise the standard of living in the legal profession. Some of the State Governments, however, in the hands of Western agrarians, had been passing laws that were displeasing and that might lead to serious checks in money-making. But in 1889 this danger was laid; for in a case arising out of the Minnesota Legislature's attempt to fix railway rates, the Supreme Court decided that the reasonableness of such rates was a judicial question, and should be decided with regard to the rights of property guaranteed by the Fourteenth Amendment. This Amendment had been forced on the country at the end of the Civil War, with the plea that it was necessary to define and protect the rights of Negroes. And there was embodied in the Amendment a harmless-sounding sentence which was intended to work a revolution in the American Constitution and to defend Big Business forever from the finical interferences of State Governments. The sentence reads: 'No State shall make or enforce any law which shall abridge the privileges or immunities of citizens of the United States; nor shall any State deprive any person of life, liberty, or property without due process of law, nor deny to any person within its jurisdiction the equal protection of the laws.' To the uninitiated citizen this sounded like a tautological effort to protect the Negro; but those who realized that the word 'person' applies in law to joint-stock companies and corporations, as well as to individual men and women, knew that there was larger game afoot. Here and there an attempt was made to combat the Amendment on the ground that it subordinated the States to the Federal Supreme Court, but the public did not understand the argument, and the Amendment was forced upon the North by a humanitarian appeal for the protection of the blacks, and it was forced upon the South by the sword.[1] The story is an interesting example of the way in

[1] No Southern State being allowed to escape from military rule, or to apply for a renewal of its statehood, until it ratified this amendment.

which the authors of the Civil War used the Negro question as a cover for the economic revolution that was their primary purpose. It would be gratifying to have Lincoln's opinion of the Fourteenth Amendment, the means by which it was ratified, and the results which have followed from it.

In 1894, having won the Congressional elections as a result of the strife that Cleveland's Administration had created in his party, the Republicans boasted that they would be able to elect a rag doll to the Presidency in 1896. Actually, they elected something even more meek.

William McKinley was born in Ohio in 1843. His family were Scotch-Irish in descent and had settled in Pennsylvania in the middle of the eighteenth century, moving West to Ohio in 1814. McKinley's father was an iron-manufacturer and the boy had leisure for a school education, but was forced to withdraw from college because of ill health. The war came the next year, when McKinley was eighteen, and he enlisted as a private in an Ohio regiment. At the end of the war he was a brevet major, four years of service having transformed him into a man of outstanding strength and health. He went East, to Albany, New York, for the study of law, and in 1867 he settled in Canton, Ohio, combining his law practice with work for the local Republican Party. Four years later he married, his wife soon becoming a confirmed invalid, but nevertheless outliving her robust husband.

After serving for a time as prosecuting attorney, he was sent to the National House of Representatives in 1876, where he represented the extreme protectionist interests of his manufacturing constituency. With one brief break, he remained in Congress until 1890, finally rising to be Chairman of the Ways and Means Committee and the Republican leader in the lower House. In 1890, he sponsored a tariff with such prohibitive rates that it led to the defeat of his party in 1892. On the currency question he was inclined toward bimetallism; but his views on that subject, as on all others, were nebulous, and therefore not likely to stir hostility. From 1891 to 1895, he served as Governor of Ohio, making a record that impressed the party leaders for its paleness and tranquillity. A leading Ohio business man, by the name of Marcus Alonzo Hanna, decided that he would enjoy the job of kingmaker, and chose his friend McKinley as good plastic material for his master hand. McKinley had no enemies; he had shown that he could carry the crucial State of Ohio; and though his record was tainted with bimetallism, he was easily induced to renounce this heresy. Hanna, though personally honest, was adept at 'influencing' politicians, and he secured McKinley's nomination on the first ballot. His method of securing McKinley's election has already been described.

In return for his kindness, Hanna asked only for a seat in the Senate, and McKinley's way of obliging him was unpleasant enough to stand for a symbol of his Administration. Henry Adams, who after thirty years of observing Washington politics had learned to expect almost anything, described himself as 'shocked beyond all restraints of expression to learn that the President meant to put Senator John Sherman in the State Department in order to make a place for Mr. Hanna in the Senate.... John Sherman, otherwise admirably fitted for the place, a friendly influence for nearly forty years, was notoriously feeble and quite senile, so that the intrigue seemed to Adams the betrayal of an old friend as well as of the State Department. One might have shrugged one's shoulders had the President named Mr. Hanna his Secretary of State... but John Sherman must inevitably and tragically break down. The prospect for once was not less vile than the men.' Sherman did not last long in the State Department, which at that moment was the most important, and the hardest-worked, office in the Government; for the problems of Hawaiian annexation, of chaos in Central America, and of Cuba's revolt against Spain, all demanded immediate attention. And it was already clear that the last of these problems involved the danger of war.

Firm or even modestly sensible diplomacy could have evaded all danger of a Spanish-American war; but such diplomacy presupposed a President who could stand up to the jingoes and the new journalism at home. McKinley could stand up to nothing. There was a large humane public in America which he might have mobilized against the war-mongers; but he was afraid of splitting his party, afraid of losing the next election. With the most pacific intentions he drifted toward the needless war; and in the end his pusillanimity led him to a shameful act.

The Cuban revolt against Spain began in 1895. Inevitably some American lives were endangered and some American capital. Also, the Spanish methods of dealing with the revolt were cruel; at times, they were even more cruel than the methods of General Sherman's 'bummers' in Georgia and South Carolina. But the most dangerous factor in the situation was that a number of important people in America were eager for annexation and that others were openly eager for war. As soon as the insurrection broke out, an American Senator remarked, 'Cuba should become an American colony.' Another Senator said, 'It is time that some one woke up and realized the necessity of annexing some property. We want all this northern hemisphere.' And still another announced, 'We certainly ought to have that island in order to round out our possessions as they should be.' And the young Theodore Roosevelt, soon to become Assistant Secretary of the Navy in McKinley's Administration, was an even more dangerous influence. During the Venezuelan crisis, also in 1895, he wrote his friend, Henry Cabot Lodge, as follows: 'I do hope there will not be any backdown among our people.... Personally I rather hope the fight will come soon. The clamour of the peace faction has convinced me that this country needs a war.' And in 1898, at the critical moment in the negotiations with Spain, he came away from the White House and exclaimed disgustedly to a friend: 'Do you know what that white-livered cur up there has done? He has prepared *two* messages, one for war and one for peace, and doesn't know which one to send in!' Since there was no need for war, since Spain was finally to yield to every demand of the United States, the hesitation of the President seems reason ble — but not to a man to whom war, for its own sake, was desi able.

A responsible President, however, would have had more dangerous men than Roosevelt to combat, had he sought honestly for peace. For the year of the Cuban revolt was the year in which Mr. William Randolph Hearst arrived in New York, with a conscienceless ambition and almost eight million dollars. He bought the New York *Morning Journal*, and was ready to do what he could to distort the minds of his countrymen. His rise was rapid. Within a few years, Godkin, of the *Nation*, was lamenting a 'régime in which a blackguard boy with several millions of dollars at his disposal has more influence on the use a great nation may make of its credit, of its army and navy, of its name and traditions, than all the statesmen and philosophers and professors in the country.' And Hearst did not have to work alone. Pulitzer, of the *World*, was also in the field, ready for the most desperate efforts when there was danger of the war falling through. It was Pulitzer who later admitted that he 'had rather liked the idea of a war — not a big one — but one that would arouse interest.' Although he got exactly what he wanted — a smallish war that unquestionably aroused interest — he was ungrateful in the end. For after some months, according to his biographer, he found that 'the cost of conducting the fleet of tugs and voluminous cables had wiped out the *World*'s profits. Dealers failed to cut their orders between battles and the paper was swamped with returns. Mr. Pulitzer lost interest in war and turned to urging an earlier peace.'

McKinley, therefore, would have had to stand against the unscrupulous and the unimaginative, in Congress, in his own Administration, and in the press. But there was support in the country, had he appealed to it. Grover Cleveland, in retirement, expressed the views of many intelligent Americans when he wrote, on the day after the declaration of war: 'With all allowances I can make,... I cannot avoid a feeling of shame and humiliation.... My only relief from the sick feeling which these thoughts induce consists in the reflection that it affects no one but myself and in the hope, almost amounting to expectation, that we shall find Spain so weak and inefficient that the war will be short and that the result may not be much worse than a depreciation of national standing before the world abroad, and, at home, demoralization of our people's character, much demagogy and humbug, great additions to our public burdens and the exposure of scandalous operations.'

The demands that McKinley made upon Spain, during the negotiations preceding the war, were reasonable: that Spain should give an armistice to the rebels, should break up the concentration camps where thousands of men were confined, and should consent to American mediation between Spain and Cuba. Spain was dilatory in acceding; but as American pressure remained steady, she gave way little by little, and finally, in April, 1898, she capitulated. She revoked the concentration policy, she granted an armistice, and the American Minister in Madrid cabled to McKinley that if he would refrain from humiliating Spain, he could obtain a settlement on the basis of Cuban autonomy, or independence, or even of cession to the United States. The day after receiving this cable, McKinley sent a message to Congress which contained nine pages of inflammatory remarks written on the assumption that Spain had made no concessions. 'I have exhausted every effort,' he wrote, 'to relieve the intolerable condition of affairs which is at our doors.' Then at the end of this war message, McKinley added: 'Yesterday... official information was received by me that the latest decree of the Queen Regent of Spain directs General Blanco, in order to prepare and facilitate peace, to proclaim a suspension of hostilities, the duration and details of which have not yet been communicated to me.' This ungracious conclusion to a stirring account of America's wrongs was ignored by Congress, which promptly declared war.

The explanation of McKinley's conduct is simple. During the negotiations with Spain, two sensational incidents had been used by the pro-war press to arouse public opinion to a point where it seemed to be demanding war. Early in February, the press had published a letter written by the Spanish Minister at Washington to a friend in Cuba. The letter had been stolen from the mails in Havana. It had nothing to do with the Spanish Government, but it contained unflattering comments on McKinley and was made into a national insult by the Hearst-Pulitzer papers. And a few weeks later, the American battleship, *Maine*, which had been sent to Havana on an ostensibly friendly visit, exploded and sank To this day, no one knows whether the *Maine* was destroyed by an internal explosion or whether it was blown up by a mine from without; and no one had ever explained why the Spaniards should have blown it up, since the most likely result was war and the loss of all their colonies. Nevertheless, it was good material for the war press; and it would have taken firmness to stand against the excitement caused by the disaster to the *Maine*. Therefore, when McKinley suddenly found that the Spaniards had given in, that he was offered a peaceful diplomatic triumph if he had the courage to seize it, he showed that he had no courage at all. Fearful of the country's clamour, fearful of disrupting his party and losing the autumn elections, he sent his discreditable message to Congress and let the war come.

A year later, he himself admitted in an interview that 'if he had been left alone, he could have concluded an arrangement with the Spanish Government under which the Spanish troops would have been withdrawn from Cuba without a war.' If he had been left alone! The man in the position once held by Washington and the Adamses complains that if it had not been for the noise of empty men he might have led his country in an honourable path!

Cleveland's predictions were fulfilled to a word. Spain was weak and inefficient; the war was short, and the result was not much worse than demoralization, demagogy, and humbug. In the long run, some good may result from the war; for when the story becomes generally known it should dispel the illusion that democracies tend to be pacific. The reverse is true. A democracy, like any other country, fights certain inevitable wars. In a clash of civilizations, such as that between North and South in the United States, the stronger side presses for mastery until the weaker has to choose between submission or war. If the civilization is vital, the choice will be war. No nation can sidestep such crises. And occasionally, as in the Mexican War, a nation is offered so rich a booty that it is most unlikely to resist. If it fails to resist, the form of government need not be blamed. But a democracy is peculiarly liable to such wars as the Spanish-American: wars in which there is no aim envisaged, no principle at stake, and no *casus belli* unless the truth be huddled over or suppressed; wars that are demanded by the clamour of a press-fed public, and created by officials who live in terror of the next election. It is the curse of democracy that it breeds rulers who dare not trust the people. As was clearly shown in the debates over the peace treaty, the frothy hysteria of the Hearst press did not represent the whole United States. There was an influential public that would have responded to honest leadership. But from the Civil War to the time of Woodrow Wilson, Cleveland was the only President with both the brains and the courage to give such leadership. Roosevelt had the courage, but he was a boyish jingo and could never think when there was fighting in the air. And the rest were nothing. No nation can do itself justice with such rulers. And no democracy has ever, over a long period, produced better rulers.

Largely as a result of Roosevelt's foresight and energy, the American navy was ready, when the war came, to strike Spain in the Far East as well as in the Caribbean. The result was that Manila, in the Philippines, fell to the Americans, and in the peace treaty the United States took over the whole group of islands, paying Spain twenty million dollars in compensation. Having put an end, with much self-congratulation, to an oppressive war against a native population in Cuba, the United States found that it had undertaken to carry on a similar war in the Pacific, for the eight million Filipinos were displeased with their new masters, and subduing them involved a far harder and longer fight than the war with Spain. However, as McKinley justly remarked, 'The march of events rules and overrules human action.'

Meanwhile Hawaii had also been annexed. 'We need Hawaii,' said McKinley to his Secretary, 'just as much and a good deal more than we needed California. It is Manifest Destiny.' McKinley's gift for phrases was notable; but he surpassed himself in the instruction issued to the peace commission that was to treat with Spain: 'It is my earnest wish,' he wrote, 'that the United States, in making peace, should follow the same high rule of conduct which guided it in facing war. It should be as scrupulous and magnanimous in the concluding settlement as it was just and humane in its original action.'

Cuba, as a result of the war, was established in nominal freedom, but really in a state of dependence on the United States similar to that of Egypt on Great Britain. But the most far-reaching effect of the war was that it made the United States into a world power. In 1899, a few months after the close of the war, the firm of Morgan and Company floated a large issue of bonds for the Mexican Republic. This was the first important foreign loan ever issued in America. Two years later, the United States lent fifty millions to England, and a few years after that she helped finance the Russo-Japanese War. At the opening of the twentieth century, America entered the last phase of her capitalist development: she became a colonial power with growing foreign investments.

In 1900, the Republicans nominated McKinley for a second term, and chose Theodore Roosevelt for the Vice-Presidency. Roosevelt had been a picturesque and popular figure during the war, and at its close he was elected Governor of New York State. In that office he fought corruption so strongly and with such success that the State politicians, thinking to be rid of him once and for all, manœuvred his nomination for Vice-President, an office that was usually synonymous with dignified retirement from public life. Six months after re-election, however, McKinley was shot and killed by an anarchist. Roosevelt, at the age of forty-three, was President of the United States. The one thing that might upset the Republican Party had happened. A brave and popular man, with the sense to see what was going on about him, and the decency to resent it, had been accidentally pushed into the Presidency.

CHAPTER IX

ROOSEVELT, TAFT, WILSON, AND HARDING

I

ROOSEVELT was the fifth Vice-President to be lifted to the Presidency as the result of a death. The records of his four predecessors were ominous. Not one of them had later been given the Presidency in his own right, and the two who were strong men and who tried to assert themselves while in the White House had been driven out of public life by their outraged parties. A Vice-President was meant to be seen and not heard, and he was expected to remember this humbling fact even if chance put him in the Presidency. Roosevelt, however, had one advantage over the other four: in spite of his culture and prominent social position,[1] he had a personality which was charming both in personal and public relations. The contrast between his zestful gaiety, his versatile talents (as writer, naturalist, soldier, politician), and the heavy, colourless men who had preceded him for a generation, was so pleasing that good will and hopefulness seized the public mind. But no such feelings were experienced by the Old Guard in the Republican Party.

Roosevelt was born in New York, in 1858. On his father's side the family was Dutch, being descended from a Martenszen van Roosevelt who had settled in New York (then New Amsterdam) in 1649. Roosevelt's mother was Martha Bullock, a Georgian of Scotch-Irish and Huguenot descent. Her brothers fought for the Confederacy and she herself was a passionate Southern sympathizer; but her husband was on the side of the North, and as young Roosevelt grew to know what was going on, he shared his father's feelings with an irrational violence which must have been amusing in a boy of five, but which became embarrassingly silly by the

[1] Since the Jacksonian revolution, in 1828, no man possessing both these advantages had been elected President.

time Roosevelt was middle-aged. In 1904, when he was President of the United States, Roosevelt wrote, 'Right was exclusively with the Union people, and wrong exclusively with the secessionists.' And again, 'Jefferson Davis was an unhung traitor. He did not, like Benedict Arnold, receive money for his treachery, but he received office instead.' Roosevelt, who was an historian of some merit, knew that Jefferson Davis could have had all he wanted in the way of office without encouraging the secession movement; but the knowledge, characteristically, was kept isolated in Roosevelt's mind, having no influence on his opinions, which were the mirror of his emotional life.

In this matter of thoughtfulness, the contrast between Roosevelt and Lincoln is illuminating. Lincoln had comparatively little information, but what he knew was made a part of his whole nature. He could not refrain from thought or ignore his own knowledge; the result was wisdom, sympathy, and lifelong growth in maturity. But Roosevelt, who loved to know things, to acquire facts on a wide range of subjects, never appears to have thought at all. He had knowledge without wisdom, enthusiasm without sympathy, and so far from growing more mature all his life, he never really surpassed his adolescence. He was 'too rash, too unadvised, too sudden,' but with the childlike lovableness that often goes with those failings. Henry Adams wrote of him: 'Power, when wielded by abnormal energy, is the most serious of facts, and all Roosevelt's friends knew that his restless and combative energy was worse than abnormal. Roosevelt... was pure act.' When pure act is undirected by wisdom, it may be useful or pernicious; it is never likely to be of the highest value. It was Roosevelt's good fortune, throughout most of his career, to be useful to his countrymen; it was his misfortune that his last ten years were an unkind caricature of his better self.

Roosevelt was a sickly child, and his early education was carried on by foreign travel supplemented by tutors. Influenced by his father, he set himself the task of building up his strength; and by the time he went to Harvard College he had made himself almost robust. This was a triumph of will; but unfortunately it did not free Roosevelt from the self-assertiveness, the overemphasis on physical prowess, which often results from the struggle to overcome a bodily failing. This quality, like too many others, Roosevelt had in common with William II of Germany; it is fearful to think what havoc might have resulted had this war-loving youth, this 'mercurial and care-free firebrand' (as a Detroit newspaper described him in Spanish War days), ever been in control of such a weapon as the German army.

At Harvard College, Roosevelt did moderately well in his studies and unusually well as a boxer — a hazardous occupation for a youth whose eyesight was faulty.[1] He graduated in 1880, and in the same year married Alice Hathaway Lee, of Boston. After visiting Europe and climbing mountains in Switzerland, he returned home to take up the study of law. Within a year, however, he abandoned this in order to enter the New York State Legislature as a Republican. His family was shocked, for politics — especially State politics — was not the sort of thing that was expected of a Roosevelt. He was told that his associates would be grooms, liquor-dealers, and low politicians. 'In that case,' he told his relatives, 'they belong to the governing class, and you do not. I mean if I can to be one of the governing class.' The naïveté of this remark is typical of Roosevelt, and explains some of his hold on the popular mind. Because he was an instinctive democrat, responding with delight to the idea of a nation that was run by its simplest citizens, its grooms and liquor-dealers, he believed (apparently without effort) that the United States was such a nation. By believing it, he almost, for a few years, made it true. But he failed in the end, for the reason that he could never bring himself to admit how far the United States had grown away from his democratic dream. He treated the rule of Big Business as a temporary accident in the life of America, instead of as the foundation fact of its politics. All he accomplished, therefore, was to interrupt

[1] Roosevelt was never able to overcome this disability, and in middle age he lost the use of one eye.

this rule for a few years, leaving the business men ready to carry on as if he had never been.

For three years in succession Roosevelt was elected to the State Legislature, and in 1884 he was a delegate to the Republican National Convention. This was the Convention that nominated Blaine. Roosevelt fought the nomination, making it quite clear that he knew how undesirable Blaine was; nevertheless, he supported the party after the nomination, refusing to secede with the Mugwumps. He justified himself on the ground that the only way to do anything in American politics is by working within the party organization, and that if every honest man in politics abandons his party each time it does anything of which he disapproves, he is merely, with a false show of virtue, handing the country over to the dogs. But the main reason for Roosevelt's 'regularity' and for much of his subsequent success is that by nature he was an intense partisan. He did not have to make allowance for his party, any more than a boy has to make allowance for his school team; he instinctively felt that Republicans, at least as compared with Democrats, were always in the right.

Although he had stood by the party, Roosevelt was not popular with the Blaine faction. His political future was insecure, so he wisely decided to retire from the field, for the time being. In the summer of 1884, he went West to a cattle ranch he had recently bought in North Dakota. The underlying motive for this flight from the world was the personal tragedy that had come upon him the previous winter. His wife had died in February, 1884, a few days after giving birth to a daughter, and only a few hours after the death of Roosevelt's mother. His exuberance was temporarily quenched by the double blow. 'Black care rarely sits behind a rider whose pace is fast enough,' he wrote a few years later; but the sudden ending of his romantically happy marriage could not be escaped by any forcing of the pace. He needed time to recuperate and reorganize — which is what he found for himself in North Dakota.

In Roosevelt's autobiography there is no mention of his first wife. It is in keeping with the childlike, unthoughtful quality in his nature that he should have met this bitter experience by trying to forget and to deny it. He always had an imperious way with unwelcome facts. In the world of action, however, his courage was complete. Six days after the death of his wife and of his mother, he was back at the legislative job in Albany. It was not until the session was over, and work at the Republican Convention was over, that he took refuge in his wilderness. There, for two years, he lived the life of a rancher, enjoying himself thoroughly, completing the work of building up his health, and increasing his self-respect by winning the friendship and approval of the 'Wild Western' community in which he lived. Roosevelt was always in need of reassurance that he was really a strong, grown-up man, entitled to swagger among other men and in no danger of being mistaken for the feeble child of his early experience. He got great comfort therefore, from his two years in the 'Bad Lands,' rounding up steers, serving as deputy sheriff, showing drunken bullies the advantages of a college course in boxing. Unfortunately, he was never entirely comfortable with his strength; he could never quite wear his virility as if it belonged to him and there were no need to call attention to it. Even in his last years, after acquiring world fame and world flattery, he would, if he were ignored and thwarted, give way to a quality of rage that recalled the kickings and screamings of an infant.

The defeat of Blaine, in 1884, was good for the political reputations of the men who had opposed his nomination without quarrelling with the party. In 1886, Roosevelt was invited to return East and stand for Mayor of New York. He did so, and was defeated — whereupon, for the second time, he retired from politics. In December, 1886, he married Miss Edith Carow, whom he had known since early childhood, and then tried to persuade himself that he was settling down to a career as author. Although this second marriage was thoroughly happy, and Roosevelt's temperament made it impossible for him to be bored with life, nevertheless, he was discontented to be out of politics, and his literary work during these years was below the level of his best writing.

In 1889, his exile from public life was ended by President Harrison, who appointed Roosevelt Civil Service Commissioner at Washington. In this post he served for six years, showing his genius for publicity by attracting general attention to the prosaic subject of Civil Service Reform, and managing to get twenty thousand positions transferred from the spoils system to the permanent Civil Service. In 1895 he was called to New York to serve as President of the Board of Police Commissioners. His flamboyant, publicity-seeking methods in dealing with corruption attracted nation-wide attention, but accomplished little.

During the campaign of 1896, Roosevelt was an ardent McKinley man, and a supporter of the gold standard. He did not trouble, however, to discover what the gold standard was, or even to look up his own party's record on the subject. As a result, he made some very silly statements during the campaign, a fact which passed unnoticed during that storm of calumny and mass-hatred. One of these statements, at least, deserves to be remembered: free silver, according to Roosevelt, would not injure the rich, with their lands, factories, and houses, and their habit of paying bills by cheque; the poor, who used cash, were the people who would suffer.... Such vague flummery was characteristic of Roosevelt, who, though a man of wide interests and knowledge, never seemed to know when he was talking nonsense.

When McKinley became President, Roosevelt returned to Washington as Assistant Secretary of the Navy. From McKinley's point of view it was a bad choice, for the gentle President really hoped to preserve peace with Spain, whereas Roosevelt, in the words of Representative Butler of Pennsylvania, 'came down here looking for war. He did not care whom we fought so long as there was a scrap.' And Mrs. Bellamy Storer said he was 'as innocent as Toddy in *Helen's Babies* who wanted everything to be "bluggy."' Childish, rash, and sanguinary, Roosevelt was a representative within the Administration of the mood of the new journalism. He did not have to wait long for his war, and when it came he resigned the assistant secretaryship in order to raise a regiment of volunteer cavalry. This outfit, which came to be known as the 'Rough Riders' (although its active service was on foot), was made of cowboys, ranchmen, city clubmen, college athletes, and members of the New York City police force. It was a cross-section of Roosevelt's career. As unmilitary a unit as was ever brought together, it expressed a boy's dream of martial adventure, and was well suited to this journalists' war, where press-boats were to follow the fleets into action and pressmen to hold up the landing operations while they made sure they had some future hero's name correctly spelled.

Roosevelt served as lieutenant-colonel in his regiment. He was brave, colourful, and accustomed to dealing with journalists. He and the Rough Riders received so much publicity that it seemed to a grateful country that they were the land forces of the United States. By the end of the war Roosevelt was a popular hero; but professional soldiers regarded him with mistrust — partly because of his success in holding the limelight, partly because of the gross indiscipline of his political appeal, over the heads of his superior officers, to have this regiment transferred home immediately on the close of hostilities. This was done to save the men from yellow fever, which had begun to sweep the camps. It was a humane act, and in that comic-opera war it may have been justified; but it was not forgiven by the military men. It rose against Roosevelt twenty years later and was partly responsible for the greatest disappointment of his life.

On returning home to New York, Roosevelt was nominated for the governorship of the State. His war popularity elected him, and his attack on the corruption in the Republican machine at Albany was responsible for his being pushed upstairs into the Vice-Presidency. An assassin's bullet promoted him to the position from which his party leaders would have kept him at any cost.

2

Roosevelt brought three main ideas to the Presidency: first, a belief in centralized authority, which fitted the whole drift of

American politics, for ever since the Civil War the National
Government had been growing in power at the expense of the
States; second, a belief that within the central government the
Executive should regain much of the prestige that had been lost to
Congress; third, a determination to break the corrupt control
exercised by the very rich. The last two points were popular with
the people; the first was a mere acceptance of what was bound to
happen in an era of Big Business. All the great corporate 'persons' whose rights were protected by the Fourteenth Amendment
were interstate concerns, and therefore only a highly centralized
National Government could even pretend to control them. So
Roosevelt met little opposition in seeking to aggrandize the power
of the National Government, and little effective opposition in seeking to aggrandize that of the Executive — for his popularity, and
his skill in using the press, made it easy for him to arouse the public against obstructionist tactics in Congress. It was only when he
came to the third, and the most popular, item on his programme,
to his attempt to curb the super-government of the very rich, that
he found real trouble.

The essence of Roosevelt's attitude toward Big Business is contained in a speech he made in 1905. 'The great development of
industrialism,' he said, 'means that there must be an increase in the
supervision exercised by the Government over business enterprise.' Government, he continued, must be strong enough to ensure that the power of wealth is 'used for and not against the interest of the people as a whole.... We do not intend that the Republic shall ever fail as those republics of olden times failed, in
which there finally came to be a government by classes, which resulted either in the poor plundering the rich or in the rich... exploiting the poor.' And in the following year he wrote to Taft that
'the dull, purblind folly of the very rich men, their greed and arrogance... and the corruption in business and politics, have tended
to produce a very unhealthy condition.' This is a statement of the
problem; but the weakness of Roosevelt's position was that he regarded it as in some sense a statement of the solution as well. He

appeared to believe that if the evils of Big Business were curbed by an honest President, such as himself, all its benefits would remain, resulting in an America with simple Jeffersonian virtue and Astorian wealth. In this, he represented the American public, which continued to hanker after the best of two worlds (while receiving the best of neither), and to be unwilling to face the dilemma presented by triumphant capitalism.

In the realm of politics and economics the two great changes that had come over America since the time of Washington were the rise of democracy and of unfettered capitalism. The first was unplanned, and came as the result of westward expansion and the influence of the frontier States. The second was carefully planned, and was opposed with equal care. It triumphed because it was the natural economic development, and because economic determinism will always operate unless it be met by one of two forces: a religious ideal, such as that which set limits to business enterprise during a part of Europe's Middle Ages, or a social ideal, such as that which developed in the South between 1820 and the Civil War. This social ideal, being held by a minority section, was destroyed by force; and the religious ideal has never, since the formation of the United States, been strong enough to stand against the lure of prosperity. The United States is a Protestant country, founded at the end of the eighteenth century when Protestantism was already losing its effective force and breaking into groups for the furtherance of moral uplift or of humanitarianism. The country has known many churches, but no Church. Never has the steady triumph of Big Business, with all its moral and social implications, been threatened by the rival claims of a Christian way of life. Once the Southern dissent had been crushed, the capitalist knew no rival.

With the rise of Roosevelt there came to the White House, for the first time since Johnson, a man who protested against many of the assumptions of the business man's world. Unhappily, the so-called Progressive Era of Roosevelt, Taft, and Wilson represented little more than protest. The Progressives thought all they had to do was to repair the machinery of democratic government and the country would thrive. Actually, democracy is powerless in a world of Big Business. If it can ever succeed, it must be in Jefferson's world of free farmers, or Bryan's world of the business man of the crossroads store. The Progressives passed laws purporting to give the people greater control of the Government; they awakened the conscience of the country, creating a brief demand for better things. And the end of all their effort was the Presidency of Warren Harding. Democracy, in the giant world-cities of today, is as unreal as the democracy of the Roman Empire.

The choice before the United States, the dilemma which the Progressives failed to define, is the choice between saving traditional American democracy at the cost of economic retrogression (by creating a simpler society in which social democracy would be thinkable), or else of creating a new social order (and presumably a new form of government) suitable to a super-industrialized, urbanized society, and capable of administering a modern capitalist state in the common good and in accord with the Christian moral code.[1] Clearly, the first choice is unacceptable. Only a religious ideal would reconcile a nation to turning away from the deadly charms of industrial progress. And the second choice will not be made until American political leaders convince themselves that Jacksonian democracy and the cosmopolis-state of Big Business are as incompatible as slave-based aristocracy and the frontier life.

Because of his failure to face these problems, Roosevelt's famous war on Big Business was only an interruption to the natural development of capitalism. He would not allow the trusts to reach their full stature because that would mean the final transformation of America into a plutocracy; but neither would he hamper the trusts too far because that might interfere with prosperity. His attitude was summed up by Mr. Dooley as follows: ' "Th'

[1] Communism, of course, is a third possibility, and will become a probability if present tendencies are left unchecked.

trusts," says he, "are heejous monsthers built up by th' enlightened intherprise iv th' men that have done so much to advance progress in our beloved country," he says. "On wan hand I wud stamp thim undher fut; on th' other hand not so fast." ' Roosevelt prosecuted some of the trusts and caused their formal dissolution, though this had little effect on their power; he strengthened the Interstate Commerce Commission, which had power to regulate railway rates; and he created the Department of Commerce and Labour, with powers of supervision over interstate corporations. The subsequent history of the United States is proof that this did not seriously hamper the power of business, or revive anything which even the most hopeful person could describe as true democracy.

One of Roosevelt's popular and useful deeds was his stand for the conservation of the nation's natural resources. Now that most of the damage had been done, the people, under Roosevelt's lead, woke to the folly of handing the nation's resources over to a few rich men, who had gained control of the lumber, coal, and oil that had once belonged to the Government. It was too late to return to J. Q. Adams's dream of an instructed and want-free nation; but at least Roosevelt induced Congress to preserve many of the remaining forests, mines, and sources of water-power. This is probably Roosevelt's most lasting contribution to the good of the nation. His most exciting exploit was the taking of Panama.

Panama belonged to the Republic of Colombia, and when the United States had at last chosen the isthmus as the site for the proposed canal, in preference to the Nicaraguan route, endless chances for fraud were created. A French company already had rights in the canal, and the United States proposed to buy the company off. In the three-cornered negotiations which followed, the legislators of Colombia had a tendency to dive for gold in troubled waters. As always when there was a chance of his being thwarted, Roosevelt's patience gave way. 'Those contemptible little creatures in Bogotá,' he wrote to his Secretary of State, 'ought to understand how much they are jeopardizing things and imperiling their own future.' The latter phrase is ominous, in view of subsequent history. For in November, 1903, Panama had an opportune revolution.[1] American naval vessels appeared at Panama City and off Colon, preventing any incivility from the Colombian troops. Perhaps it was with that act in mind that Roosevelt said the United States had shown 'a spirit, not merely of justice, but of generosity in its dealings with Colombia.' The new State of Panama was recognized an hour and fifteen minutes after it reported its existence to Washington, and four days later Panama sent commissioners to sign the treaty that 'the contemptible little creatures in Bogotá' had been delaying. Years afterward, in a public speech, Roosevelt summed the whole thing up: 'I took Panama and left Congress to debate, and while the debate goes on the canal does also.'

When Wilson became President, he drew up a treaty offering Colombia an apology and twenty-five million dollars. Roosevelt was furious, and his friend Henry Cabot Lodge blocked the treaty in the Senate. But in 1921, when Harding was President, Lodge helped secure the ratification of a treaty offering Colombia her twenty-five million dollars. The explanation of this change of heart was an appropriate one for the Harding Administration: oil had been found in Colombia.

Though unspectacular as compared with Panama, or with his mediation to end the Russo-Japanese War, or even with his espousal of reformed spelling, one of Roosevelt's most important acts was the logical extension he gave to the Monroe Doctrine when he justified his intervention in the affairs of Caribbean countries as follows: 'If we are willing to let Germany or England act as the policeman of the Caribbean, then we can afford not to interfere when gross wrong-doing occurs. But if we intend to say "Hands off" to the powers of Europe, sooner or later we must keep order ourselves.'

By 1904, Roosevelt had such a hold on the American people that the politicians could not prevent his nomination, and that au-

[1] Roosevelt described it as a 'most just and proper Revolution.'

tumn he was easily elected to the Presidency. Four years later his popularity had grown even wider, and he could have been nominated for a third term. The nation thoroughly enjoyed him — enjoyed his zest for life, his fits of impatience, his world-celebrity, his boisterousness, and his dogmatic opinions on life, letters, and the future world. He had said, however, that he would not accept a third term, and when the time came he used his influence to force the nomination of his friend, William Howard Taft.

Roosevelt was fifty years old in 1909, when he left the Presidency. His strength and vitality were at their highest. It was his tragedy that he could find nothing to occupy him, and that the American political system offered him no dignified position in public life. There was talk of his being given the Presidency of Harvard University; but Henry Lee Higginson, one of the most influential Overseers, was sceptical. 'We need a man of judgment,' he stated; 'and is judgment to be found coupled with such enormous energy?' If Roosevelt's past career were not a sufficient answer, his remaining ten years would convince anyone that Higginson's query was a wise one.

3

Two weeks after Taft's inauguration, Roosevelt sailed for Africa, where he spent a year in the wilds. During the spring and summer of 1910 he travelled through Europe, collecting honorary degrees and giving his opinions on all subjects known to newspapermen. On his return to America he found that Taft, though professedly carrying on the Roosevelt policies, was widely believed to have made a truce with Big Business. After trying for a brief while to refrain from criticism, Roosevelt was drawn back into public life under circumstances which made most of his old friends turn against him.

William Howard Taft was a genial, unambitious man who never got over his surprise at finding himself President. His real interest was in the legal profession — a taste which ran in the family, since both his father and his grandfather were judges. The Tafts had emigrated from England to Massachusetts in the seventeenth century, remaining in New England until 1839, when William Howard's father — a distinguished man, although he was to serve for some time in Grant's cabinet — moved to Ohio. There the future President was born, in 1857.

After making a first-class record at Yale University, Taft studied law at Cincinnati and was admitted to the Ohio bar. From the beginning he was a distinguished lawyer, and at the age of thirty he became a judge of the Superior Court of Ohio. The year before this advancement, he had married Miss Helen Herron, who was later to be one of the most popular hostesses ever known to the White House. In 1890, under President Harrison, Taft was appointed Solicitor-General of the United States, and before the end of Harrison's term Taft was a United States Circuit Judge. In 1900, he was appointed President of the Philippine Commission, which led to his becoming Governor of the islands during the troubled period between 1901 and 1904. Bland, conciliatory, and with a deep kindliness of nature, Taft did all that was possible to reconcile the Filipinos to having civilization and progress applied to them. On one occasion he referred to these actively hostile people as 'little brown brothers' — to which the American soldiers replied with the refrain,

> He may be a brother of Big Bill Taft,
> But he ain't no friend of mine.

In 1904, Taft returned to the United States to become Secretary of War under Roosevelt. In spite of the bellicose title to his job, the rotund and gentle Taft managed to remain a pacifying influence in American public life. In 1906, he took temporary charge of Cuba, when that island had managed its affairs so badly as to provoke American intervention. In 1907, Taft visited the Philippines to open the first legislative assembly, and then went on to Japan, where he made assuaging speeches at a time when American-Japanese relations were at dangerous tension.

Roosevelt was fond of Taft, and he knew that Taft shared his own vaguely liberal doctrines; therefore, he forced Taft's nomination in 1908. The Democrats again offered Bryan, with a rival (but scarcely distinguishable) set of liberal panaceas. The business community's traditional distrust of the Democratic Party was enough to secure Taft's election by about seven and a half to six and a half million votes.

Roosevelt had taken the view that the President's powers extended to anything not expressly forbidden by the Constitution — an interpretation that suited his forthright nature and his love of battle. During his seven years in the White House there was constant strife between Congress and the Executive. With the inauguration of Taft the initiative passed to Congress — where it had been, except for the Roosevelt years, ever since the defeat of President Johnson. Taft had little combativeness in his nature and no experience in the rough work of politics, his reputation having been made on the bench and in administrative tasks. He took the view that the President had only those powers that were specifically granted him — which is good constitutional law, but bad practice, since the vast extent of the United States cannot be governed by a disorderly mob in Congress.

Taft's modesty was so pronounced that he found it hard to assert even those powers which he knew himself to possess. 'When I am addressed as "Mr. President," ' he wrote to Roosevelt, 'I turn to see whether you are not at my elbow. When I read in the newspapers... of a conference between the Speaker and the President, or between Senator Aldrich and the President, I wonder what the subject of the conference was.' In view of such self-distrust, it is surprising how much Taft accomplished. Never trying to bully Congress, he was able, on several important matters, to persuade it. His affection for humanity was so inclusive that he could treat Congress as if it were composed of big white brothers, and there were times when Congress did not bite the hand that stroked it. There were other times, however, when it did — with the result that in May, 1910, Taft wrote sadly to Roosevelt: 'It is now a year and three months since I assumed office and I have had a hard time — I do not know that I have had harder luck than other Presidents, but I do know that thus far I have succeeded far less than have others. I have been conscientiously trying to carry out your policies, but my method of doing so has not worked smoothly.'

This view of his own accomplishments was unjustified. Taft had been as successful in carrying out Roosevelt's policies as Roosevelt himself had been. A parcels-post service and a postal savings bank (both opposed by business interests) had been established; New Mexico and Arizona had been admitted as the forty-seventh and forty-eighth States; the prosecution of trusts had been continued; the Interstate Commerce Commission had been strengthened; and two constitutional amendments had been forced through Congress: [1] the Sixteenth Amendment, authorizing a Federal income tax, and the Seventeenth, transferring the election of United States Senators from the State Legislatures to the people, and so completing the long process by which the constitutional safeguards against democracy have been defeated. All this was 'Progressive,' and if it produced no useful results, that was because something was wrong with the Progressive policies, not because Taft was failing to implement those policies.

While winning these favours from Congress, Taft had been defeated on several important points. He had summoned Congress in special session for the purpose of lowering the tariff, and Congress, as usual, had raised it. He had negotiated arbitration treaties with France and England, and the Senate had so mutilated them that he had been forced to withdraw them from consideration. He had arranged for tariff reciprocity with Canada — the legislatures of the two countries being intended to adopt identical acts — but the wild words spoken in Congress while the bill was being forced through so incensed the Canadians that their legislators rejected the agreement. But there was nothing in all this to excuse the charge that Taft had betrayed the Progressive cause. All that had happened was that Progressives were awakening to the fact that their vaunted efforts to curb the power of wealth and

[1] These were not ratified by the States until 1913.

to restore the Government to the people had accomplished little. There was less corruption at Washington, fewer purchased Senators and hungry Congressmen about the Capitol; the logical development of Big Business had been held up; but nothing positive had been done. The Progressives had failed in creative thought. They had no planned society which they wished to build, being stultified by their faith that the existing society was, at bottom, healthy. They believed that if they removed the worst of the evils which were corrupting that society, the result would surely be gratifying. When the result was almost unnoticeable and completely ungratifying, they expressed their disappointment blaming Taft.

R. A. Ballinger, the member of Taft's Cabinet who had charge of the Government's conservation policy, was accused of dishonest practices. Taft asked for an investigation by the House of Representatives; when the House exonerated Ballinger, the President dismissed the man who had accused him. This man was Gifford Pinchot, the Government's chief forester and an ardent Roosevelt man. Out of this incident the Progressives made a grievance, using it to symbolize the Administration's so-called betrayal of the Roosevelt programme. Within a few months of Roosevelt's return he was countenancing this faction, with the result that he was gradually led into open war on his old friend. As always with Roosevelt, this war was unqualified and bitter.

It was at this time that Roosevelt evolved a doctrine which he called the New Nationalism — a combination of his old fight against the money-power with what amounted to a demand for State socialism. The New Nationalism, said Roosevelt, called for 'far more governmental interference with social and economic conditions than we have yet had.' But what sort of State did Roosevelt wish to build with all his regulation? Did he want to destroy Big Business and return to a simpler economics? Did he wish the Government to take over Big Business and run it for the general welfare? Did he imagine that Big Business would go happily forward by itself, while the State confiscated its profits and distributed them in social service? Since he never answered these questions, he never brought his New Nationalism to life.

By the time of the Republican Nominating Convention of 1912, Roosevelt was the open rival of Taft and had declared that he wanted a third term. The Republican machine backed Taft; but in many States there were groups of Roosevelt Republicans, with the result that a number of these States sent two sets of delegates to the Convention. But the Convention, as always, was in the hands of the 'regulars,' who made short work of the Roosevelt men. Taft delegates were awarded almost all of the contested seats, and Taft was nominated on the first ballot.

As soon as the Convention had nominated Taft, Roosevelt and his followers prepared to found a new party. In August they held a Convention which nominated Roosevelt in an atmosphere of hysterical enthusiasm. 'We stand at Armageddon and we battle for the Lord,' said Roosevelt, with somewhat blasphemous exaggeration. The actual result of their battling was the election of Woodrow Wilson, the man whom Roosevelt was soon to hate with the whole force of his adolescent spleen.

Taft retired from the Presidency with relief, returning to the form of work for which he was suited and in which he excelled. He was appointed Professor of Law at Yale University. During the World War, he used his genius for conciliation by serving on the board for the arbitration of labour disputes, and he supported Wilson and the League of Nations during the fight over the Treaty of Versailles. In 1921, President Harding appointed him Chief Justice of the Supreme Court, and his real career had reached its culmination. The Presidency was merely an interruption in Taft's life, a painful interruption to an otherwise enjoyable and placid career. After years of service at the head of his profession, Taft died in 1930. He was the most lovable man who had ever ruled in the White House, inspiring a personal devotion that must have made the bitterness of political hatreds seem — at least in retrospect — trivial.

4

The Progressive Era in American politics came to its full fruition in Wilson. He represents American liberalism at its best, and most of its positive achievements were his work. That the achievements proved vain, that the end of the Progressive Era was Warren Harding and Coolidge Prosperity, is the result, not of the personal failure of Wilson, but of the insufficiency of liberalism before the problems of the twentieth century.

It is an interesting fact that Wilson's rise to power was promoted by the very men whom he thought it his life's work to frustrate. With cynical realism, these men decided that a liberal in the White House might be a nuisance, but would never be really dangerous. He would express, and satisfy, the people's demand for 'reform'; he might pass some irritating laws; but then the whole thing would blow over and the rich could return to their traditional work of growing richer. But unless the people were given this mild vent for their discontent, something unpleasant, something effective, might happen. Bryan, with his disturbing currency notions, was still the chief force in the Democratic Party; Roosevelt, who probably did not know what he was saying, was pleading for socialist doctrines with his New Nationalism; and in the West, La Follette, who well knew what he was saying, was backing the same cause. Wilson himself, in the spring of 1911, put the situation with clarity: 'There is a tremendous undercurrent of protest,' he said, 'which is bound to find expression. Taft will be renommated by the Republicans; unless the Democrats nominate someone whom the people can accept as expressing this protest, there will be a radical third party formed and the result of the election may be little short of a revolution.'

Five years before Wilson made this speech, a little group of men representing the real centre of power in the country had come to the same conclusion about the danger of something 'little short of a revolution,' and had begun to look about for a safe, milk-fed liberal to head the Democratic Party. Their choice, to their subsequent sorrow, fell on Wilson, then President of Princeton

University, a student of history and politics with no experience in practical affairs, but with a reputation as a public speaker and as a man of charm and force. In February, 1906, after a dinner at the Lotos Club in New York City where Wilson was guest of honour, Colonel George Harvey rose and proposed him for President of the United States.

Harvey was a political journalist and the friend and confidant of the great men of Wall Street. He had been head of Harper and Brothers, the publishing house, which was then financed by J. Pierpont Morgan, and he was editor of *Harper's Weekly*. According to his own account, Wilson's candidature was 'interesting' to such men as Thomas F. Ryan and August Belmont, from the world of Big Business, and to Ochs, of the New York *Times*, and Laffan, of the *Sun*. What these men feared, in 1906, was that the choice at the next election might be between Roosevelt and Bryan; Wilson appealed to them because in his writings and his speeches he seemed to be appealing for a return to a simpler, more Jeffersonian form of society, and for putting more power in the hands of the people. Big Business feared neither of these ideas. The simpler society it felt to be the dream of a 'Presbyterian priest,' as 'Boss' Smith of New Jersey called Wilson; and it had long ago learned that the more power there was given to the people, the less responsible control was exercised by anybody. What they feared was state supervision at the hands of the erratic Roosevelt, or the money heresies of Bryan. But when Roosevelt abdicated voluntarily, in favour of placid Taft, the danger appeared to have blown over and the 'Presbyterian priest' was put back in his box.

Colonel Harvey, however, soon began preparing for 1912. Taft was a comforting interlude; but the political passions stirred by Roosevelt were not to be allayed without at least the appearance of action, and the Princeton Professor seemed to offer the best hope for the appearance without too much of the reality. In May, 1909, *Harper's Weekly* was announcing, 'We now expect to see Woodrow Wilson elected Governor of the State of New Jersey in 1910 and nominated for President in 1912 upon a platform demanding tariff revision downward.'[1] And early in 1910, Harvey began working on ex-Senator James Smith, Jr., Democratic 'Boss' of New Jersey, pointing out all the reasons why Wilson should be nominated Governor of that State. Smith represented everything that is worst in American politics. He ruled New Jersey in secret alliance with the Republican 'Boss,' dividing the spoils and giving orders to mayors and governors as if they were office-boys. Smith was sceptical about Wilson, but Harvey persuaded him that the Democratic 'machine' in New Jersey was in such evil odour that the one chance for victory was to nominate a man who was unquestionably honest. This sounded like a desperate measure; but Smith finally gave in. The scene is an interesting comment on American politics: the New York business interests wanted some safe man built up into a Presidential possibility, in case they should need him to head off Roosevelt or La Follette; Smith wanted a Democratic Governor, and was even willing, if necessary, to put up with an honest one. So they chose Wilson, it never occurring to anybody that a college professor might have a will of his own after he had been placed in office. They were resigned to his being honest, but they thought of course he would be a fool.

Once Smith was won over, the nomination of Wilson was assured. Few of the State's politicians knew him, and none of them wanted him. At the nominating convention there was protest and bitterness at the way the machine was forcing this political outsider on the State. But the 'Big Boss' had given his orders, and Wilson was chosen on the first ballot.

It was not long before the New Jersey bosses and the New York bankers repented of their work; but by that time it could not be undone. Once Wilson was given his chance, he quickly became the leader of that very branch of the party which he had been put forward to defeat. His Eastern backers deserted him as soon as he showed that he had the zeal to force liberal laws on New Jersey

[1] As Wilson's biographer, Mr. Ray Stannard Baker, points out, 'Harvey's backers, the great bankers of the nation, were not unwilling to see the tariff revised downwards.'

and the courage to outface the bosses who thought they owned him. But the Bryan Democrats of the West and South turned to Wilson for the same reasons that the Easterners turned from him. At the 1912 Convention it was William Jennings Bryan who secured Wilson's nomination, in the face of bitter opposition from New York. He could never, of course, have been elected (since he did not even win as many votes as Bryan himself had won) but for the split in the Republican Party.... Such was the chain of accident and misunderstanding that brought this college professor to the White House, giving the Progressive Movement the chance to show what it was worth. It was all so quick, so improbable, and so unanticipated, that Wilson may be forgiven for imagining that it showed the hand of God.

5

Thomas Woodrow Wilson was born in Staunton, Virginia, in 1856. He was Scotch-Irish on one side of the family and pure Scotch on the other. Both his grandparents had been immigrants to the United States — Wilson and Jackson being the only two Presidents who did not have a long line of American forbears. Shortly after Wilson was born, his father, who was a Presbyterian Minister, was transferred from Virginia to Augusta, Georgia, and it was there the boy lived during the Civil War. At first he had no regular schooling; but his father had culture and wisdom and character, and the relation between the two was of lifelong value to both.

When Wilson was fourteen, the family moved to Columbia, South Carolina, where Dr. Wilson was to be professor in a theological seminary. This was during the misery of Reconstruction, which bore most heavily on South Carolina. Wilson, who was of course a Southern sympathizer, was young enough to escape the bitterness of the Southerners who knew what was being done to their world, and old enough to profit by an environment of simple living and hard work. In 1873 he went to Davidson College in North Carolina. The following year his family moved to that

State, and Wilson, whose health was poor, spent a year at home, resting and studying. In 1875 he went north to Princeton College, where he took his B.A. degree. He was undistinguished as a scholar, but was already a good public speaker and debater.

Throughout his youth it was Wilson's fixed purpose to go in for politics, in defence of liberalism and the simple, virtuous society of his childhood. When he was sixteen his cousin asked him whose picture it was that hung above his desk. 'That is Gladstone,' he answered, 'the greatest statesman that ever lived. I intend to be a statesman, too.' The choice of Gladstone for hero is appropriate — the two men being much alike in character, in quality of mind, and in their intimate knowledge of God's hopes and plans. On leaving college, Wilson studied law at the University of Virginia, presumably because law is the highroad to advancement in American politics. He practised for a time in Atlanta, and then, being very poor and finding the profession little to his taste, he decided to alter the whole plan of his life, to abandon politics and take up college teaching. Instead of dealing with public affairs at first hand, he determined to become an influence through his books and students. He went to Johns Hopkins College, in Baltimore, for graduate study in government and politics, taking his Ph.D. degree in 1886. The previous year he had married Miss Ellen Louise Axson, of Savannah, Georgia — a woman who, by her almost idolatrous belief in his greatness, by her care for his feeble health, and by the serenity and charm of the background she gave his life, was one of the chief causes for Wilson's success.

After taking his advanced degree, Wilson taught history for a time at the woman's college of Bryn Mawr, then at Wesleyan University in Connecticut. Finally, in 1890, he was appointed Professor of Jurisprudence and Political Economy at Princeton. In his academic work, Wilson was never distinguished as a scholar. His books, though interesting in the light of his later career, are unimportant. He made no contributions to knowledge, and his five-volume popular history of the United States is commonplace. The slow, exacting work of scholarship did not attract him and his mind was not notably original or profound, so he could not use the findings of other men as the basis for historical thought which is of value to the adult world. As a teacher of undergraduates, however, he excelled. He could dramatize and make exciting the issues of politics and law. He could infuse his subject with moral energy — for, in spite of a tendency to dilute reality with abstractions, he passionately felt that a crisis in American politics was approaching and that he knew the one way in which his country could be preserved from ruin. Lastly, there was nothing about his mind to dismay the undergraduate — no unpredicted depths or subtleties. Knowledge, humour, self-confidence, moral purpose — all these reassuring qualities were present, and were employed in giving a view of politics which was just far enough above their own to be stimulating to college students. But there were none of the distressful probings to which Henry Adams had subjected his students at Harvard, none of the horrifying suggestion that the teacher himself might not have the answer to every problem. For the same reasons that explain his success as a college teacher, Wilson was in demand on the lecture platform. After he had been for a dozen years at Princeton, there were influential men all over the country who had studied under him, whose minds he had stirred and who had a proper gratitude and respect for him. And there were earnest lecture-audiences who thought him a prophet. He had done exactly what he set out to do — had made himself an indirect influence on the political thought of the country. Then, in 1902, he was appointed President of Princeton College.

Since Princeton was regarded as one of the three leading institutions of learning in America, its Presidency was a post of great honour and considerable news-value. To be sure, no important scholar or writer would be likely to accept a college presidency in America, for the position requires constant diplomatic entertaining and speech-making, continual efforts to raise money from the reluctant rich alumni, and much executive work. Such a job would make scholarship or creative thought impossible; but it suited Wilson's plan of life, for it enlarged his potential public and gave new publicity to all he had to say. He did not want the artist's or the scholar's leisure; he wanted wide attention for his politico-moral sermons.

Princeton was a rich man's college, and since this was a period of rapid growth in all the leading American colleges, it was steadily in need of money, which had to be raised from graduates and from the parents of students. Wilson's appointment as head of such an institution shows, therefore, that the trustees regarded him as 'safe.' His exhortations for greater democracy in American life, for the control of vast wealth, for the purification of politics, had been made in general terms, so that he was vaguely felt to be a moral force, but not to be anything so disturbing as a reformer. He soon showed, however, that to him at least his generalities had meaning. He revolutionized the teaching methods of the college, and then set to work to democratize Princeton by breaking up an exclusive club system and altering the whole social atmosphere. At once he met strong resistance; and then, for the first time, he showed the weakness that was to mar his life, leading him to a tragic end. Convinced, as throughout his career, that all right was on his side, he made his opponents into evil-doers who were conspiring to cheat the truth. He failed to distinguish between the ideas, which it was his privilege to hate and to fight, and the men and women who were his old friends and to whom it was ludicrous to impute vicious motives. The result of his conduct was that the little academic village was split with passions that would have seemed exaggerated for the Trojan War. Ten years after Wilson had resigned from Princeton, the bitterness he left behind him was not healed. A further result, of course, was that Wilson failed to put through his plan. He could never win over the opposition, since he began on the assumption that his opponents were morally deformed. In 1910, when he stood for Governor of New Jersey, he left his work at Princeton undone.

Among the many farcical and tragical examples of Wilson's treatment of the friends who disagreed with him, the most instructive, for an understanding of his future career, is the story

of his relations with Mr. John Grier Hibben, who succeeded him
as President of the University. Wilson and Mr. Hibben had been
more than friends; there was a devoted intimacy between them
which, on Wilson's side, was so exaggerated as to suggest the in-
stability that underlay his character. 'He must see them [the
Hibbens] every day,' writes Wilson's biographer; 'he made no
plans, came to no conclusions, without talking with "Jack" Hibben.
His letters to Hibben and to Mrs. Hibben were addressed "My
dear, dear Friend," "Dearest Friend," and often signed "Yours
devotedly," or "Your devoted friend."' [1] Mr. Hibben was a man
whose genius was for kindness and tact — the least quarrelsome,
the least dictatorial of men. Yet even this friendship ended, on
Wilson's side, in an explosion of bitterness. Years later, when Wilson was about to be nominated to the Presidency, he wrote to a
friend: 'The worst has happened at the University. Hibben has
been elected President!' As Governor of New Jersey at the time,
Wilson was *ex-officio* president of the board of trustees, and as a
matter of form, in accordance with all precedent, he was supposed
to be present at Mr. Hibben's inauguration. He refused to attend.
... It is hard to reconcile such self-righteousness with the humour
which Wilson undoubtedly possessed and which made him an
entertaining companion when surrounded by people he liked.

As soon as he was elected Governor, Wilson had an open fight
with 'Boss' Smith, which resulted in the defeat of Smith and the
frustration of his hopes to return to the United States Senate.
Then, having shown his strength and his determination, Wilson
began to force through the Legislature the laws that he had promised to sponsor: a Direct Primaries law; [2] an Employers' Liabil-
ity Act; an act creating a Public Utilities Commission, etc. By
securing such laws in the boss-ridden State of New Jersey, Wilson
won a national reputation and at the same time lost the support

[1] Ray Stannard Baker, *Woodrow Wilson*, III, 160.
[2] Whereby candidates for office were nominated at a 'primary' election, by the
registered voters of a party, instead of by the party caucus. The device is intended
to help the people to choose their own candidates, but, though it has been adopted in
many American States, it has not diminished the 'machine' control over politics.

of the men who had brought him forward and who now did all in their power to head him off. But in spite of the fact that his second year as Governor was not a success, that the personal difficulties that had marred his career at Princeton were beginning to appear again, he was the party's strongest candidate. Bryan had been defeated three times, and there was no one else who could match Wilson's vigour, oratorical power, earnestness, and ability to please an audience. In the spring of 1911 he made a successful political tour through the West, showing that he had become a genuine national figure. In the summer of 1912, after a long deadlock in the Convention, Bryan decided to give his full support to Wilson (chiefly because the business interests of the East were opposing Wilson so strongly), and the nomination was his. The Taft-Roosevelt split had already taken place, so everyone knew that the Democratic nomination was as good as election.

6

Wilson was the second Democratic President to be elected since 1856, the reason for the party's weakness during all these years being lack of an issue. The Civil War had settled the old issue between the agrarians and the business men. After 1865, anyone who suggested reverting to a policy that might diminish the profits of industry would be a political suicide. The Democrats, therefore, while pretending still to cherish the interests of the farmer, had no important policy to offer which was an alternative to that of the Republicans. The Democratic Party was not an opposition — it was merely a substitute. It was an amorphous coalition of all who were dissatisfied with the Republicans, but who did not know what they wished to do about it: Western farmers, whenever money became too expensive and their debts too burdensome; Southern farmers no matter what their financial status, since Reconstruction had left the Republican Party an object of hatred in the South; Southern industrialists (when, toward the close of the century, industry began to develop in the South) for the same reason; the new immigrants, who felt that their capitalist rulers were against them and who therefore turned against the party in power; a few rich Easterners, who had risen from among the new immigrants, or whose interests were chiefly commercial so that they disliked the ever-rising Republican tariffs. Such a group had no economic or political unity, had nothing in common but a distaste for the Republicans, and a desire to get them out of office and to get themselves in. When Bryan forced a real issue on the Democrats, the party split in two. When Cleveland was elected, as the result of the nomination of Blaine, he could not even get his Congress to reduce the tariff, although such reduction was the only one of their old measures that the Democrats still pretended to favour. Meanwhile, the Progressive Movement arose within both parties. Except for his demand for free silver, Bryan's doctrines were almost the same as Roosevelt's, and since Wilson repudiated free silver there was no sharp issue between him and his leading opponent.

Wilson, however, was temperamentally a Jeffersonian — and in this respect, rather than in their legislative programme, he and Roosevelt clashed. Wilson believed in democracy as a religious dogma. He believed that in crises of the national life the people were divinely inspired, and that their decisions had a supernatural sanction. And he desired a far simpler society than that of twentieth-century America. His vision was of a land of farmers and small business enterprises. While he and Roosevelt were advocating the same measures, it was Roosevelt's temperament to press on toward paternalism and a socialist State, it was Wilson's temperament to turn back toward individualism and a pre-industrial America. But neither was willing to face the fact that a revolution would be required before the America of his desire could come into being. Both vaguely trusted that all would be well if some of the more forthright thieveries of Big Business were frustrated and if the people were given still more power.

One of Wilson's plans for increasing the people's power was to restore the Presidency to its full ancient prestige, making of the President the immediate interpreter of the people's will, in which capacity he should have complete control over Congress. His conception of the office was not very different from that of a Greek tyrant — and the tyrant, as Plato points out, is the usual successor to inchoate democracy. Such was Wilson's solution to the problem of the growing leaderlessness and irresponsibility of American government. His first book [1] advances the thesis that 'the President is at liberty, both in law and conscience, to be as big a man as he can.' He criticized Taft for not being more of a leader, saying that the people 'clearly long for someone to put the pressure of the opinion of all the people of the United States upon Congress.' In 1913, he wrote to a friend that the President 'must be a Prime Minister, as much concerned with the guidance of legislation as with the just and orderly execution of law.' On one occasion during his first term, he was planning, if an important bill failed, to appeal to the people — presumably by a plebiscite — to declare whether they wished him to resign or whether they wished Congress to give in and pass the bill.

For his first eighteen months in office, Wilson carried all before him. His only concession to the politicians was in the matter of patronage. He had hoped to consider each executive appointment, and in each case to choose the best man available. He found that if he did this, it would take his whole four years in office and would so antagonize the Congressmen (each of whom regarded certain appointments as his personal privilege) that he could never get any of his measures made law. Wilson's Postmaster-General describes an interview in which the President was taught this lesson. 'I am going,' said the Postmaster-General, 'to make fifty-six thousand appointments. I will see honest and capable men in every office. But I will consult with the men on the Hill.... If they are turned down, they will hate you and will not vote for anything you want.' Wilson gave in. But in all other matters, during this early period, he had his way. Just as in his first years in the Princeton presidency, and his first months in the governorship, he seemed unbeatably self-assured and strong. So long as he had an enthusiastic following to whom he could appeal, he made

[1] *Congressional Government*, published in 1885.

short work of his opponents. It was when the following began to lose interest, when the first excitement died down, that his inability to meet opposition became clear.

Wilson's first demand on Congress was for an honest lowering of the tariff. At once the old game began. If Congress had been left to itself, there would have been months of dark bargaining followed by a bill in which all the important rates were higher than ever. The tariff lobby had never been defeated. There had been no real reduction since before the Civil War. Wilson waited until matters looked very bad, then issued a statement to the press. 'Washington,' he said, 'has seldom seen so numerous, so industrious, or so insidious a lobby.... There is evidence that money without limit is being used to sustain this lobby and to create an appearance of a pressure of opinion antagonistic to some of the chief items of the tariff bill.... Only public opinion can check and destroy it.' Public opinion, throughout the West and South, responded so violently that Congress was coerced. In the East, Wilson was criticized for demagogy. 'Is it possible,' asked the New York *Times* with solemn absurdity, 'that the President had mistaken for lobbying the ordinary, usual, and perfectly legitimate measures taken by protected interests to present their case to Congress?'

The triumph was complete. A Washington correspondent wrote that Wilson had 'destroyed an ancient industry, and smoked out of corners a horde of vermin, little and large. Someone here today likened the process now going on to the washing of a dog. "The fleas are entirely opposed to it," he said. "The dog does not like it much either, but will be more comfortable himself afterward, and immeasurably more agreeable as a member of the family."'

The same use of public opinion to coerce Congress was made by Wilson in support of all his important measures. After the lowering of the tariff came the Federal Reserve Act. In 191:, Wilson had stated, 'The plain fact is that the control of credit... is dangerously concentrated in this country. The large money resources of the country are not at the command of those who do not submit to the direction and domination of small groups of capitalists.... The great monopoly in this country is the money monopoly. So long as that exists, our old variety and freedom and individual energy of development are out of the question.' Seeking to deal with this problem, Wilson and his advisers evolved the Federal Reserve Act, providing machinery for the automatic expansion and contraction of the currency in relation to the business needs of the different sections of the country. The Act represents a skilful compromise between the Republican policy of creating a money monopoly and the cheap-money, decentralizing policy of the Democrats before the Civil War.

Following the Federal Reserve Act came a new anti-trust act. Next came the struggle over the Panama Canal tolls. Congress had passed a bill giving American coastwise shipping free passage through the canal — a reasonable provision except for the fact that it was in violation of the Hay-Pauncefote treaty with Great Britain. But when Wilson sought to repeal the act, he met strong opposition both within and without the party. It was during this fight that he contemplated appealing to the country if he were beaten. But he was not beaten; he forced the bill through a resentful Congress. When he went on, however, to demand from the Senate the ratification of a treaty apologizing to Colombia for the theft of Panama and paying twenty-five million dollars in compensation, he found that he had gone too far. The Senate held the treaty up, and before Wilson was able to concentrate public opinion back of this new demand, the World War broke out in Europe. American interest began to veer away from Progressive reforms at home; new passions and new alignments began to make themselves felt. Wilson's great days were over. He had become the master that he planned to be; he had passed the laws that he promised. During that first year of his Presidency it must have seemed to him that the whole Progressive dream was realized. And to what did it all come? Within a few years the country had relapsed into a slough more malodorous than that from which the Progressives had lifted it. Liberalism was clearly not the answer to the American dilemma. It was too tentative, too lacking in the courage to go boldly to the right or to the left.

In the last days of Wilson's authentic greatness, he lost the wife who had done so much to make that greatness a reality. In August, 1914, Ellen Axson Wilson died.... Sixteen months later, Wilson married Mrs. Edith Bolling Galt, of Washington.

7

The clarity and success of Wilson's domestic policy is a contrast to the feebleness of his handling of foreign affairs. He had no programme in foreign relations, only a diffuse idealism. The result, as in the case of his hero, Gladstone, was an uncertainty of touch which made trouble in spite of the most altruistic and moral plans.

When dealing with the sordid revolutions and counter-revolutions in Mexico, Wilson was at his weakest. But his intentions were laudable. In November, 1913, Sir William Tyrrell said to him, 'When I go back to England, I shall be asked to explain your Mexican policy. Can you tell me what it is?' Wilson replied, 'I am going to teach the South American Republics to elect good men!' This was a new note in foreign affairs. Neither the South American Republics, nor the interested nations of Europe, nor the perplexed American people, understood what was happening. The result was ambiguity, hard feeling, an intervention that was not an intervention, and loss of prestige. It seems unlikely that the South Americans learned how to elect good men; but the North Americans, to judge by Wilson's successor, clearly forgot how to do so.

The same hopefulness and pedagogic benevolence can be seen in Wilson's dealings with Europe. In the spring of 1914, he informed Congress that 'signs multiply about us... of an age of settled peace and good-will.' And when, a few months later, the World War began, Wilson thought the American people could be induced to preserve neutrality in thought as well as deed. In sections of the Middle West, where the indifference to Europe was almost as complete as the indifference to Africa or to Central Asia, such neutrality was at first a fact. But even in the Middle West there was a large German population which sided passionately with the fatherland; and along the three seaboards, where the inhabitants were aware of the outer world, there was never a genuine neutral feeling. The Irish were strongly pro-German; but within a few months of the outbreak of war it was clear that the native Americans sympathized with the Allies. In part this was the result of the brilliance of the English propaganda and the stupidity of the German efforts to counter it; but chiefly it was the working of racial feeling. In spite of the millions of immigrants from all the corners of Europe (7,753,816 immigrants entered the country between 1900 and 1910, and there had been twenty-seven and a half million immigrants since Washington's inauguration), America was still an Anglo-Scotch nation. The family relationship was too close for neutrality. In a crisis, the Americans had either to hate the English or to side with them. By September, 1914, it was clear that along the seacoasts of the country public opinion had chosen the latter course. The Government, to be sure, was soon quarrelling with England over questions of contraband and the freedom of the seas; but public indignation centered on the quarrel with Germany over her methods of submarine warfare.

Roosevelt, whose temperamental distaste for Wilson had turned to hatred as a result of the Colombian treaty, began to urge America to arm with a view to intervention on the side of the Allies. After the sinking of the *Lusitania*, in May, 1915, he became contemptuous with Wilson for not taking a firmer hand with Germany. But the majority of the country was behind Wilson, seeing no reason why it should be drawn into the fight. The election of 1916 was a referendum on this question — the Republicans passing over Roosevelt (who had returned to the party in order that there might be unity at this crisis) and nominating Charles Evans Hughes, the Democrats renominating Wilson.

Roosevelt's support of Hughes, and the attitude of the Republicans toward Wilson's diplomacy, made it probable that the

United States would move toward war if Hughes were elected. 'He kept us out of war,' was the Democratic campaign-slogan. The ferocity of Roosevelt's feeling toward Wilson is shown by a speech he made just before election day. Wilson had spent the summer months, whenever he could be away from Washington, at a place called Shadow Lawn. 'There should be shadows now at Shadow Lawn,' cried Roosevelt; 'the shadows of the men, women, and children who have risen from the ooze of the ocean bottom and from graves in foreign lands; the shadows of the helpless men whom Mr. Wilson dared not protect lest he might have to face danger;... the shadows of deeds that were never done; the shadows of lofty words that were followed by no action; the shadows of the tortured dead.'

Wilson was re-elected by so narrow a margin that the newspapers first announced Hughes as the next President and it was several days before the result was certain. Germany should have learned from the election that it would take only a little further pressure to bring America into the war. Yet less than three months later, Germany announced that she intended to renew unrestricted submarine warfare, and there seems reason to believe that her rulers were surprised when Wilson dismissed the German Ambassador and began at last to prepare for war. That surprise, that failure to understand Wilson or the motives for his diplomacy, explains why America was finally brought into the war. That a man who was not a pacifist, who was not frightened, who led a nation that had shown itself as easily roused to belligerency as any nation in history — that such a man could show the patience that Wilson had shown was too subtle a thought for the Potsdam mind. After the *Lusitania* sinking, Wilson had argued and reasoned with Germany. Ten months later, after the sinking of the *Sussex*, he had argued and reasoned again, and finally had won a promise that no further merchant ships would be sunk without warning and without provision for saving the lives of those on board. But when it became convenient to retract the promise, the Germans appeared to believe (in spite of the warnings of their Ambassador at Washington) that Wilson would do nothing but write further notes. They might have chosen another course had they known for certain that this one would bring America into the war. And they would have known this for certain had they troubled to understand Wilson. It was conscience and a sense of duty that had made Wilson forbearing — not patience or gentleness, of which he had little. When finally he saw that he was to be flouted, all the moral wrath of the Scotch Covenanter rose within him, making him the most effective war-President America has had.

The work of presenting the war to the people as a noble moral effort came naturally to Wilson, and he did it supremely well. The people responded with enthusiasm. Though the United States has usually been disarmed, and has always thought itself pacific, it has fought six wars in less than a hundred and fifty years. The combative instinct is not lacking in the American people, and now at last it could be indulged in an honourable foreign war. There was no theft intended, as in 1812 and 1845; there was no diplomatic chicanery involved, as in 1898. The issue seemed clear and satisfying. Wilson, who had so recently been teaching the South Americans how to vote, was now convinced that he and his countrymen were destined to teach the whole world how to govern itself. What other motive could the Deity have had in permitting all this carnage? Wilson's zeal and conviction of high purpose were felt by the nation, which entered the war united and with delight.

Knowing the harm that had been done in previous wars by political interference with military affairs, Wilson determined to leave his General Staff and his Commander-in-Chief unhampered. This is a hard task in a democracy; but Wilson succeeded, and in doing so he came sharply and for the last time in conflict with Roosevelt. Though fifty-eight years old, it was intolerable to the forever-adolescent Roosevelt that his country should be at war and he himself be left out of the fighting. He asked to be allowed to lead a division of volunteers to France. The idea appealed to the nation; two hundred and fifty thousand men offered to go with him; Congress passed a bill authorizing two divisions of volunteers; and Clemenceau wrote to Wilson: 'You are too much of a philosopher to ignore that the influence on the people of great leaders of men often exceeds their personal merits, thanks to the legendary halo surrounding them. The name of Roosevelt has this legendary force in our country.... You must know, Mr. President, more than one of our *poilus* asked his comrade: "But where is Roosevelt?"' Wilson had an interview with Roosevelt, remarking afterwards, 'he is a great big boy. I was... charmed by his personality. There is a sweetness about him that is very compelling.' Sweetness and boyishness, however, do not make a divisional commander. Marshal Joffre, who was then in America, said that it cost about ten to fifteen thousand lives to train a major-general, and even assuming that Roosevelt learned quickly, ten thousand lives seemed a high price. Also, his presence in France would inject politics into the whole handling of the American army. Nevertheless, Wilson referred the matter to the General Staff. But the army had once experienced Roosevelt's amateurishness and insubordination; the General Staff advised unhesitatingly against the exploit. Roosevelt was deprived of his last adventure. Naturally, but unfairly, he blamed Wilson, and throughout the war he attacked the Administration for lethargy and lack of vigour. Meanwhile, he himself was weakening. When in the summer of 1918 his youngest son was killed in France, Roosevelt's friends noticed that for the first time the exuberance, the boyishness, seemed to have died in him. He was tired. On the day of the armistice he was taken ill, and though he made a brief recovery he soon relapsed. He died on January 6, 1919.

Wilson, too, had entered the dark days of his life. The armistice was concluded on the understanding that peace was to be based on Wilson's Fourteen Points — minus Point Two, which provided for the freedom of the seas. A few of these points were specific and clear — such as that on the restoration of Belgium and that on the return of Alsace-Lorraine to France. Others, however, were little more than affirmations of moral purpose, such as Point Eleven, which declares that the Balkan problem should be settled by 'friendly counsel along historically established lines of allegiance and nationality.' Since there are no such lines in large parts of the Balkans, the point reduces itself to a plea for 'friendly counsel,' which is hardly a basis for negotiation. To Wilson himself, the supremely important point was the Fourteenth, which called for the creation of a League of Nations. He appears to have felt that if only the League were created any injustices in the treaty would soon be rectified, and that if the League were not created the great moral uprising of peoples (which he considered the war to have been) would have taken place in vain. Therefore, he was tempted to bargain for the League by conceding other points. However, Germany had been promised that peace would be made on the basis of Thirteen Points, and Wilson saw that the moral uprising must not be allowed to end in the breaking of this promise. It was here that the vagueness of the Points did its fatal work. For Wilson, in fact, made concessions on other points in order to get his League of Nations, and then (to judge by his subsequent speeches in America) deceived himself into believing that he had made no concessions, that the promise to Germany had been kept. The strain had been too great. Events had conspired, in 1917 and 1918, to make him feel that he was the moral dictator of the world. Then suddenly it turned out that he was nothing of the sort, that his orders were not obeyed, that the world in its invincible ignorance had other plans. He had either to face this fact and admit that he had failed in his new rôle of spiritual conqueror, or else he had to persuade himself that he had really succeeded, that the treaty was all he had said it was going to be, that it *was* a new world even if it did have shabby edges. He chose the latter course, and thereafter his ruin was swift.

Before he sailed for Paris, he had already ensured an unpleasant reception for whatever treaty he brought home. Before the autumn elections of 1918 — at which the whole House of Representatives and a third of the Senate were to be chosen — he had

appealed to the country to return a Democratic Congress, putting
his plea in such a way as to suggest that Republicans could not be
trusted to behave themselves in a world-crisis. The country, per-
versely, had returned a Republican Congress, with the result that
the new chairman of the Senate Committee on Foreign Relations
was Henry Cabot Lodge, a lifelong friend of Roosevelt and a sardonic critic of Wilsonian uplift.... In addition to this unwise appeal to the country, Wilson had made a further political blunder
in the appointment of the Peace Commissioners. He made the
Commission into an almost wholly partisan group, containing only
one Republican member and that one a man who in no sense represented his party.

These two mistakes of Wilson's were the result of his chief
character-defect: his failure to remember that opponents could be
honest, decent men. It was wicked to make the world's peace into a party issue, but Wilson was driven to do this by the same weakness that had driven him, so many years before, to turn against his
old friend, Mr. Hibben. Nevertheless, had Wilson kept his head
clear, had he returned home with his treaty and urged it on the
country for what it was — a poor thing, but the best that he could
get — he could have roused the country to support him once
again, and his treaty, League and all, might have been accepted.
But it was a new Wilson who returned from Paris. His enemies had
always accused him of hiding from the truth among his florid
phrases. It had never before been true, for back of his phrases (at
least in domestic politics) there had been clarity of purpose. But
now the old taunt appeared to be justified, and, having alienated
the partisan Republicans, Wilson proceeded to alienate his natural liberal supporters as well, by declaring that the treaty was a
wholly good thing, that it embodied the Thirteen Points, that it
was a true foundation for universal peace.

In the summer of 1919, the Senate having refused to accept the
treaty without important reservations, Wilson began a tour of the
country to win popular support. The strain and shock of the last
six months had been too much for him. In September he collapsed,

and for months was almost wholly incapacitated. He did not resign the Presidency, but the Administration was left without a
leader. The treaty was kept waiting, since the Democratic Senators would not ratify it with reservations, and the Republicans
would not ratify it without.

Wilson, from his sick-bed looked forward to the election of 1920,
when the people would have a chance to come to his support.
His policies were sure to be the issue, and his old faith in the di-
vine inspiration of the electorate was undimmed. He may have
been a little daunted when his party nominated a hack politician
from Ohio; nevertheless, the important point was that here was a
plebiscite on the question of the League of Nations and the new
reign of righteousness. Fortunately, the Republicans — as if to
keep the issue clear — had nominated another hack politician from
Ohio, a man who was nobody's superior. The people would declare for or against the Wilson policies. For the stricken Jeffersonian democrat in the White House not only a life's work but a life's
faith was at stake. The people elected Warren Harding.

After his retirement, in March, 1921, Wilson lived quietly in
Washington. He was a very sick man. On Armistice Day, 1923,
he made a brief speech from the balcony of his house. This was his
last public appearance. He died the following February.

Wilson had outlived President Harding, who succeeded him.
He had lived long enough to see the country relapse into conditions as disgraceful as those of the seventies, and to see that the relapse was unlamented. It is not known whether this affected his
views of democracy, or his faith in progress, whether, at the end,
he would have subscribed to his statement made in the brave days
before he first held public office: 'All through the centuries there has
been this slow, painful struggle forward, forward, up, up, a little
at a time, along the entire incline, the interminable way.'

8

Warren Gamaliel Harding was born in Ohio in 1865. His father was a farmer, and later became a physician. Harding attended

the local school and the Ohio Central College — which was an advanced secondary school, not an institute of higher learning. After trying, and abandoning, the study of law, Harding got a job on one of the weekly newspapers in Marion, a town of about four thousand inhabitants. A little later he and a friend bought a moribund weekly paper for three hundred dollars, and within a few years Harding had made this a paying venture.

In 1891, Harding married Mrs. Florence Kling De Wolfe, a widow. Her father was a banker, and apparently a man of some discernment, for he opposed the match. Harding, by this time, was a strikingly handsome man — tall and strong-looking, good-natured, affectionate, and weak. He had a reputation for dissipation, but that is probably too strong a word to use for his activities. Shortly after his marriage, Harding transformed the *Star* from a weekly into a daily paper. It continued to prosper, and Harding became a man of some importance in the little town, and also in the local Republican Party. He was soon a director of the Marion County Bank, a trustee of the Baptist Church, a Mason, and an Elk.

In addition to his good looks, Harding had a strong, effective voice. As a result of these physical assets, and of the political position that his editorship gained him, he began to take part in local campaigns. At the close of the century, he was sent to the State Senate, and at about the same time he met Harry Daugherty — the man who was to make him President and then to ruin him. In 1902, Harding was elected Lieutenant-Governor of Ohio. In 1910, he was the Republican candidate for Governor, but was defeated. In 1914, with the help of Daugherty and his political 'gang,' he was elected to the United States Senate.

In the Senate, Harding was 'regular' and safe. He never said or did anything that attracted attention, but he was a friend of Big Business and a partisan anti-Wilson man. Also, he was a good friend of the Anti-Saloon League, supporting the Eighteenth Amendment (which was passed on the wave of moral uplift that accompanied the War) and the Volstead Act, and making useful suggestions for overcoming opposition to these measures. Aside from his official record, Harding was soon known to be an enthusiastic drinker and gambler, and a man of genuine good-nature who made friends quickly among the unexacting. What was not so well known was that in 1917 a woman named Nan Britton became his mistress, and that in 1919 Harding and Nan Britton had a daughter. This, however, is probably the reason why he was elected President a year later.

It was in 1919 that Harry Daugherty, political organizer, spoilsman, and head of the 'Ohio Gang,' began to push Harding for the Presidency. He had no popular support in the primaries, not even winning the entire delegation from his own State. Yet Daugherty insolently predicted that after a long deadlock in the Nominating Convention, at two o'clock some morning, a little group of the real Republican leaders would meet in a smoke-filled hotel room and would decide to make Harding the party's nominee. And this is exactly what happened. In the early ballots at the Convention, Harding was nowhere; but after a long struggle there was an early morning meeting in the hotel room of Colonel George Harvey, and it was decided to give Harding the nomination. His qualifications were that he was good-looking, that he sounded significant, that he meant nothing, and that he came from Ohio. The last point was important. Grant, Hayes, Garfield, Harrison, McKinley, Taft — most of the Republican Presidents had come from Ohio. It is not, unhappily, that only Ohio can produce the typical President; it is simply that Ohio, since the Civil War, has been a crucial State. Farther east, the Republicans felt safe; farther south, the Democrats were invincible; the West voted chiefly on the price of wheat, which could not easily be changed for the sake of the election; but Ohio was fairly evenly divided between the two parties, so the Republicans usually chose a man who had shown that he could carry that State.

Before committing themselves to Harding, Harvey and his fellow-oligarchs showed their knowledge of Washington gossip by calling their prospective candidate before them and asking if there were any reason in his past life why he should not be nominated. Rightly considering that Nan Britton and her daughter belonged to his present rather than his past life, Harding answered no. He was nominated the same day. Harvey's comment was, 'He was nominated because there was nothing against him, and because the delegates wanted to go home.' In judging that there was nothing against Harding, Colonel Harvey showed the same acumen that had led him to pick Wilson as an easy man to use.

The League of Nations was the ostensible campaign issue. In fact, the League was a symbol for the high purpose, the whole atmosphere of effort and uplift, for which the Progressives had stood, and of which the nation was tired. The return to national isolation, which the repudiation of the League involved, was felt to mean a return to the old days of slackness and *laissez-faire* which had preceded Roosevelt. Senator Brandegee remarked that the time did not require 'first-raters.' Harding, with his one creative effort in the realm of the spirit, coined the word 'normalcy' to express the general desire. 'Back to normalcy' was the phrase that summed up the American temper. Harding was elected by a huge majority.

The new Cabinet contained some respected men, like Hughes, Mr. Hoover, and Mr. Mellon, and some cheap politicians like Daugherty and Fall. Below the Cabinet officers there were evil, disquieting figures, such as Charles R. Forbes, the head of the Veterans' Bureau, and Colonel Miller, the Alien Property Custodian. And below them there was a worse group still: hangers-on and go-betweens of whom the public as yet knew nothing. Within a month of Harding's inauguration, the whole atmosphere of Washington had changed. Both officially and socially, the tone became relaxed, care-free, abandoned.

The chief Administration policies were dictated by the Senatorial clique and by the three leading men in the Cabinet. The adoption of a National Budget — a reform which had been brought almost to completion under Wilson — and the Washington Conference are the achievements of which the Administration could be most proud. Meanwhile, behind the scenes, there was taking place a series of steals more wild, quick, brazen, and bizarre than anything that had yet happened in America. Harding, being a man without courage or character, was powerless. The 'Ohio Gang' owned him. With Daugherty as Attorney-General and Fall as Secretary of the Interior, and with Nan Britton and the baby to use in blackmailing Harding if, having learned too much of what was going on, he tried to interfere, they seemed safe. It is a sign of the grade of character these men possessed that they soon overplayed their hands so grossly that suicide, murder, or jail was the end of many of them.

Two months after his inauguration, Harding signed an order transferring the naval oil reserves from the control of the Navy Department to that of the Department of the Interior, over which Fall ruled. The game was under way. A little later, when leases of great value were made to the Doheny and Sinclair oil interests, and the Senate threatened an investigation into why this had been done, Harding announced that he entirely approved of the acts of the Department of the Interior. Meanwhile, the Department of Justice was blackmailing violators of the Prohibition law, making them pay bribes as an alternative to prosecution; and the Director of the Veterans' Bureau and the Alien Property Custodian were looting on a scale and with an openness that suggested insanity. The quality of what was going on may be suggested by the subsequent history of the chief actors: Attorney-General Daugherty was twice tried upon criminal charges but the juries failed to agree on a verdict; Secretary Fall was sent to prison; Forbes and Miller were sent to prison; Jess Smith, chief collector of blackmail for the Department of Justice, committed suicide (or possibly was murdered); C. F. Cramer, the attorney for the Veterans' Bureau, committed suicide; Thurston, an attorney who helped expedite the Alien Property Custodian cases, died suddenly; John T. King, indicted with Miller and Daugherty in an Alien Property Custodian case, died suddenly; C. F. Hateley, undercover agent for the Department of Justice and special emissary for Daugherty, died suddenly.

The strangest of these sudden deaths, however, was that of President Harding. In June, 1923, he and his wife and a large party left Washington for a trip to Alaska.[1] Newspapermen accompanying the party noticed that the President was worried and anxious. In Kansas City he had an interview with the wife of Secretary Fall, after which his anxiety was noticeably greater. While in Alaska he received a long code message from Washington, and for the next two days he appeared to be on the verge of a collapse. Shortly after this, he asked some of his friends among the reporters what a President could do when he had been betrayed. On returning to the United States, he was said to be suffering from ptomaine poisoning. Five days later, in San Francisco, he died suddenly. The cause was said to be an embolism, but the newspaper accounts at the time were confused and contradictory — even on the question as to whether General Sawyer, Harding's personal physician, was with him at the time of his death, or whether Harding was alone with his wife.[2]

Had Harding lived a few months longer, he would have been impeached, and the scandal would, for the time at least, have destroyed the Republican Party, and would have dragged down several of the important men who sat in the Harding Cabinet and who spoke no word, although all Washington suspected what was happening. Harding undoubtedly knew what lay before him. It has been alleged that he told his wife he intended to escape with Nan Britton and the child, and that she, to save his reputation and the party, and to serve her own jealousy, murdered him. It has also been suggested, with more likelihood, that Harding had the courage to kill himself. Or he may have died of a timely embolism.

The important point about the Harding régime is the indifference of the American public to the scandals that resulted. Vice-

[1] Shortly before starting on this trip, he is alleged to have told his sister that he did not expect to return.

[2] It is an interesting fact that about a year later, when Mrs. Harding was visiting General Sawyer at his home in Ohio, he, too, died suddenly — the New York *Times* commenting that 'General Sawyer's death was almost identical with the manner of death of the late Warren G. Harding.'

President Coolidge, who sat mum while the evil work was done, was elected President in 1924. And the man who succeeded him, in 1928, had been a member of Harding's Cabinet, and had not felt called upon either to draw attention to what was going on about him, or to resign from the little group of thieves to which he had been appointed.

$$\frac{311}{307}$$

CONCLUSION

'DEMOCRACY and plutocracy are the same thing under the two aspects of wish and actuality, theory and practice, knowing and doing. It is the tragic comedy of the world-improvers' and free-dom-teachers' desperate fight against money that they are *ipso facto* assisting money to be effective.... The freedom of public opinion involves the preparation of public opinion, which costs money; and the freedom of the press brings with it the question of posses-sion of the press, which again is a matter of money; and with the franchise comes electioneering, in which he who pays the piper calls the tune. The representatives of the ideas look at one side only, while the representatives of money operate with the other.... So it runs in every last act of a Culture-drama, when the megalo-polis has become master over the rest.' [1] Spengler's comments, made at the end of the modern democratic era, are no more caustic than those made at the beginning by the founders of the United States, who did all in their power to save the new country from the anticipated blight. Their effort was defeated, partly by geography and partly by the movement in world history which began with the French Revolution. The defeat was so nearly in-evitable that it might be called the doom of America, rather than its deserts.

One feature of a money-bossed democracy is that good men learn to refrain from public life. The time comes when there seems to be no relation between the Government and the country that it betrays. But it is wrong to blame those who hold aloof: their action is the result, and not the cause, of the degradation in politics. Since the Civil War, for example, good men have merely been wasted in Washington. The system which arose immediately after that war (a system with roots as far back as Van Buren, but which needed the funds of Big Business to make it complete) could

[1] *The Decline of the West*, II, 401–02.

not be broken until it had time to show its full evil. To alleviate that evil, as the Progressives did, was only to prolong the pain; yet it was too soon to try and kill the system itself. Not even its victims would admit that fundamentally all was unsound. It was a time for tinkering, for liberalism; good men merely showed their good sense by staying out of politics. But at last the days of cynical waiting are over. The tinkering has been tried, and has failed. The nation has undergone Harding, racketeering, the gangster, the slump. The number of Americans who are in need is greater than the whole population of the country that fought the Civil War. It is time for a decisive movement to the Right or to the Left.

Democracy normally culminates in dictatorship: the money-anarchy makes way for the tyrant-state. The reason is obvious. Discipline, subordination to the common good, can only be imposed in two ways: in the name of religion or in the name of the State. But no country decays into plutocracy until its religious faith is waning. Recovery, therefore, can only come by demanding sacrifice, and subordination, to the State. This presupposes a State whose will has moral worth and whose rulers compel obedience even at the cost of obliterating the individual. To build such a State on the ruins of democracy is work for a dictator. Must such work be the next stage in America? The time is coming when no man can be so shameless as to defend the present system. The Left stands ready with its remedy. Communism is prepared to play the dictator's old part of liquidating the mean disorder of plutocracy. What of the Right? Have conservatives anything to offer? 'Conservative,' in America, has come to mean one who favours the politics of Big Business — which suggests that Americans feel they have nothing worth saving but their money. If the suggestion is unjust, the time has come to prove it.

The early story of the Republic gives the example of a State served by its best men. The writings of those who built, and first administered, that State are an education in political thought. When America was young and had a soul, she knew that freedom from autocracy must be bought at a heavy price in responsibility and effort. Is it too late to return to that knowledge, to those traditions? With a century of experience for warning, is it possible to cancel the Jacksonian revolution, to go back to the days before the excesses of democracy instead of pushing forward to communism or to some alternative tyrant? History suggests that once the franchise has been given, it can only be withdrawn by revolution. But in the days when America could still be proud, it was her boast that she was able to initiate, that she need not always follow the old course to the old conclusion. Can she purge her Republic? Or must she stumble on until everything she has stood for is discredited?

If the conservative attempt be made, the task should be simplified and given added appeal by the increase in real wealth which the machine is offering. Few nations have ever found a second chance, but it seems likely that with wise administration the well-taught, well-nurtured America of J. Q. Adams's dream has again become possible. Will these new communal riches be wasted like the old? Will they be seized for the advantage of a Marxian State which, whether good or bad in itself, would be the end of the American effort? Or will those who believe that there was much merit in that effort take this new, this last, chance to build a genuine commonwealth, a government that is neither tyrannous nor venal?

THE END

BIBLIOGRAPHY

BIBLIOGRAPHY

PART ONE gives a few of the best general histories and interpreta-
tions of the United States, and then some of the most interesting
books on topics treated in the present volume. This is merely a
reading list, based on personal preference. Part Two is an attempt to list the best book, or books, on each of the Presidents.
Where the best is notably unsatisfactory, attention is called to this
fact. Mention is made of biographies of a few of the men who
overshadowed the Presidents between Jackson and Lincoln.

PART ONE

A. Bibliographies
1. Channing, Hart, and Turner. *Guide to the Study and Reading of American History.* Boston, 1912.
2. G. G. Griffin. Annual: *Writings on American History.* 1912–1917, Yale University Press; subsequently, American Historical Association.

B. General
3. Edward Channing. *History of the United States.* 6 vols., New York, 1905–25. (From the Discovery through the Civil War.)
4. Charles A. Beard and Mary Beard. *The Rise of American Civilization.* 2 vols., New York, 1927.
5. S. E. Morison. *Oxford History of the United States, 1783–1917.* 2 vols., London, 1927.
6. Willis M. West. *The Story of American Democracy.* Boston, 1922.
7. James Truslow Adams. *The Epic of America.* Boston, 1931.
8. Mark Van Doren (editor). *An Autobiography of America.* New York, 1929.
9. Allan Nevins. *American Social Life as Seen by British Travellers.* New York, 1923.
10. Vernon Louis Parrington. *Main Currents in American Thought. An Interpretation of American Literature from the Beginnings to 1920.* (Completed to 1900 only.) 3 vols., New York, 1927–31.
11. Charles A. Beard and William Beard. *The American Leviathan.* New York and London, 1931. (An account of the American Government today.)

C. 1763 to 1789.
12. G. L. Beer. *British Colonial Policy, 1754–1765.* New York, 1907.

13. A. M. Schlesinger. *The Colonial Merchants and the American Revolution, 1763–76.* New York, 1918.

14. A. M. Schlesinger. *New Viewpoints in American History.* New York, 1922. (Chapter Seven.)

15. C. H. Van Tyne. *A History of the Founding of the American Republic.* Vol. I: *The Causes of the War of Independence.* Boston and London, 1922. Vol. II: *The War of Independence, American Phase.* Boston and London, 1929.

16. J. Franklin Jameson. *The American Revolution Considered as a Social Movement.* Princeton, New Jersey, 1926.

17. Thomas Anburey. *Travels Through the Interior Parts of America, in a Series of Letters.* 2 vols., London, 1791 (2d ed.) (Anburey was with the Convention troops, before and after their capture, and so travelled from Quebec to Charlottesville and north again.)

18. C. H. Van Tyne. *The Loyalists in the American Revolution.* New York, 1902.

19. Allan Nevins. *The American States, 1775–89.* New York, 1924.

20. Gaillard Hunt and J. B. Scott (editors). *The Debates in the Federal Convention of 1787, which Framed the Constitution of the United States of America.* Reported by James Madison. International edition, 1920.

21. Charles A. Beard. *An Economic Interpretation of the Constitution of the United States.* New York, 1923.

22. *The Federalist,* by Hamilton, Madison, and Jay. Edition with notes, etc., by P. L. Ford. New York, 1898.

D. *1789 to 1829*

23. Charles A. Beard. *Economic Origins of Jeffersonian Democracy.* New York, 1915.

24. Henry Adams. *History of the United States During the Administrations of Jefferson and Madison.* 9 vols. New York, 1889–96.

25. Julius W. Pratt. *The Expansionists of 1812.* New York, 1925.

26. A. G. Bradley. *The United Empire Loyalists.* London, 1932. (The War of 1812 as seen from Canada.) (Published in New York, 1932, under title of *Colonial Americans in Exile: Founders of British Canada.*)

27. Frederick Jackson Turner. *The Rise of the New West, 1819–1829.* (American Nation Series, vol. 14.) New York, 1906.

28. Frederick Jackson Turner. *The Frontier in American History.* New York, 1921.

29. F. L. Paxson. *History of the American Frontier, 1763–1893.* Boston, 1924.

E. *1829 to 1861*

30. Claude G. Bowers. *Party Battles of the Jackson Period.* Boston, 1922.

31. W. E. Dodd. *The Cotton Kingdom.* New Haven, 1920. (Vol. XXVII of *Chronicles of America.*)

32. C. S. Boucher. '*In Re* That Aggressive Slavocracy,' *Mississippi Valley*

Historical Review, VIII, 13–79. (Denies there was ever unity in Southern opinion.)

33. C. S. Boucher. *Nullification Controversy in South Carolina*. University of Chicago Press, 1916.

34. Ulrich B. Phillips. *American Negro Slavery*. New York, 1918.

35. R. C. H. Caterall. *Second Bank of the United States*. University of Chicago Press, 1903.

36. N. W. Stephenson. *Texas and the Mexican War*. New Haven, 1920. (Vol. XXIV of *Chronicles of America*.)

37. Justin H. Smith. *The War with Mexico*. 2 vols., New York, 1919. (An ingenious justification which should be read in a watchful temper.)

F. The Civil War

38. James Ford Rhodes. *History of the United States from the Compromise of 1850 to ... 1877*. 7 vols., New York, 1893–1906. (Vol. 8, 1877–1896. New York, 1919.)

39. See above, item No. 3, volume 6.

40. Lieutenant-Colonel T. A. Dodge. *Bird's-Eye View of our Civil War*. Revised edition, Boston, 1897.

41. G. C. Eggleston. *The History of the Confederate War: Its causes and its conduct*. 2 vols., New York, 1910.

42. W. H. Russell. *My Diary North and South*. London, 1863. (The *Times* Correspondent.)

43. Henry Adams. *The Education of Henry Adams*. An autobiography. Boston, 1918.

G. 1865 to 1923

44. Louis M. Hacker and Benjamin B. Kendrick. *The United States Since 1865*. With a foreword by D. R. Fox. New York, 1932.

45. W. A. Dunning. *Reconstruction, Political and Economic, 1865–77*. New York, 1907. (Vol. 22 of *The American Nation* series.)

46. Claude G. Bowers. *The Tragic Era. The Revolution after Lincoln*. Boston, 1929.

47. Don Carlos Seitz. *The Dreadful Decade. Detailing Some Phases in the History of the United States ... 1869–1879*. Indianapolis, 1926.

48. Henry Adams. *Historical Essays*. New York and London, 1891. (Includes *The Legal Tender Act, The New York Gold Conspiracy*, and *The Session, 1869–70*.)

49. Ida M. Tarbell. *History of the Standard Oil Company*. 2 vols., New York, 1904.

50. C. E. Russell. *Stories of the Great Railroads*. Chicago, 1912.

51. F. E. Chadwick. *The Relations of the United States and Spain*. 3 vols., New York, 1909–1911.

52. Don Carlos Seitz. *Joseph Pulitzer: his Life and Letters*. New York. 1924.

53. Walter Millis. *The Martial Spirit.* Boston, 1931. (The Spanish-American War as farce.)

54. S. J. Buck. *The Agrarian Crusade. A Chronicle of the Farmer in Politics.* New Haven, 1920. (Vol. XLV of *Chronicles of America.*)

PART TWO

1. *Washington*

55. William R. Thayer. *George Washington.* Boston and London, 1922.

56. Rupert Hughes.
> I. *George Washington, the Human Being and the Hero, 1732–62.* New York, 1926.
> II. *George Washington, the Rebel and the Patriot, 1762–77.* New York, 1927.
> III. *George Washington, the Savior of the States, 1777–81.* New York, 1930.

57. Bernard Faÿ. *Georges Washington, gentilhomme.* Paris, 1931. Translation, *George Washington, Republican Aristocrat.* Boston. 1931.

58. William E. Woodward. *George Washington, the Image and the Man.* New York, 1928.

59. P. L. Haworth. *George Washington: Farmer.* Indianapolis, 1915.

60. *The Diaries of George Washington, 1748–99.* Edited by John C. Fitzpatrick. 4 vols., Boston, 1925.

2. *John Adams*

61. J. Q. Adams and C. F. Adams. *The Life of John Adams.* 2 vols., Philadelphia, 1871. (Begun by J. Q. A. and completed by C. F. A.)

62. James Truslow Adams. *The Adams Family.* Boston, 1930.

63. C. M. Walsh. *The Political Science of John Adams.* New York, 1915.

64. A. D. Morse. 'The Politics of John Adams.' *American Historical Review*, IV, 292.

65. *Familiar Letters of John Adams and his Wife.* Compiled by C. F. Adams. Boston, 1875.

66. *Correspondence of John Adams and Thomas Jefferson, 1812–1826.* Indianapolis, 1925.

3. *Jefferson*

67. Francis W. Hirst. *Life and Letters of Thomas Jefferson.* New York, 1926.

68. See above, item No. 24.

69. John T. Morse, Jr. *Thomas Jefferson.* Boston, 1883. (*American Statesmen* series.)

70. John Taylor of Caroline. *An Inquiry into the Principles and Policy of the Government of the United States.* Fredericksburg, 1814. (Invaluable for understanding 'Jeffersonian democracy.' Has never been reprinted, but is well summarized in No. 23 above, from which the quotations in this book are taken.)

71. Claude G. Bowers. *Jefferson and Hamilton.* Boston, 1925. (Not only geese, but practically all early American fowl, are swans to Mr. Bowers. But his books are lively and useful.)

4. *Madison*
    72. Gaillard Hunt. *Life of James Madison.* New York, 1902.
    73. See above, item No. 24.
    74. Charles E. Hill. *James Madison.* New York, 1927. (Vol. III of *The American Secretaries of State.*)

5. *Monroe*
    75. Julius W. Pratt. *James Monroe.* New York, 1927. (Vol. III of *The American Secretaries of State.*)
    76. Daniel C. Gilman. *James Monroe.* Boston, 1883. (*American Statesmen* series.)
    77. George Morgan. *The Life of James Monroe.* Boston, 1921.

6. *J. Q. Adams*
    78. John T. Morse, Jr. *John Quincy Adams.* Boston, 1882. (*American Statesmen* series.)
    79. See item No. 62, above.
    80. Dorothie Bobbé. *Mr. and Mrs. John Quincy Adams.* New York, 1931. (Although written with a horrifying sweetness, this book contains valuable material and occasionally brings J. Q. A. to life.)
    81. *Diary of J. Q. Adams.* Edited by Allan Nevins. New York, 1928. (A good selection, in one volume, from the *Memoirs* in twelve volumes.)

7. *Jackson*
    82. John Spencer Bassett. *Life of Andrew Jackson.* 2d ed., New York, 1916.
    83. G. W. Johnson. *Andrew Jackson.* New York, 1927.
    84. D. Karsner. *Andrew Jackson.* New York, 1929.

8. *Van Buren*
    85. E. M. Shepard. *Van Buren.* Boston, 1883. (*American Statesmen* series.)

9. *Some dominant figures of the Middle Period*
    86. Gaillard Hunt. *John C. Calhoun.* Philadelphia, 1908.
    87. W. E. Dodd. Essay on Calhoun in his *Statesmen of the Old South.* New York, 1911.
    88. Henry Cabot Lodge. *Daniel Webster.* Boston, 1888. (*American Statesmen* series.)
    89. Carl Schurz. *Henry Clay.* 2 vols., Boston, 1887. (*American Statesmen* series.)
    90. Ulrich B. Phillips. *Life of Robert Toombs.* New York, 1913.
    91. Allen Johnson. *Stephen A. Douglas.* New York, 1908.

10. *Harrison*
   92. Dorothy Burne Goebel. *William Henry Harrison.* Indianapolis, 1926.

11. *Tyler.* There is no adequate biography of Tyler.
   93. L. G. Tyler. *Letters and Times of the Tylers.* Richmond, 1884.

12. *Polk*
   94. Eugene Irving McCormac. *James K. Polk.* University of California, 1922.

13. *Taylor.* There is no adequate biography of Taylor.
   95. O. O. Howard. *Zachary Taylor.* New York and London, 1892. (Vol. 2 of *Great Commander Series,* edited by J. G. Wilson.)
   96. See No. 37 above.

14. *Fillmore.* There is no good biography of Fillmore. The best account of his life is the brief article by Julius W. Pratt in the *Dictionary of American Biography.*
   97. W. E. Griffis. *Millard Fillmore, Constructive Statesman, Defender of the Constitution, etc.* Ithaca, New York, 1915. (The subtitle is a warning of the tone in which the book is written.)

15. *Pierce*
   98. Roy F. Nichols. *Franklin Pierce, Young Hickory of the Granite Hills.* Philadelphia, 1931.
   99. J. R. Irelan. *History of the Life, Administration and Times of Franklin Pierce.* Chicago, 1888.

16. *Buchanan*
   100. St. G. L. Sioussat. *James Buchanan.* New York, 1928. (Vol. V of *The American Secretaries of State.*)
   101. See item No. 38 above, vols. I and II.

17. *Jefferson Davis*
   102. W. E. Dodd. *Jefferson Davis.* Philadelphia, 1907.
   103. H. J. Eckenrode. *Jefferson Davis.* New York, 1923.
   104. Mrs. V. J. Davis. *Memoirs of Jefferson Davis.* 2 vols., New York, 1890.

18. *Lincoln*
   105. Carl Sandburg. *Lincoln, the Prairie Years.* 2 vols., New York and London, 1926.
   106. N. W. Stephenson. *Lincoln.* Indianapolis, 1922.
   107. W. E. Barton. *Lincoln.* 2 vols., Indianapolis, 1925.
   108. *The Political Debates Between Abraham Lincoln and Stephen A. Douglas in the Senatorial Campaign of 1858.* 2d printing, New York, 1924.

19. *Johnson*

109. Robert W. Winston. *Andrew Johnson, Plebeian and Patriot*. New York, 1928.

110. Lloyd Paul Stryker. *Andrew Johnson. A Study in Courage*. New York, 1929.

20. *Gran'*

111. L. A. Coolidge. *U. S. Grant*. Boston, 1922.

112. W. E. Woodward. *Meet General Grant*. New York, 1928. (An interesting and useful book, in spite of the title.)

113. *Personal Memoirs of U. S. Grant*. 2d ed., edited, with a preface, by F. D. Grant. 2 vols., New York, 1895.

21. *Hayes*

114. Charles Richard Williams. *Rutherford B. Hayes*. 2 vols., Boston, 1914.

22. *Garfield*

115. Theodore C. Smith. *James A. Garfield*. 2 vols., New Haven, 1925.

23. *Arthur*. There are no biographies of Arthur. See the general histories of the period, and the article on Arthur, by Frederic Logan Paxson, in the *Dictionary of American Biography*.

24. *Cleveland*

116. Robert McElroy. *Grover Cleveland*. 2 vols., New York, 1923.

117. Denis Tilden Lynch. *Grover Cleveland. A Man Four-Square*. New York, 1932.

25. *Benjamin Harrison*. There is no life of Harrison; but one by Albert T. Volwiler is in preparation. See the general histories of the period, and the article on Harrison, by Albert T. Volwiler, in the *Dictionary of American Biography*.

26. *McKinley*

118. C. S. Olcott. *Life of William McKinley*. 2 vols., Boston, 1916.

27. *Roosevelt*

119. *Theodore Roosevelt, an Autobiography*. New York, 1913.

120. Henry F. Pringle. *Theodore Roosevelt*. New York and London, 1932.

121. H. Hagedorn. *Roosevelt in the Bad Lands*. Boston, 1921.

122. *The Letters of Roosevelt to Henry Cabot Lodge*. 2 vols., New York, 1925.

28. *Taft*

123. Herbert Smith Duffy. *William Howard Taft*. New York, 1930. (Uncritical, and gushing in its enthusiasm and affection, this is the only biography to date.)

29. *Wilson*

   124. Ray Stannard Baker. *Woodrow Wilson, Life and Letters*. Vols. I and II, New York and London, 1927. Vols. III and IV, New York and London, 1932. (Volume IV ends with August, 1914. Further volumes to come.)

   125. W. E. Dodd. *Woodrow Wilson and his Work*. New York, 1920.

   126. J. P. Tumulty. *Woodrow Wilson as I Knew Him*. New York, 1921. (By Wilson's private secretary.)

   127. William Gibbs McAdoo. *Crowded Years*. Boston and London, 1932. (An autobiography by a member of Wilson's Cabinet who became Wilson's son-in-law.)

   128. *The Intimate Papers of Colonel House Arranged as a Narrative* by Charles Seymour. 4 vols., Boston and London, 1926 and 1928.

30. *Harding*. There are no reliable books on Harding. But there is a good article on him, by Allan Nevins, in the *Dictionary of American Biography*. A trustworthy biography is improbable for some time, both because of the natural distaste inspired by the subject and because Mrs. Harding, before her death, destroyed Harding's papers.

   129. Nan Britton. *The President's Daughter*. New York, 1927. (The interesting 'revelation' in Nan Britton's book is that of the cultural and intellectual quality of Harding.)

   130. *The Strange Death of President Harding*. From the diaries of Gaston B. Means, as told to May Dixon Thacker. New York, 1930. (The book is clearly untrustworthy, and its most important charges cannot be checked. Yet it is worth attention as giving local colour for the period.)

INDEX

INDEX

Adams, Brooks, quoted, 103

Adams, Charles Francis, 96, 106, 225; on John Quincy Adams, 97; introduction to Lincoln after his appointment as Minister to Great Britain, 187; his changing opinion of Lincoln, 187, 188; his diplomacy, 192

Adams, Charles Francis, Jr., quoted on the Negro, 183; on the building of the Union Pacific Railroad, 229

Adams, Henry, 97; as an historian, 35; quoted on Jefferson, 50; quoted on J. Q. Adams, 106; on the Southern statesmen, 194; on the breakdown of the old American system in Grant's administration, 197; on Congress in the late sixties, 212, 213; on the Gould-Fisk scandal, 217; on President Grant, 219; on the submission of the American people to capitalism, 250; on John Sherman and Hanna, 259; on Theodore Roosevelt, 268

Adams, James Truslow, quoted, 36, 60, 95, 204

Adams, John, 22; causes the election of Washington as Commander-in-Chief, 13, 40; inaugurated as President, 30; resented Washington's pre-eminence, 32; contrasted with Washington, 32, 33; moral courage and intellectual power, 34; inheritance and early life, 35, 36; moral fervour against English trade laws, 36–38; sees war a necessary outcome, 38; defends authors of the 'Boston Massacre,' 38, 39; in the Continental Congress, 39–43; heads movement for independence, 40; as a public speaker, 40; opposition to democracy, 40–42; his *Discourse of Davila*, 41; representing the United States in Europe, 43; successful work in the peace conference, 43, 44; the last of his unclouded triumphs, 44; minister to England, 44; chosen Vice-President, 44; political struggles with Hamilton, 45–48; disinterestedness, 74, 58; elected President under unfavorable auspices, 47, 48; his theory of government, 55; difficulties of his administration, 55–60; foreign affairs a major issue, 56–58; stands out against war with France, 57, 58; his unsuccessful campaign for re-election, 59; leaves Washington before Jefferson's inauguration, 60; his final act as President the appointment of Marshall to the Chief-Justiceship, 60; last years, 71

Adams, John Quincy, 55, 80, 85, 114, 117; on James Monroe, 87; Secretary of State, 88; in the election of 1824, 90, 91; early life of, 91–93; Minister to Berlin, 93, 94; Washington's commendation, 93, 94; personal characteristics, 94, 95; in the Massachusetts Senate, 95; United States Senator, 95; Minister to Russia, 95; presides over the American peace commission at Ghent, 95, 96; Minister to Great Britain, 96; Secretary of State, 97–99; his principles of public service, 97; secures the purchase of the Floridas, 98; originator of the Monroe Doctrine, 99; as President he makes Clay his Secretary of State, 99, 100; attacked by Jackson's party, 100; his plans for the public lands opposed by Jackson's men, 101, 102; in the losing campaign of 1828, 103, 104; attacked by Bostonians, 104; his answer, 104; indefatigability, 104; ends his career in Congress, 105, 106; on the slavery question, 105 and n.; last years, 106; on Van Buren, 130; on W. H. Harrison, 135; and the Oregon controversy with England, 145

Adams family, the, 34, 35

Alien and Sedition Acts, 67, 75

American Party, 158 and n.

Ames, Fisher, quoted, 41

Anderson, Maj. Robert, 172, 173

Arbitration treaties, 282

162, 215; Lincoln on, 162; decision on the Tenure-of-Office Act, 208; powers under the Constitution, 215; and the Interstate Commerce Act, 257

Sussex, sinking of the, 300

Taft, William Howard, 286, 295; nominated and elected President, 279; ancestry and previous career, 279, 280; his administration, 281–83; renominated by the 'regulars' in the Republican Convention of 1912, 284; defeated in the election by Wilson, 284; later service, 284; Chief Justice, 284; death, 284; the most lovable President, 284

Talleyrand, 57

Tariff, the, of 1816, 1820, and 1824, 89, 90; the issue in 1888, 246; the McKinley Act, 248, 249; raised again under Taft, 282; reciprocity with Canada defeated, 282; Wilson and, 296

Taylor, John, 41, 55; his *Inquiry into the Principles and Policy of the Government of the United States*, 51, 52

Taylor, Zachary, in the Mexican War, 149, 151, 152; his administration overshadowed by Clay, Webster, and Calhoun, 150; ancestry and early life, 151; his campaign for the Presidency as a military hero, 152; an honest man but inadequate for the crisis, 152, 153; death, 153

Tenure-of-Office Act, 206–08

Texas, the annexation of, 142, 143; under Mexico and as a republic, 143; the annexation struggle, 143, 144; in the Mexican War, 147–50

Tilden, Samuel J., nominated for the Presidency, 235; Electoral Commission decides against, 235

'Tippecanoe and Tyler too,' 134

Todd, Mary, 181

Turner, F. J., his *The Rise of the New West*, 80 n.

Tweed Ring, 240

Tyler, John, candidate for Vice-President, 133; elected Vice-President as a Whig but as President not amenable to party discipline, 138, 139; early life, 138, 139; insists on being actual President, 139,

140; vetoes Whig legislation, 140; his wife dies and he remarries, 141; his cabinet, 141; goes completely over to the Democrats, 141; in the campaign of 1844, 143; retirement, 143; and secession, 143; death, 143

Tyrrell, Sir William, 298

Union Pacific Railroad, 217–19, 229

University of Virginia, 71, 89

Upshur, Abel P., 141

Van Buren, Martin, one of three who first developed the spoils system, 117; becomes a Jackson man, 117; on removals, 118; and the Eaton scandal, 121; becomes Vice-President, 127; nominated for President, 128; inaugurated, 129; personality, 130; ancestry and early life, 131, 132; administration, 132; in the campaign of 1840, 132–35; last years and death, 135; loses the Democratic nomination in 1844, 145, 146

Van Tyne, Claude H., quoted, xvii

Venezuela, boundary dispute with Great Britain, 249–51

Virginia, opposition to British policy in, xvii; planter society of, 33, 34; slavery in, 144

War of 1812, 76–79

Ward, Ferdinand, 226, 227

Washington, George, a conservative President, xix, xx, vilified by Paine and others, xx; quoted on the militia, xx; letter to Henry Lee quoted, xx; boyhood and education, 3–5; the first 'American,' 4; religious life, 5; in the French and Indian War, 6, 7; love of Sally Fairfax, 7, 8; suppression of emotions, 8, 9; marriage, 9, 10; life at Mount Vernon, 10, 11; attitude towards England, 11, 12; made Commander-in-Chief of the Continental forces, 13, 14; his conduct of the war, 14–19; his part in the formation of the government, 19–21; not a politician, 21, 22; becomes President, 22, 23; his dream of an agricultural United States, 23, 24; policies of his administration, 24–28; temperamental affinity with Hamilton, 28: